CHINA'S NEW SPATIAL ECONOMY

This book had its genesis in Workshops sponsored by the Academy of the Social Sciences in Australia at the Flinders University of South Australia, Adelaide and by the Chinese Academy of Sciences at the Institute of Geography, Beijing.

China's New Spatial Economy

Heading Towards 2020

Edited by
Godfrey Linge

Contributors
Chen Cai, Christopher Findlay, Dean Forbes,
Li Shantong, Li Wen-yan, Godfrey Linge, Liu Yi,
Rong Chao-he, She Zhixiang, Noel Tracy,
Wang Huijiong, Wang Li, Andrew Watson,
Harry X. Wu, Xu Guan, Yuan Shu-ren, Zhang Lei

HONG KONG
OXFORD UNIVERSITY PRESS
OXFORD NEW YORK
1997

Oxford University Press

Oxford New York

Athens Auckland Bangkok Bogota Bombay
Buenos Aires Calcutta Cape Town Dar es Salaam
Delhi Florence Hong Kong Istanbul Karachi
Kuala Lumpur Madras Madrid Melbourne
Mexico City Nairobi Paris Singapore
Taipei Tokyo Toronto Warsaw

and associated companies in
Berlin Ibadan

Oxford is a trade mark of Oxford University Press

First published 1997
This impression (lowest digit)
1 3 5 7 9 10 8 6 4 2

Published in the United States
by Oxford University Press, New York

© Oxford University Press 1997

British Library Cataloguing in Publication Data available

Library of Congress Cataloging-in-Publication Data available

ISBN 0-19-587666-0

Printed in Hong Kong
Published by Oxford University Press (China) Ltd
18/F Warwick House, Taikoo Place, 979 King's Road,
Quarry Bay, Hong Kong

Acknowledgements

Chen Cai, Yuan Shu-ren, and Wang Li wish to thank Li Xiumin, Wang Lianqing, and Liu Li of the Department of Geography, and Ding Sibao, Director of the Russia Research Institute, Northeast Normal University, for their assistance in the preparation of Chapter 7.

Godfrey Linge particularly wishes to thank Li Wen-yan for his many acts of kindness and friendship over more than a decade. He also greatly appreciates the continuing support and hospitality of many people in China, including Wang Huijiong, Lu Da-dao, Li Shantong, Rong Chao-he, Liu Yi, Zhang Lei, Wu Wei, Pang Xiaomin, Dong Suocheng, Chen Yimei, Chen Cai, Yuan Shu-ren, Ma Ji, Zhu Junmin, and Wang Li. He is also grateful for the interest shown in the early stages of this project by Dean Forbes, and the assistance of Merle Ricklefs (Director of the Research School of Pacific and Asian Studies, the Australian National University) and Gerard Ward. The line drawings prepared by Neville Minch, the research assistance provided by Sandra Davenport, Elanna Lowes, and Christine Tabart, and the computer wizardry of Daniel Fritsch all added much to the appearance and content of this book. His greatest debt, however, is to his wife, Jan, who not only made very significant editorial contributions but was a tower of strength during the many vicissitudes that beset this book.

Liu Yi and Zhang Lei wish to thank Professors Jin Feng-jun and Zhang Wen-chang, Institute of Geography, Beijing for their assistance in the preparation of Chapter 6.

Rong Chao-he and Li Wen-yan thank Zhang Xiaoxue and Lu Yongzhong who helped during the preparation of Chapter 3.

Andrew Watson, Harry X. Wu, and Christopher Findlay would like to express their gratitude to the Australian Research Council and the Australian Centre for International Agricultural Research for their support. Parts of this study draw on Wu, Watson, and Findlay, *Economic Decentralisation in China: a Provincial Perspective*, a report prepared for the World Bank, China and Mongolia Operations Division, June 1995.

Preface

The enormous problems facing China are usually discussed in terms of their impacts on the economy as a whole. This book differs. It views China not as a single space but as an assemblage of regions which, in terms of transport and communications, are being linked more closely but in other ways have different agendas.

Chapter 1 points to the interrelatedness of the overwhelming environmental, human, and economic issues facing this country and demonstrates that the path towards a sustainable form of development will be hard to find, and even more difficult to follow. Some of the tensions involved in trying to match national goals with spatial outcomes in a country as large and diverse as China are explored in Chapter 2, and this leads to an analysis in Chapter 3 of the infrastructural challenges posed by the need to provide modern freight and communication linkages between the regions of a country which, not so long ago, gave priority to waterways and regarded railways as being disruptive of the harmony of both man and nature.

Chapters 4 through 7 then examine the problems and potential of the four main economic regions stretching from Heilongjiang in the north-east to Guangdong in the south. They are not an amorphous mass but have characteristics of their own and different potentials. Rural China, too, as Chapter 8 carefully explains, is trying to accommodate and adapt to market reform in different ways in various parts of the country. The final chapter first examines some of the practical issues that will help determine China's direction and then reflects on the two main spatial conundrums facing this country: the seaboard versus the vast interior, and the rise and fall of the coastal areas.

Space restrictions have meant that not all possible topics could be included. Disappointingly, however, a chapter which was to have examined developments in the remote south-west of the country did not materialize.

Some editorial decisions should be explained. First, the Pinyin system of romanization for Chinese words and names (see *Beijing*

Review, 1979, 21(1), 18–20) has been used. Where features are known by an alternative name, such as the Yangtze River, the use of Pinyin has been retained but the alternative has been included in brackets on first usage in each chapter. Second, some of the detail included may seem a little pedantic (e.g. the length of railways and highways), but this has been done deliberately to try to draw attention to the sheer size of the country and the scale of the investment and effort involved in building and upgrading infrastructure. Third, 'ton' is 1,000 kg. Fourth, as sources like the *China Statistical Yearbook* use both yuan (Y) and US$ currencies, this book cites US$ values using the Bank of China rate of exchange for the year concerned: in 1995 and 1996 this was approximately 8.3 yuan to the US dollar.

Contents

Tables

Figures

Contributors

CHEN CAI, BS, Ph.D., is Director of the Northeast Asia Research Center and Professor, Department of Geography, Northeast Normal University, Changchun.

CHRISTOPHER FINDLAY, Ph.D., is Co-Director, Chinese Economies Research Centre, University of Adelaide.

DEAN FORBES, BA, MA, Ph.D., FASSA, is Professor, Department of Geography, Flinders University of South Australia, Adelaide.

LI SHANTONG is Senior Research Fellow, Development Research Centre, State Council of the People's Republic of China.

GODFREY LINGE, B.Sc. (Econ.), Ph.D., FASSA, is Professor, Department of Human Geography, The Australian National University, Canberra.

LI WEN-YAN, B.Sc., is Professor (and Deputy Director 1983–91) of the Institute of Geography, Academia Sinica, Beijing.

LIU YI is Professor and Assistant Deputy Director, Institute of Geography, Academia Sinica, Beijing.

RONG CHAO-HE, M.Ec., Ph.D., is Professor, College of Economics, Northern Jiaotong University, Beijing.

SHE ZHIXIANG, B.Sc., is Professor, Nanjing Branch of Academia Sinica.

NOEL TRACY, BA, is Lecturer, Politics Department, Flinders University of South Australia, Adelaide.

WANG HUIJIONG is Research Professor, Development Research Centre, State Council of the People's Republic of China.

WANG LI, BS, MS, Ph.D., is Vice-Director of the Northeast Asia Institute and Associate Professor, Department of Geography, Northeast Normal University, Changchun.

ANDREW WATSON is Professor and Co-Director, Chinese Economies Research Centre, University of Adelaide.

HARRY X. WU, Ph.D., is Research Fellow, Chinese Economies Research Centre, University of Adelaide.

Xu Guan, M.Sc., is Assistant Professor, Nanjing Institute of Geography and Limnology, Nanjing Branch of Academia Sinica.

Yuan Shu-ren, BS, MS, is Vice-Director of the Northeast Asia Research Center and Professor, Department of Geography, Northeast Normal University, Changchun.

Zhang Lei is Assistant Professor, Institute of Geography, Academia Sinica, Beijing.

1 An Overview: Towards Sustainable Development?

GODFREY LINGE

The People's Republic of China (PRC) is popularly perceived to be an economic superpower, with vast natural resources and a burgeoning consumer market, striding ahead and soon to become by far the largest economy in the world. Such an image was boosted in 1992 by the publicity given to suggestions by the chief economist of the World Bank that China's Gross Domestic Product (GDP) would overtake that of the US by about 2003 (Summers, 1992: 17). Many commentators thought it plausible in view of the single-minded way short-term 'growth' was being given priority—ahead for example of environmental protection which seemed to be regarded as a luxury for rich countries. In reality, China has been running up against a series of significant population, resource, and environmental problems which, in addition to all the other difficulties, are forcing it to examine long-term models of sustainable development—a change of emphasis highlighted in March 1994 when the State Council approved a White Paper on population, environment, and development in the twenty-first century, known as 'China Agenda 21'.

This chapter provides an overview of these and other interlocking bundles of constraints that have implications for China's future growth and, as illustrated in subsequent chapters, its spatial organization. It begins, however, with a cautionary note about the availability and interpretation of the data, not only within China but also by outside commentators. A good illustration is the way that the above-mentioned GDP estimate for China was originally calculated and later re-evaluated. It was based on the Chinese per capita income, using the purchasing power parity (PPP) concept, being 10 per cent of that in the United States, or about US$2,310. However, towards the end of 1996, in an evaluation of poverty in China, the World Bank reduced its estimate to US$1,800 (citing simply 'better data') thus slashing the size of the economy by over 20 per cent (*The Economist*, 12 October 1996: 27). This latter report

also raised the income level below which the Bank deemed a
person in China to be poor to US$1 (Y8.3) from 60 cents per day,
thus by a stroke of a pen raising its estimate of the numbers in
poverty from less than 100 million to more than 300 million.
Arguably, both definitions of poverty may be correct: the lower one
may be a useful guide within China (though it is nearly six times
the official benchmark used there), whereas the US$1 a day figure
may be the more appropriate for international comparisons affected by exchange rate considerations. (Ironically, too, this reminder
that China is less well-off than previously imagined may advantage
its quest to join the World Trade Organization because poorer
countries are under less immediate pressure to liberalize their
trade rules.) Care has to be taken, too, in interpreting published
data, illustrated by the narrow definition of 'unemployment' (discussed below) and the way industrial output (and hence national
growth statistics) are inflated as they include the poor quality,
unsaleable products still being turned out by some state enterprises. In China itself concern about the reliability of data being
provided to government led to amendments to the Statistical Law
in mid-1996 to discourage leaders of areas, departments, and units
from 'abusing power to falsify data' (*Xinhua News Agency*, 22 May
1996). These caveats need to be borne in mind throughout this
book.

Natural Resource and Environmental Constraints

In absolute terms China appears to be rich in a wide range of
natural resources, although the vast reserves cited often include
inferior grades (the average iron grade, for example, is only half
that of internationally traded ore: Michalski et al., 1996: 15). When
considered in per capita terms, however, the picture changes. Thus,
Deng (1995: 30) has noted that China's water resources per head
amount to only 28 per cent of world average; arable land, 32 per
cent; and forested areas, 14 per cent. Making matters worse is the
lack of congruence between resource-consuming and resource-
providing regions. About 64 per cent of the arable land lies north
of the Changjiang (Yangtze) River but the water resources there
amount to only 17 per cent of the national total (Deng, 1995: 30).
Most energy-rich areas lie 1,000 km or more from the core economic regions (Li and Fan, 1993: 71), with some 70 per cent of

the coal resources being in Shanxi and Shaanxi Provinces and Nei Mongol Autonomous Region (AR), over 80 per cent of the oil resources in north-east and north China, and more than 68 per cent of hydro-power potential in the south-west (mainly in Sichuan and Yunnan Provinces) and Xizang AR (Tibet). This, as explained in Chapter 3, places an enormous burden on the transport system which itself, by international standards, is still poorly developed.

Water

China's average per capita water availability is about $2,300 m^3$ but in its nine northern provinces it is only $500 m^3$ (*Xinhua News Agency*, 21 July 1996). Droughts curb grain production by about 20 million tons a year, create recurrent water shortages in cities and widespread rural areas, and restrict hydro-power generating capacity in some regions. One of the worst examples of mismanagement is the Huang He (Yellow) River, the second longest in China: so much water is being stored upstream in hydro-power reservoirs or diverted for irrigation that the last 1,000 km dried up completely for three months in 1995 and five months in 1996. By 2000, claims the Ministry of Water Resources, China will need at least 60,000 million m^3 more water for human and livestock consumption, hydro-power generation, anti-desertification projects, industrial use, and crop irrigation. Of the 64 million hectares of land considered suitable for irrigation only two-thirds have been utilized in this way. Half the nation's 600 medium to large cities are affected by water shortages and 108 are regarded as being 'badly' in need (*Xinhua News Agency*, 21 July 1996). In Beijing, where the average per capita water availability is only $400 m^3$, the local reservoirs cannot keep pace with demand and the overuse of underground water has lowered the water table from 5 m below sea level in 1950 to 50 m below in 1993: the resulting subsidence, occurring over an area of some $2,100 km^2$, is causing major structural faults in buildings and infrastructure. The northern seaport city of Tianjin has a mere $155 m^3$ of water available per capita, while at others along the coast, including Qingdao, Yantai, and Dalian, water usage is restricted, as it is in such large inland cities as Datong, Taiyuan, and Xi'an. Most of these places have water supply projects in train, but questions remain as to whether some of their development plans can be achieved in a sustainable way unless very large investments are forthcoming for projects to channel water from one part of the country to another. As the *China Daily* (10 August 1996: 4) commented: 'the shortage of fresh water is bottlenecking the social and economic development in North-west China, the middle and southern parts of Liaoning Province and coastal areas'.

A great deal can and needs to be done to reduce wastage. The price of water to domestic users is generally so low that there is little incentive to curb consumption or maintain plumbing. Pricing mechanisms are, however, being introduced, as in Shandong Province where the charge for extracted groundwater has been raised to encourage its use exclusively for drinking. Only 20 to 30 per cent of industrial water is recycled compared with 70 to 80 per cent in developed countries where, in any event, factories use five to ten times less water per unit of output than comparable ones in China. The suggestion has been made, too, that plants using large volumes of water for cooling and other purposes could turn instead to seawater if relocated near the coast (see Chapter 6).

Much is being wasted because of pollution, with more than 100 million tons of sewage and dirty waste, 80 per cent untreated, being discharged daily into rivers and lakes (*Xinhua News Agency*, 22 July 1996). Of the 532 rivers monitored by the Ministry of Water Resources, 436 are polluted—some so badly, like the Huaihe (Anhui Province), Songhua (Jilin Province), and Liao (Liaoning Province), that the people living beside them need to drink bottled supplies. Despite the environmental laws and administrative fiats promulgated by the central government since the early 1990s, the situation continued to deteriorate because these were all but ignored by small enterprises and local administrations in pursuit of growth. Then August 1996 saw a more forceful nationwide campaign aimed at closing all the paper-mills, tanneries, coking works, dyeing mills, and other small enterprises polluting rivers: reportedly, 57,000 (80 per cent of those blacklisted) were shut down during the first three months (*Legal Daily*, 26 December 1996). The message, of course, is that local initiative is to be encouraged but not now at any price. The reduction of output and loss of jobs that this entails is unclear, but the financial institutions now faced with the bad debts have received little sympathy from the National Environmental Protection Agency (NEPA) which sees it as a warning to anyone who finances polluting enterprises (Korski, 1996).

Environmental Issues

In the space available here, it is impossible to discuss the many other environmental issues facing China, many of which have been comprehensively considered elsewhere (e.g. World Bank, 1992). Among the more serious are soil erosion, shifting sand, grassland degradation, and air pollution: half the rainfall of Guangdong Province is acid rain, and in the Zhujiang Delta the figure is nearer 90 per cent. All require expensive remedial action even if, in the long-term, net gains may be obtained through increased production and greater efficiency. Moreover, new problems are emerging. Oceanographers have warned that rising sea levels related to global warming could soon affect areas like the Huang He Delta and other parts of the Bohai Sea Rim: the cost of repairing the 'weak and fragile' embankments along China's 18,000-km coastline has alone been put at US$300 million (So, 1996). Significantly, the growing problem of car emissions was pointed up for the first time in the 1995 annual report of NEPA, which noted that these had now become the leading source of winter-time airborne pollution in Beijing and Guangzhou.

Although environment protection has been a national priority since the early 1980s—with 1.5 per cent of GNP (Gross National Product) being set aside for this purpose from 1997 through 2000—the policing of pollution and other legislation has been weak. As Ye Ruqiu, Deputy Director of NEPA, has noted (1996):

for many years, many local governments and departments have been following the traditional development strategy which primarily focused on tremendous resource consumption and extensive economic pattern. Attention was often given to the speed and quantity of development rather than to the efficiency and quality, external production expansion instead of internal production improvement, and natural resource exploitation instead of resource conservation. The industrial structure formed over years of economic development was characterized by the high percentage of industries with high energy and resource consumption. A considerable portion of technologies was still at the level of the 60s and 70s or even earlier.

From this point of view, foreign direct investment (FDI) has proved to be something of a double-edged sword. As anticipated, some overseas investors not only introduced sophisticated manufacturing technology but also modern environmental control and protection systems. Others, noting that China's environmental standards were lower and not as well enforced as in other (mainly developed) countries, saw an opportunity to save on establishment and running costs. Ye Ruqiu (1996) reports that in 1991, of the 11,500 manufacturing enterprises (with a total foreign investment of US$8,770 million), as many as 3,350 (US$3,220 million) were 'heavily polluting' ones.

Population and Employment Constraints

Population

The population has grown from an estimated 550 million when the PRC was formed in 1949 to 1,224 million in December 1996, and is increasing by about 13 million annually. Although the growth rate is slowing, the total is expected to top 1,272 million by 2000 and continue to rise to between 1,500 and 1,600 million by 2050. Since 1949, improvements in nutrition, health care, and living standards have almost doubled life expectancy in 1996 to seventy-one years and, along with the rigorous family-planning programme introduced in 1956 (Hull, 1990), this has moved China from being a high birth-rate and high mortality country to a low birth-rate and low mortality one. The absolute number of people is one problem: the ageing of the population is another.

Since 1990 the rate of increase of people aged over sixty has been triple that of the population as a whole, and the aged are expected to number 132 million by 2000 (about 10 per cent of the population) and 374 million in 2040 (25 per cent) (*Xinhua News Agency*, 19 December 1996). In some places the 'greying' process has become even more marked, as in Shanghai where 15 per cent of the population is already aged sixty or more. Although this ageing phenomenon is occurring in many countries, most had a higher per capita income and a stronger economic base to support the elderly by the time they made up a tenth of the population. Furthermore, not only is China's traditional household caring system being eroded by demographic and social change, but the long-standing cradle-to-grave workplace welfare system is no longer sustainable if state-owned enterprises (SOEs) are to operate competitively without massive government subsidies (see later). As the 10:1 ratio of workers to dependants will change to 4:1 in little more than three decades, several experiments are in hand to try to develop a sustainable social security arrangement. Arguably, a strongly regulated privately funded welfare system would ease the burden on the state (and enable it to concentrate more on the needs of the disadvantaged); it would also provide the basis for a domestic savings infrastructure that would reduce China's dependence on inflows of overseas capital, the demand for which is becoming more competitive globally as countries like India emerge as attractive options for investors.

Various statistics can be quoted to show that the people's quality of life has generally been improving. Thus, the number of rural dwellers living below the official poverty line (set at Y530 in 1995, or about US$64 a year) has declined to 65 million, many of whom are in remote mountainous areas in the central-west; the number of illiterate or semi-literate people has been reduced to 145 million; and considerable efforts are being made to upgrade urban housing standards (as illustrated in Chapter 5 in relation to Shanghai). The other side of the coin is that unemployment rates are growing and income disparities within and between urban and rural areas are increasing.

Unemployment

It is difficult to obtain a clear picture of the unemployment situation. Officially, close to 3 per cent of the 176 million working-age people in urban areas have no job, but this does not include those *xiagang* workers—sometimes half or more of the 'payroll'—who are still on the books of an enterprise but are paid a small living allowance to stay at home. Revealingly, the Central Bank governor admitted in mid-1996 that, over and above the 5 million urban workers who were registered as unemployed, a further 7 million had been sent home by their SOEs; the root cause, he argued, was not tight monetary policy, which has often been blamed, but 'the irrational economic structure and the low efficiency of companies' (Dickie, 1996b). Indeed, some estimates suggest that 15 per cent of state workers could be sacked with virtually no impact on production and that, if these and the unregistered unemployed are taken into account, the real level of urban unemployment may be closer to 20 per cent. The picture about employment and income levels is further muddied because of the extent of 'moonlighting' by residents and the large numbers of migrants from rural areas who are working illegally as labourers or in other unskilled jobs.

Until recently, the non-urban population tended to be categorized simply as 'farmers' or 'peasants', but new estimates suggest that, of the 460 million in the countryside labour force, 250 million are farmers and 100 million work in township and village enterprises (TVEs) (*Xinhua News Agency*, 23 December 1996). The remainder are migrant workers, nine-tenths of them young and unmarried, seeking jobs in urban areas, initially within their own province but later moving further afield and, in particular, to the larger coastal cities. Exact numbers are not known. The government adheres to a figure of 80 million, but plausible estimates put the real total for 1996 at between 120 million and 140 million. Officially it has been admitted that by 2000 the rural labour force becoming surplus—mainly by the introduction of more efficient farming methods and the loss of farm land to urban uses and encroaching deserts—will probably reach 140 million (*Zhongguo Xinwen She News Agency*, 11 October 1996).

In effect, China is caught between the blades of several pairs of scissors. Even to hold the official urban unemployment rate at around 4 per cent, 40 million new jobs will need to be created by the end of 2000 to keep pace with the numbers of school leavers entering the labour market and at least 14 million (and probably many more) workers who need to be transferred from SOEs to enable them to restructure their operations, eliminate their cradle-to-grave social obligations, and compete with joint ventures (JVs) and TVEs using modern technology. In places like Shanghai, where SOEs in traditional industries (like textiles) are the first to be closed or restructured, the workers made redundant (especially women) tend to be older and less well-educated so cannot easily transfer to the new high-tech and information-orientated industries being sought by government. The influx of rural migrants compounds the problem, although without their readiness to do jobs not wanted by the increasingly sophisticated residents, the burgeoning cities would be even less able to cope with the development pressures upon them.

Faced with these mounting urban unemployment problems, the government is trying to find ways of circumventing an influx there of the additional 40 million or more rural labourers who will become surplus by 2000. Fostering development in the Central and Western Regions (Figure 1.1) has long been a goal espoused by the central government but, as is made clear in Chapter 2, it has been made a centrepiece of the Ninth Five Year Plan (1996–2000). The

Figure 1.1: The threefold division of China introduced in 1986 as part of the Seventh Five Year Plan.

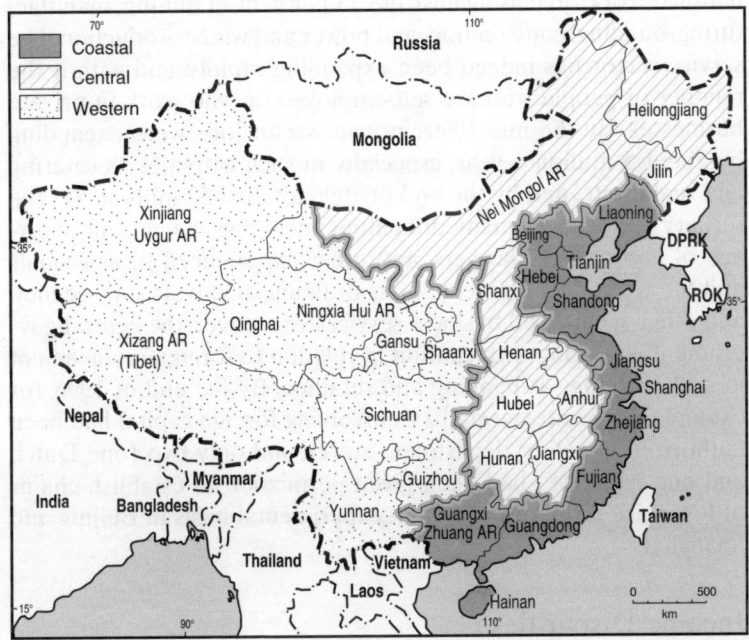

Source: based on Linge and Forbes, 1990b: 11.

opening up of natural resources, the provision of infrastructure, and the encouragement of industry based on local raw materials (such as by transferring 500,000 cotton spindles from the coastal areas to Xinjiang Uygur AR) will in due course improve living standards and increase and diversify job opportunities. Yet, quicker and more decisive action is clearly needed. Thus, by 2000 the Ministry of Construction intends to relocate 30 million of the surplus rural labourers to small country towns where it will create jobs upgrading housing and building public health, education, and cultural facilities. If this ambitious scheme succeeds, it would help boost the population of China's 50,000 small towns to 200 million and give the 10,000 places to be selected for 'priority treatment' a chance to become more economically viable (*China Daily*, 16 December 1996). There are also ongoing government-subsidized projects ranging from the reclamation of wasteland to the operation of vocational schools and skilling programmes.

The main source of new jobs is likely to be the service sector, which at the end of 1996 employed 24.8 per cent of the 691 million national workforce as against the 23 per cent in mining, manufacturing, building, construction, and power and water production. The service sector has indeed been expanding rapidly, and with it the number of people who are self-employed or who work in private businesses. By the mid-1990s, private sector jobs were expanding by about 5 million a year, especially in such activities as catering and real estate, and by the end of 1996 totalled 52 million. Yet the tertiary sector faces many difficulties, including the chronic shortage of accountants, lawyers, and other experienced professionals and the weak development so far of financial, advertising, agency, and other specialized business services. Moreover, the central government is moving with caution in relation to foreign involvement in such activities as banking and retailing. By the end of 1996, for example, only sixteen retail JVs involving foreign capital had been authorized to set up department stores, and only two (one Dutch and one Japanese) had been given permission to establish chains of low-price retail outlets on an experimental basis in Beijing and Shanghai.

Income Disparities

The growing disparity between the per capita incomes of urban and rural dwellers, and the social tensions this creates, have long been of concern to the central government, but detailed discussion is deferred to Chapter 2 because this problem continues to dominate China's approach to regional planning and development strategies. In fact, such simple comparisons now have little meaning, not least because of the growing disparity in urban incomes. A State Statistical Bureau survey of thirty-five main cities published in October 1996 (Roell, 1996) showed that half the urban households had annual incomes of between Y10,000 and Y20,000 (41 per cent received less and 9 per cent more), and that the incomes of as many as 40 per cent of them had been declining in real terms during the previous year. Although the average per capita urban income was Y3,250, many households, pensioners, and workers in SOEs were reportedly 'facing difficulties'—hardly surprising in view of the incidence of urban unemployment and under-employment.

Given the range of climate, topography, soils, and other physical conditions, it is not surprising that the per capita incomes of peasant farmers have long varied markedly between different parts of the country. In addition, as Watson, Wu, and Findlay stress in Chapter 8, rural China embraces many different organizational structures and practices. Hence, the practice of quoting per capita averages for the Coastal, Central, and Western Regions (actually Y1,350, Y1,120, and Y810 in 1995) has little utility. The income of farmers in rural Shanghai averaged Y3,595 in 1996, whereas a farmer out west in Guizhou Province would be lucky to receive a fifth of that amount. Even within the more economically advanced parts of the country some farmers are benefiting from the new industrial-urban development pulses, whereas those more distant from them still lack even sealed roads. Jiangsu Province, regarded as one of richest in China, has earmarked some of its budget for infrastructure and industrial projects in its twenty-seven northern counties which remain economically backward (*China Daily*, 9 March 1995). Differences are emerging at even smaller geographical scales. In 1994, farmers around places like Suzhou, Wuxi, and Changzhou in Jiangsu Province earned 65 per cent more per head than those elsewhere in its riverine region (*Xinhua News Agency*, 12 May 1995). Moreover, income figures have to be set against outgoings—including the levies, taxes, and fees imposed not only by local administrations but often also by petty rural officials all too eager to line their own pockets (Lam, 1997)—and the presence or absence of education, health, and other amenities that count towards living standards.

The central government has been giving agriculture greater priority because of longer-term concerns about possible future food shortages and the more immediate need to stabilize—even raise—rural incomes to try to ensure that farmers continue to grow grain rather than turning to more lucrative cash crops. Following another record harvest in 1996 (480 million tons), growers have been assured that grain prices will not again be allowed to fall as they did after the 1995 bumper harvest (466 million tons): 'we must tighten grain purchasing and make sure the peasants will have higher income as a result of higher output so as to preserve their enthusiasm to develop agricultural production', Vice Premier Zhu Rongji said in January 1997 (*Xinhua News Agency*, 9 January 1997). A couple of months earlier he had spelled out the government's priorities: the higher prices of cotton and grain, and higher energy and transport costs 'represent a transfer of profits from the industrial sector to the agricultural and other sectors' (Kwang, 1996).

State-owned Enterprises

Zhu's statement was a clear warning that the central government was no longer prepared to be a milch cow propping up loss-making SOEs, the problems of which form a recurrent theme through this book. When the shortage economy became a market environment governed increasingly by supply and demand, the SOEs simply lacked the experience necessary to adapt to the new circumstances brought about by the changing needs of a more liberalized domestic market and competition from foreign multinationals. Many simply continued 'blind production'—turning out goods without specific orders—so that products with a notional value of US$80,000 million that no one wants have continued to pile up in warehouses (*Nikkan Kogyo Shimbun*, 21 January 1997: 5). Lack of cash flow led to inter-enterprise chains of unpaid accounts and this, in turn, caused them to use bank loans to cover current outlays such as wages rather than purchases of the up-to-date equipment needed to break the vicious circle. As explained earlier, they were also saddled with surplus labour and with small armies of ex-employees and their dependants to whom they owe 'social responsibility' dating back in some instances to the 1950s.

The SOEs are engaged in a wide range of activities—manufacturing, coal mining, and trading, for example—and the larger ones form the core of the economic system. Of the 380,000 or so SOEs, less than 15 per cent are large and medium-size firms, but these account for 82 per cent of the total assets. The number involved in mining and manufacturing activities declined from about 95,000 in 1985 to 80,000 in 1996 and their share of the gross output value of industry during this period fell from 65 to 32 per cent. More revealingly, the number of people employed by this group of SOEs declined from 56 million in 1985 to 44 million in 1990 and—despite rationalization attempts—remained at this same level in 1995 (State Statistical Bureau, 1996a: 402).

In October 1996, total SOE indebtedness—including bad bank loans and inter-industry triangular debts—amounted to US$410,000 million. During 1996 about 44 per cent of the SOEs accumulated losses totalling US$7,420 million (despite cuts in interest rates on their accumulated bank loans), a year-on-year rise of 20 per cent (Korski, 1997). This situation was being exacerbated as the government raised rail freight charges and the artificially low prices of inputs like coal, cotton, and grain to reflect their real production costs. This deteriorating situation, along with criticism that the agricultural and industrial sectors are being allowed to get out of balance, is forcing the government to harden its resolve, tackle the SOE issue more firmly, and allow only the survival of the fittest.

Such a stance has become more possible because a series of experiments in selected cities, sectors, and enterprises since about 1993 has led to a better understanding of the financial, employment, and other ramifications involved. Thus, as part of a wider progamme to improve the efficiency of its SOE sector (outlined in Chapter 5), the Shanghai Municipal administration has been closing textile plants since the early 1990s and trying to find ways of coping with the employment and other needs of the 300,000 people made redundant. The older heavy industry SOEs are only one side of the problem; there are also many medium and small provincial enterprises left over from the Mao era of central planning. Almost every province has small factories making similar products, such as domestic appliances and televisions, with cross-border competition sometimes being prevented by restrictions on the sale of 'foreign' brands.

The solutions are complicated by the ideological importance attached to state ownership of the means of production. The goal, encapsulated in the slogan 'seize the large and release the small', is for the state to maintain tight control of perhaps 10,000 key enterprises while shedding responsibility for the others in ways that minimize social dislocation. Thus, Premier Li Peng disclosed in October 1996 that the central government would no longer provide financial support for enterprises owned by provincial, city, and prefectural governments. Rather, its immediate priorities are to increase the number of pilot enterprise groups from the 57 that existed at the end of 1996 to about 120, and sort out the affairs of the 1,000 or so key enterprises. This is no small task as many have scores of productive and non-productive subsidiaries, often at scattered locations.

All this, however, requires concomitant changes to administrative, legal, social, and financial structures and practices, an example being the setting up of separate policy banks to make loans to the key state sectors so that the other financial institutions can be empowered to extend loans to SOEs only on commercial terms. The previous practice of lending based on policy decisions made the banks little more than conduits for pumping funds into state firms regardless of their prospects. The 90,000 or so small and medium-size industrial SOEs are now having to confront more starkly such possibilities as selling to their workers or outside investors, sale by auction, mergers, take-overs, leasing, transformation into stockholding co-operatives, or bankruptcy. This latter option is becoming less easy as the banks are now fighting creditors who ignore bankruptcy rules and use various devices to try to walk away from their debts (Mu, 1996).

To encourage mergers and take-overs, Zhu Rongji has indicated that the new owners would not be required to pay off outstanding debts until after five years, during which interest payments would be waived (*Xinhua News Agency*, 14 January 1997). The state banks will thus have to continue shouldering the burden, and this in turn may hinder progress on much-needed banking reforms. Importantly, too, the new owners will not be compelled to take over the social responsibilities of the enterprises they acquire as this obligation will be assumed by local governments and their various re-employment projects, even though these in many cases are still at an embryo experimental stage.

Adding to the problem of SOE reform are the defence-related plants that, as explained in Chapter 2, were set up during the 1966–75 period in remote inland areas (Figure 2.2), and now form part of the loose network of perhaps 20,000 companies—involved in activities ranging from telecommunications to massage parlours—developed by the People's Liberation Army (PLA) since the early 1980s. Profits from these commercial activities helped to make up for the 40 per cent reduction (in real terms) in the PLA budget between 1978 and 1989, and since then for the effects of inflation. Considerable efforts have been made to refocus the production of the ordnance factories from military to civilian needs but with varying success because of their remoteness, conservative management style, and increasing competition from foreign JVs and TVEs. Their importance for this analysis is that they have provided development nodes away from the Coastal Region, as is the case with most of the 40 factories and 140,000 civilian employees of the PLA's Xinxing (New Prosperity) Group—making clothes, electronics, pharmaceuticals, petrochemicals, textiles, vehicles,

Figure 1.2: Regional boundaries as defined for this book. Liaoning Province has been cross-hatched because, as discussed in Chapter 7, some analysts prefer to include it as part of the North-East while others believe it should be considered as a component of the Bohai Sea Rim.

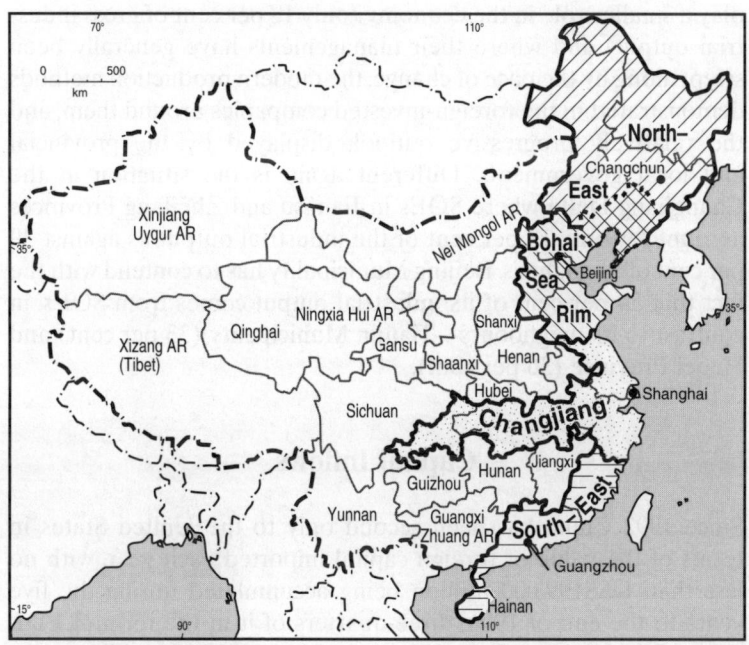

Source: author's compilation

shoes and steel products (O'Neill, 1996a). Or again, 80 per cent of the total output of the High and New-Tech Development Zone at Xiangfan in the north of Hubei Province comes from converted military plants (*BBC Monitoring Service*, 5 November 1996). They have also attracted foreign capital to inland locations, as in Guizhou Province where fifty-five relatively small-scale JVs have been established by Japanese, South Korean, German, and Hong Kong firms to make electronics, machinery, and motor vehicle parts.

As is demonstrated in several chapters in this book, the extent and nature of SOE activities have been, and remain, a significant influence on the prosperity and potential of urban and regional economies. Thus, in the North-East (Figure 1.2), where they contributed 52 per cent of total gross industrial output in 1995, they have had a particularly depressing effect because of their domination of the local economy, their continuing resistance to change, and the massive impacts that any adjustments they do make have on employment levels. This contrasts with the South-East where they play a smaller role in the economy (only 18 per cent of gross industrial output) and where their managements have generally been swept along by the pace of change, the modern production methods demonstrated in the foreign-invested companies around them, and the relatively progressive outlook displayed by the provincial and local governments. Different again is the situation in the Changjiang Delta where SOEs in Jiangsu and Zhejiang Provinces account for only 18 per cent of the industrial output as against 39 per cent of Shanghai's. Beijing Municipality has to contend with the fact that 54 per cent of its industrial output comes from SOEs, in contrast to its neighbours—Tianjin Municipality (33 per cent) and Hebei Province (36 per cent).

Capital Inflows

Since 1992 China has been second only to the United States in terms of the value of foreign capital imported each year, with no less than US$199,000 million being accumulated during the five years to the end of 1996, three-quarters of it in the form of FDI. Of the US$55,000 million utilized in 1996, US$13,000 million came in the form of overseas loans which were used for infrastructure facilities and basic industries, with special emphasis being given to the Central and Western Regions.

Following Deng Xiaoping's advocacy in 1991–92 of further economic liberalization and even greater opening up to the outside world, the inflow of utilized FDI jumped from an annual average of US$3,600 million in the four years 1988 through 1991, to US$11,000 million in 1992, and an average of US$35,000 million for each of the next four years. The 1997 figure is expected to be about US$40,000 million. Impressive though these figures are, on a per capita basis they amounted in 1995 to a mere US$32, far below Malaysia's per capita FDI intake of US$297 and less even than Thailand's US$39 (Lu, 1996c).

By the end of 1996, 17 million people (10 per cent of the urban workforce) were employed by the 140,000 overseas-funded enterprises that had become operational (*Xinhua News Agency*, 17

Table 1.1: Foreign capital in registered enterprises by main regions, percentage of total China, and average value of investment per enterprise, 1995

Region	Number of enterprises (per cent)	Foreign direct investment (per cent)	Average value of investment per enterprise (US$000)
North-East[a]	8.0	8.3	801
Bohai Sea Rim[b]	18.0	13.5	823
Shanghai Mun.	6.2	9.1	1,608
Changjiang Delta[c]	4.6	10.3	777
Changjiang Valley[d]	6.4	4.8	830
South-East[e]	36.3	47.3	1,434
Other[f]	10.5	9.1	960
Total China	100.0	100.0	1,099

[a] Liaoning, Jilin, and Heilongjiang Provinces.
[b] Beijing and Tianjin Municipalities, Hebei and Shandong Provinces.
[c] Jiangsu and Zhejiang Provinces.
[d] Anhui, Hubei, Hunan, and Jiangxi Provinces.
[e] Guangdong, Fujian, and Hainan Provinces.
[f] The Central and Western Regions (see Figure 1.1).

Source: State Statistical Bureau, 1996a: 601.

January 1997). Although the data are rather imprecise, most of the FDI seems to have been used in the industrial and mining sector (46 per cent in 1993, 68 per cent in 1995), and in real estate, hotels, and tourism (39 per cent in 1993, 19 per cent in 1995). There is some uncertainty, too, about the actual origin of FDI, some three-fifths of which comes through various channels from the 55 million-strong Overseas Chinese diaspora in Hong Kong, Taiwan, Singapore, and other South-East Asian countries. As Tracy notes in Chapter 4, much of this has been invested on the basis of *guanxi* (connections), especially family ones in Guangdong and Fujian Provinces which were the destinations for nearly half the FDI in 1995 (Table 1.1). Another element—unmeasurable but believed to be significant—is the flow of 'black' money being recycled back to the mainland to gain tax and other advantages. Apart from these movements from and through Hong Kong, the largest investors are the United States, Taiwan, and Japan, but Singapore and South Korea are now showing an awakening interest in specific projects, especially in the Changjiang Delta and Bohai Sea Rim areas, which are illustrated later in this book. Despite the attempts by government to encourage overseas investors to consider inland locations, the three Municipalities of Beijing, Tianjin, and Shanghai and the nine provinces making up the Coastal Region (Figure 1.1) attracted some 87 per cent of the FDI during each of the years from 1992 through 1995.

The 'quality' and 'longevity' of FDI have generally been given only limited attention by commentators, yet there are discernible differences even within regions. The eastern and western sides of the Zhujiang (Pearl) River Delta provide a good illustration. After 1984, the eastern side became increasingly attractive to Hong Kong investors seeking cheap land and labour as the corridor from Shenzhen to Guangzhou was opened up alongside the existing railway. Many of the businesses were small and footloose and, being motivated by quick profits, fitted in well with the short-term horizons of the rural towns and villages. In contrast, development in the west was slowed by the more difficult terrain and, in particular, the lack of bridges across the many south-flowing tributaries of the Zhujiang River. The western side already had many large cities which, being more familiar with modern development, had a longer time-horizon and sought foreign investment for quality rather than quantity (Economist Intelligence Unit, 1995).

In 1996, however, investors and the Chinese authorities both began to adopt new approaches to FDI. Much of the industrial investment until then had been aimed at reducing costs to make competitive exports, and this is borne out by the fact that foreign-invested enterprises (FIEs) accounted for 43 per cent of China's exports in 1996 and 47 per cent of the country's total trade. South Korean and Japanese firms setting up plants at places like Dalian in Liaoning Province, stress that the availability of cheap labour near their home markets was, and for the moment remains, the chief attraction. There is plenty of evidence, too, that smaller investors in south China cut corners by erecting premises and installing machinery with little concern for the health and safety of workers or environmental standards. However, wages and other costs have been rising, labour has become less docile, all manner of regulatory codes have been established and more actively enforced, and export platforms elsewhere in the Asian region (such as India and Indonesia) have become more attractive.

For its part, the central government is becoming more selective about the uses to which FDI should be put and the sorts of firms it wants to see operating in China as part of its drive to replace the fixation about quantity with the goals of quality and efficiency. Guidelines published in June 1995 listed the kinds of projects in which FDI would variously be encouraged, permitted, restricted, or banned, and these lists were subsequently further refined by the individual industry ministries. In general, there has been a move away from geographically focused inducements (other than in the inland areas) in favour of promoting key sectors that will help drive the economy without destabilizing it, such as agriculture, petro-chemicals, electronics and other high-tech industries, and environ-mental protection technology.

FIEs are also now expected to fit in with the government's aim of developing 'pillar' industries, although this is not without its casualties. From mid-1995 the design and production of a 'People's Car' was promoted as one such industry and was used to spearhead moves to restructure each of the leading manufacturing sectors into a handful of enterprise groups that would co-ordinate the activities of hundreds of factories scattered around the country. The car plan, however, was based on hopelessly optimistic assessments of the potential market (see Chapter 3), and by September 1996 had been quietly relegated in favour of housing reform. This was considered a more appropriate pillar because it could simultaneously achieve several objectives: lower the very high level of individual savings deposits (US$427,000 million by mid-1996 and growing rapidly); reduce the considerable stock of vacant residential accommodation in some cities; enable per capita urban living space to be increased from $7.9\,m^2$ to $9\,m^2$; and provide unskilled jobs.

FIEs pose a challenge. On the one side, 1996 saw people trying to sheet home the blame for the poor performance of SOEs and a growing number of TVEs to the preferential treatment afforded the FIEs and the unfair competition it created as their products in some instances were now dominating the domestic market. More-over, for some ideologues, the willingness of foreign companies to accept short-term losses in the hope of long-term profits smacked of predatory capitalism. On the other, the government is looking to overseas investors to help upgrade technology in the larger SOEs and take some of the smaller ones off its hands through mergers and acquisitions; wants to attract more large multination-als with proven records and longer-term investment horizons; and is on the brink of allowing foreign businesses to play a greater role in fields where they have been more or less restricted, such as mining, banking, retailing, and insurance. Some steps have already been taken to level the playing field by phasing out duty-free imports of capital goods; equalizing corporate income tax rates (which have been 55 per cent for domestic enterprises as against 33 per cent for FIEs); unifying transport, power, and other charges; and setting aside special arrangements, as in the brewing and chemical industries, that favoured FIEs.

China, which has been attracting about one-third of the world's FDI in recent years cannot assume, however, that funds will continue to be readily available. Its very success has led other developing countries in the region to respond by reforming their own financial systems to boost their chances of attracting capital, especially for infrastructure projects, the demand for which in East Asia alone is likely to exceed US$150,000 million annually over the next decade. China also faces the particular problem that it has already received some US$19,000 million in loans from the World Bank to say nothing of a further US$9,000 million through the Bank's 'soft' loan programme operated by the International Development Agency. At its current rate of borrowing—about US$3,000 million a year—it may, within three or four years, come up against the Bank's rule that no country may account, over a length of time, for more than 10 per cent of its total lending (*The Economist*, 13 July 1996: 26). The Bank is China's largest single source of foreign capital and, in terms of annual commitments, this country is also the Bank's largest customer. Although compromise arrangements may be possible, China might be forced to trim its development plans unless it can find the US$80,000 million or more that it needs each year from other sources—including, very importantly, domestic savings. Its power-generation programme alone, for example, depends on some US$20,000 million being available from outside sources during the Ninth Five Year Plan.

This potential shortfall has led the government to move towards allowing greater foreign involvement in infrastructural projects, particularly by expanding the use of the 'build, operate, transfer' (BOT) system whereby foreign investors are allowed to build projects and operate them for a specific period, after which ownership is returned to the host country. Previously this system had only been used by a few joint ventures—such as between Guangdong Province and Hopewell Holdings Ltd to build the Shenzhen–Guangzhou expressway—but had proved unsatisfactory because of unclear rules, inadequate property laws, and poor returns for the foreign partner as only 'artificially low' tolls were allowed on roads and bridges (Dalton, 1995). Lengthy negotiations led to a more precise set of guidelines and formed the basis of the first completely foreign-financed BOT deal in November 1996, a US$590 million agreement with the French utility company Electricité de France and GEC-Alsthom CN to expand the Laibin B power station in Guangxi Zhuang AR. Similar arrangements for highway, bridge, and water supply projects are being made on a trial basis.

Town and Village Enterprises

TVEs, which are discussed at several points in this book, are usually collectives owned by towns and villages to run everything from coal-mines to plastic flower factories (see Chapter 8). Discussion of their rise and role has been postponed to Chapter 5 because of the particularly significant part they played in the industrial development of the Changjiang Delta during the 1980s. There were about 22 million of them in 1995 producing roughly one-third of the country's industrial output and the same proportion of its exports (*Xinhua News Agency*, 12 February 1996). They are usually, as the name suggests, fairly small but about 5,000 of them have turnovers exceeding US$10 million; they have also set up over 1,000 businesses overseas with an investment of US$3,000 million. As indicated earlier, TVEs employ about 100 million people and have thus made a very important contribution to the problem of absorbing surplus rural labour. All these are positives, but the other side of the coin brings this chapter round full circle because these TVEs are a leading source of air and water pollution. Yet every 1,000 TVEs that are shut down add another 5,000 people to the army of unemployed already searching for work. As this chapter has shown several times, the authorities in China seem unable to win whichever way they turn.

2 Regional Planning: Developing an Indigenous Framework

WANG HUIJIONG, LI SHANTONG, AND GODFREY LINGE

Until 1979 the spatial economy of China was largely in the hands of central government ministries which directly controlled most of the larger enterprises, as well as the more significant agricultural and industrial inputs and outputs. These ministries tended to pursue their own particular goals without much co-ordination, either between themselves or with the provinces which, for the most part, lacked the financial resources to do much more than follow instructions from above. There were, in addition, central edicts covering the sale and distribution of some key commodities, the mobility and remuneration of workers, and the allocation of industrial investment in favour of producer rather than consumer goods. The State Planning Commission had an important co-ordinating role, but the sheer size of this geographically diverse country, and the growing complexity and heterogeneity of the economy made it increasingly difficult for the central government to maintain firm control. Even though none of the Five Year Plans from 1953 to 1980 said much specifically about regional planning, the end result of a changing mix of political, economic, social, and military strategies was a small improvement in the level of inland development.

Then, with the launch of the reform programme in the late 1970s, the emphasis began to shift towards growth-orientated regional strategies and the impacts of the mounting competition between the provinces and the local government areas within them. This rivalry was fostered by the increasing decentralization of control over matters that affected regional development—especially revenue raising and spending—and the possibilities that arose to influence the locational decisions of the incoming wave of foreign investors. By the early 1990s this opportunistic scramble, along with the side effects of various central government pricing and other controls, had led to widening economic and social disparities between (and within) coastal and inland areas. Several of the strategies included in the Ninth Five Year Plan (1996–

2000) are aimed at alleviating the resulting social and political tensions.

The Period from 1949 to 1978

Each of several episodes during these three decades left a distinct imprint on the spatial economy of China, thus contributing both to the problems and the opportunities now facing regional planners.

Phase 1: 1949 to 1958

Economic activity in 1949 was largely concentrated in a few coastal areas. About half the country's industrial output was produced in six regions: the Zhujiang (Pearl) River Delta around Guangzhou; the Changjiang (Yangtze) River Delta centred on Shanghai; Qingdao–Jinan in Shandong Province; the Beijing–Tianjin–Tang-shan triangle; and central and south Liaoning Province. Inland areas remained backward, with only a few places—like Nanjing, Wuhan, and Chongqing—being economically significant (Chen and Zhu, 1995: 43).

After three years of economic rehabilitation, the incoming government sought to redress this imbalance by opening coal-mines; thermal and hydro-power stations; and iron and steel, non-ferrous metal, chemical, and other plants near raw material and energy sources. The aim was to reduce transport costs by processing the raw materials *in situ*, thereby also opening up inland mineral deposits, while at the same time reducing the vulnerability of the economy in the event of a sea-borne invasion. In the event, only 5 of the 156 major projects undertaken with outside technology and financial assistance (mainly from the Soviet Union) during the First Five Year Plan period (1953–57) were located along the eastern seaboard. As Figure 2.1 indicates, most were built in the north-east (56), north-west (33), and north (27). Similarly, 472 of the 694 important domestically designed industrial projects initiated during the 1950s were also located away from the coast. More than 56 per cent of the total capital investment in major state-owned enterprises (SOEs) during this plan period was channelled into the hitherto neglected inland areas (Development Research Centre, 1994: 34).

Of particular importance from the present point of view was the

Figure 2.1: Location of the major civil projects initiated during the First Five Year Plan (1953–57). The remainder of the 156 projects were defence-related and their locations are uncertain.

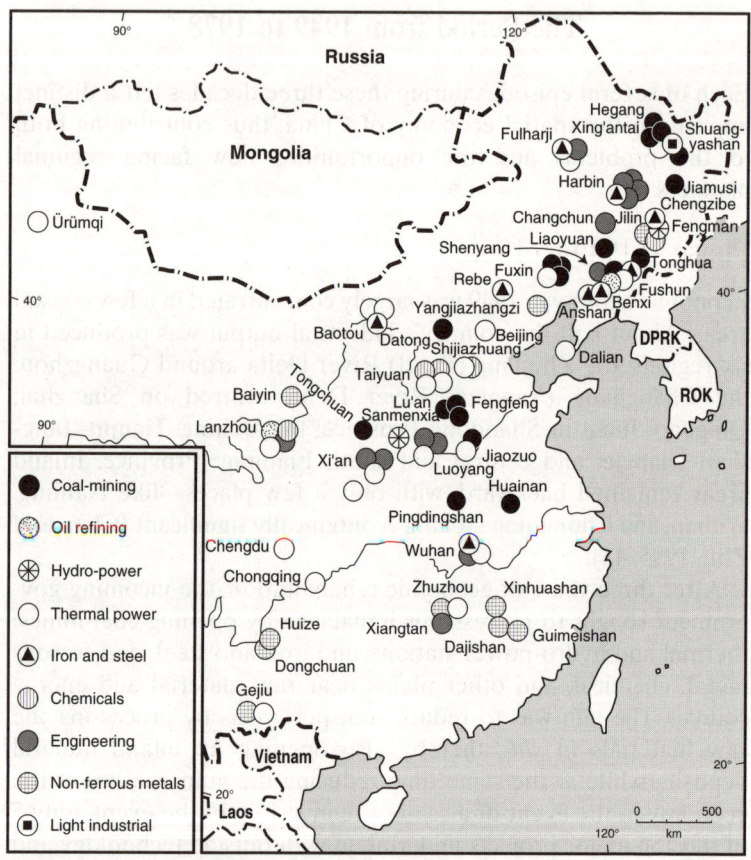

Source: authors' compilation.

re-establishment and reinforcement of heavy industry in Liaoning, Jilin, and Heilongjiang Provinces along the Dongbei Plain from Anshan in the south to Qiqihar in the north, an area which had become known during the 1930s as the 'Ruhr of China' (see Chapter 7). This already had a substantial urban infrastructure, actual and potential sources of energy, and a well-developed railway system with connections across the border to the Trans-Siberian Railway. Although the north-east benefited significantly from this early rush of investment—much of it focused around the

Anshan Iron and Steel complex—it has suffered since the mid-1980s because of the high concentration there of large heavy industry SOEs, many of which are now technologically out of date, inefficient, and unprofitable.

Phase 2: 1958 to 1963

During the period of the 'Great Leap Forward' from 1958 through 1960, an attempt was made to reform the economic system by enlarging the powers of the localities which were given control of nearly 90 per cent of the centrally owned enterprises, including many of the backbone heavy industry plants (Gao, 1984: 243). In an ill-considered attempt to make each region industrially and economically self-sufficient, more than 200,000 large, medium, and small projects were set up throughout the country irrespective of whether the resources were available or the locations appropriate. Twenty-eight of the provinces, for example, established their own iron and steel plants when only twelve had adequate iron ore resources, and countless towns and villages responded to the Great Smelting Iron and Steel Programme by digging small coal-mines and building blast furnaces—most of which produced unusable rubbish.

Then followed a period of 'readjustment, consolidation, strengthening and improvement' to correct the 'Leftist mistakes', during which the powers given to localities to control enterprises and other activities were retracted with the aim of strengthening the central management of the national economy. Many construction projects were stopped or suspended; most of the small indigenous enterprises were closed; 25 million workers were persuaded to go back to the countryside; and forty places lost their newly acquired urban status. None the less, several important industrial enterprises, such as the Baotou Iron and Steel Company (Nei Mongol AR), date from this period which also saw further development of the railway system away from the coastal fringe—notably the extension of lines from Lanzhou to Qinghai in 1959, and to Ürümqi in 1962 (Li, 1988: 102).

Phase 3: 1964 to 1975

From the mid-1960s through the mid-1970s the aim of national regional strategy changed from a 'balanced' to a 'strategic' distribution. In response to deteriorating relations with the Soviet

Figure 2.2: Approximate boundary of the 'Third-Line' region.

Source: authors' compilation.

Union, which had soured in 1960, and fears about a US-led invasion along the seaboard, a 'Third-Line' area (sometimes called the 'Third Front' or 'Defensive Heartland') was created in the remote mountainous hinterland where defence facilities could be hidden, sometimes even in caves (Figure 2.2). This operation spanned two planning periods.

Emphasis during the Third Five Year Plan (1966–70) was on projects in the south-west, such as the Chengdu–Kunming, Guiyang–Kunming, and Xiangfan–Chongqing railways; iron and steel bases at Panzhihua and Wuhan; twelve mining areas in Guizhou Province; hydroelectric power stations at Yingxiuwan and Gongzhu (Sichuan Province); thermal power stations at Jiajiang (Sichuan) and Qinshan (Hubei); and several heavy machinery and chemical plants (Chen, 1994: 11). Defence-related investment continued in the south-west during the Fourth Five Year Plan (1971–75), but more stress was put on projects in the western parts of Henan, Hubei, and Hunan Provinces. During these two planning periods at least half of all state investment was absorbed by the eleven provinces involved in the Third-Line programme (Naughton, 1988; Li, 1995a: 53–6).

By the mid-1970s some 16 million people were employed in the 29,000 Third-Line enterprises (including 600 of the country's 1,500 largest industrial plants) that had been set up at forty-five new industrial bases serviced by an array of infrastructure created more or less from scratch. Yet, despite the impressive scale of this operation, the planning, construction, and management of enterprises in the various industrial sectors were in the hands of several central ministries without, it seems, much co-ordination, so that many establishments operated at considerably less than capacity (and sometimes hardly at all) because of their remoteness, inaccessibility, or lack of an adequate power supply. The overall inefficiency is indicated by the fact that in 1975 the capital assets of the SOEs in this Third-Line region amounted to 35 per cent of the national total yet they contributed only 25 per cent of the country's industrial output value (Li, 1995a: 56).

This episode left several legacies. It gave considerable impetus to existing inland cities such as Chongqing which became the centre of a machine tool industry—adding 250,000 to its population of 2.2 million during the ten years to 1975. It also led to the creation of a score or more new urban centres, like Panzhihua which grew almost from scratch to a city of 430,000 based on the iron and steel works that began operating in 1970–71. Yet the indiscriminate location of chemical, metallurgical, and other heavy industry plants in topographically and climatically inappropriate situations has created continuing air and water pollution problems, one of the worst examples being Changshou, on the Changjiang River, which has 5 of the country's 300 most polluting enterprises. It also diverted funds that might otherwise have been used to upgrade some of the basic infrastructure in and between the coastal cities to create a better operating environment for the technologically more advanced industries (like the mass production of televisions) that were starting there. The net result of the these inland-orientated development strategies was a loss of economic efficiency, reflected in the deteriorating rate of growth of gross industrial output from

18 per cent annually during the 1953–57 period to 12 per cent (1966–70) and then to 9 per cent (1971–75).

Another significant continuing legacy is that possibly 55 per cent of the country's defence factories are still located in the former Third-Line area. In the late 1980s these accounted for between one-third and one-half of the industrial output of Sichuan Province, while in 1993 more than 130 defence-related enterprises and research institutes remained in Shaanxi Province where they employed 370,000 people (Economist Intelligence Unit, 1996). Considerable efforts have been made to convert some of these factories into civilian production, but the ageing plant and equipment and the distance from the coastal consumer markets have made this a difficult process, as is indicated by the announcement in July 1992 of a programme under which US$1,000 million would be spent well beyond 2000 to help Third-Line enterprises 'skip to the coast'.

The Fourth Five Year Plan also saw the division of China into ten 'economic cooperation' zones which were required 'to gradually establish their own industrial and economic systems with both different levels and characteristics and mutualities' (Chen, 1994: 12). In addition, the provinces, municipalities, and autonomous regions were each expected to develop their own 'Small Third-Line' (xiao sanxian) systems by further encouraging the development of coal-mines and small iron and steel, non-ferrous metal, chemical fertilizer, engineering, and cement works able to support agriculture in the event of an emergency. These factories 'made a dramatic sight among the rice fields' (Naughton, 1995: 145), but they did not absorb rural labour and were not organically connected to the rural economy; they did, however, make local cadres more familiar with industrial activities.

Phase 4: 1976 to 1978

After the death of Mao Zedong in 1976, the spatial focus of state investment began to return to the coastal fringe where much of the infrastructure needed renovation and updating to meet the demands of the more advanced forms of manufacturing. Under a ten-year development plan, originally drawn up in 1975 but deferred until after the political chaos of 1976 (Naughton, 1995: 67), stress was again put on heavy industry, using turnkey plants purchased overseas. Most of the seventeen plants imported before this over-ambitious development plan was abandoned in 1979 were set up along the coast or in nearby cities. Among them were the Baoshan Iron and Steel Complex at Shanghai which eventually came into operation in 1985 with a capacity of 6 million tons, and projects in the Changjiang Delta like the Jinling Petrochemical Complex near Nanjing which provided basic input for the Jiangsu Yizheng Chemical Fibre Plant built 30 km away at about the same time.

The oil bonanza that was expected to pay for these and other mega-projects in the ten-year plan never materialized, despite an intensive drilling programme, and this helped to precipitate the economic and planning crisis that faced the Third Plenum of the Eleventh Communist Party Central Committee in December 1978. The experiences of the previous thirty years had demonstrated the shortcomings of both over-centralization and over-decentralization of control *vis-à-vis* central and provincial governments and in the management of backbone enterprises.

Assessment

Taken overall, the three decades after 1949 probably saw a relative shift of productive activity from the coast to selected inland areas, particularly those falling within the Third-Line region (although there are problems about the comparability of the data over this period). In terms of gross value of industrial output, the share of the coastal provinces fell from about 68 per cent in 1952 to 61 per cent in 1979 (with much of the decline taking place in Shanghai Municipality—see Table 5.1), whereas that of the Third-Line provinces rose from 28 to 36 per cent (Pannell, 1988: 22; Kueh, 1989: 426).

Such raw output percentages by broad regions do not, however, indicate whether this period saw progress towards the avowedly socialist objective of greater regional *equality*, an issue that has been scrutinized, somewhat inconclusively, by several scholars employing a range of criteria and data (e.g. Roll and Yeh, 1975; Lardy, 1980; Paine, 1981; Pannell, 1988; Yang 1990; Tsui, 1991). More recently, Wei and Ma (1996) used per capita national income (also known as net material product) to show that between 1952 and 1978 the relative status of the Western, Central, and Coastal Regions did not change, with the per capita income (pci) of the latter always remaining above the national average and higher than the other two. While there was some reduction in regional inequality in terms of this measure between 1961 and 1967, the gap had become wider by 1978 than it had been in 1952, largely because the pci in the Coastal Region steadily rose between 1967 and 1976. Wei and Ma (1996: 187) also show that the fortunes of individual provinces varied considerably. In eight, the pci increased by more than 250 per cent (Beijing, Tianjin, Guangdong, Shanghai, and Jiangsu in the Coastal Region; Hubei in the Central; and Sichuan and Qinghai in the Western). At the other extreme, six achieved pci increases of less than 150 per cent: Fujian (Coastal), Jilin, Heilongjiang, Jiangxi, and Nei Mongol (Central), and Xinjiang (Western).

On the basis of these results, Wei and Ma challenge the conclusion that interprovincial inequality declined during the Maoist era. Even so, their analysis leaves open questions about intra and inter-provincial variations in welfare, living standards, and labour productivity. Indeed, Chen Yao (1994: 39) quotes Deng Xiaoping as saying towards the end of 1978 that 'since the production and people's life in the northwest, southwest and certain parts of the rest were still struggling to survive, the State should give them help in various ways, in particular, physically'.

Undoubtedly, a great deal of investment was wasted during the 1949–78 period in the various attempts to achieve immediate, if ever-changing, ideological and other aims, with scant thought being given to longer-term regional planning goals or strategies. The allocation of investment funds to inland areas in the pursuit of self-reliance and 'balance' slowed the transformation and modernization of the Coastal Region and failed to utilize the managerial and labour skills already existing there. In the absence of a well-developed transport system, the dispersal of industrial production in widely separated small plants probably made sense but also reduced even further the possibility of achieving economies of scale and encouraging technological advances through specialization. As a case in point, in 1978 almost every province had one or more of the 130 or so motor vehicle assembly plants, most of which were producing fewer than 3,000 units a year (Lyons, 1987: 81).

In some ways, China may have suffered from a lack of appreciation of the inadequacies in the Soviet approach to territorial planning, to which many of its bureaucrats had been exposed since the early 1950s. This resulted in an undue emphasis on traditional heavy industries using technologies that were rapidly getting out of date; the neglect of environmental and geographical considerations; and the attempt to develop resource-based industrial complexes in remote locations—all flaws in the Soviet model that have been noted elsewhere (Linge et al., 1978). There are also many examples of projects that went ahead without adequate feasibility studies: the construction of a pipeline to Shanghai was well underway before it was discovered that Sichuan natural gas deposits were smaller than imagined.

Most assessments of the spatial outcomes of this period have been couched almost solely in terms of whether the gap between coastal and inland areas widened or narrowed in terms of investment and output. Yet much was done to open up the interior, with railways pushing out—often through very difficult terrain—to the north-west and south-west; roads, power supplies, and other basic infrastructure were taken into remote areas; and oil, coal, and hydro-resources were explored and exploited. In turn, these developments facilitated the gradual diversification of the economies of the more remote and backward parts of the country.

While it is true that only half the inland provinces and few of the autonomous regions benefited immediately from the Third-Line investments and that, even then, some parts of them gained more than others, many of the new and enlarged settlements, industrial nodes, and supporting infrastructures have subsequently proved attractive to foreign investors. To this extent, analyses comparing geographical trends before and after 1978, based on coarse-grained provincial output data, can be misleading.

Changes in Regional Planning Concepts from 1979 to 1995

The Third Plenum held in December 1978 was a major turning point in China's economic development as it marked the beginning of a step-by-step change from a mandatory to an indicative planning system, with administrative control being gradually replaced by market mechanisms and the indirect levers of financial, fiscal, and exchange-rate policies. The priority aim of national regional strategy became economic efficiency, albeit with due regard also to equality of growth.

The 1979–95 period can thus be depicted as a more or less transitional one while progress was made from a centrally planned economic system towards the goal of a socialist market economy. *Ad hoc* and temporary economic and technical co-operation arrangements between regions became more stable and longer-term, involving not just industrial enterprises but also the construction of hydro-power stations, coal-mines, and railways (Yang et al., 1984: 237).

New regional planning concepts were introduced, including in 1979 the establishment of four Special Economic Zones (SEZs)— Shenzhen, Zhuhai, and Shantou in Guangdong Province, and Xiamen in Fujian. This was followed in May 1984 by the opening of fourteen coastal port cities (Dalian, Qinhuangdao, Tianjin, Yantai, Qingdao, Lianyungang, Nantong, Shanghai, Ningbo, Wenzhou, Fuzhou, Guangzhou, Zhanjiang, and Beihai), which were permitted to establish Economic and Technological Development Zones (ETDZs); and in May 1985 by the proclamation of the Changjiang Delta, the Zhujiang Delta, and the Xiamen–Zhangzhou–Quanzhou triangle as Open Economic Areas.

By this time, too, government officials and academic researchers were learning from local experience and extending their knowledge of overseas planning theory and practice. Concepts about regions and regional planning were still being absorbed; their relevance to China's situation and needs were being evaluated; and proposals for implementation were being evolved within the context of a traditional culture of avoiding plunges into reforms but rather, in Deng Xiaoping's phrase, 'crossing the river by feeling the stones'.

Sixth Five Year Plan: 1981 to 1985

The first explicit and systematic statement about regional planning officially published in China was contained in a special 'Regional Economic Development Plan' volume as part of the documentation for the Sixth Five Year Plan. Approved in December 1982, this began by clarifying which parts of the country should be included in the 'coastal' and 'inland' areas—terms that had long been bandied about but not precisely defined—ending the uncertainty, for example, about where Guangxi Zhuang AR 'belonged' by allocating it to the coastal zone as Mao Zedong had earlier suggested (Bo, 1991: 475).

Coastal areas. The technologically more advanced Coastal Region was seen as the foundation on which the national economy rested. It was thus important for the core areas there to be further exploited and to more completely realize their comparative advantage as well as their potential to promote the inland areas. Four goals required special attention.

First, scientific and management skills should be used to propel the manufacturing sector into technologically advanced, high-quality lines, while the production of some simpler and more commonplace items should gradually be dispersed into the inland areas. New industries should be located near raw material and energy sources rather than in the coastal areas. Second, the disruptions caused by energy shortages and transport inadequacies (see Chapter 3) needed to be eased to enable the production potential of the coastal area to be fulfilled. Third, an export-orientated strategy should be implemented, especially at Shanghai and Tianjin. Fourth, agricultural production should be developed to capitalize on the comparative advantage of the natural resources available there.

These objectives were pursued in various ways: Tianjin Municipality, for instance, provided the equipment and technology to enable calcium carbide production to be shifted to energy-rich Shanxi Province, thus reducing its annual industrial energy consumption by 3 per cent—equivalent to 50,000 tons of coal (Yang et al., 1984: 239). Such regional co-operation schemes, however, had to follow the rubric of 'one balance and two cooperations' and were not allowed to interfere with the fulfilment of central government plans.

Inland areas. The inland areas were expected to focus on accelerating the construction of transport infrastructure; exploiting further the energy and raw material resources so as to support the industrialization of the coastal areas; restructuring and reorganizing the engineering and metal-working industries; raising the level of self-sufficiency in everyday manufactured goods; and realizing the potential of agricultural production. Again, some of these objectives were pursued through co-operative ventures: thus the Tianjin Foreign Trade Carpet Company provided foreign exchange so that the Qinghai Provincial Handicraft Company could buy Japanese machinery and supply some of the increased output of woollen yarn to its partner.

Ethnic minority areas. Given the weak technological and material base of the minority areas, the Development Plan advocated that animal husbandry and agriculture be further promoted; that industries processing resources like cashmere, leather, and timber be fostered along with those making goods specifically needed by the minorities; and that trade be improved. Exemplifying how this worked in practice, a Tianjin soy sauce factory provided technical assistance enabling a Hohhot (Nei Mongol AR) food factory to launch a higher-quality product on the east coast market. In addition, these regions were to be supported by clearly defined subsidies rising annually by 10 per cent, and Y500 million (US$330 million at the then current exchange rate) a year were to be provided for a special economic development fund to assist ethnic minority and underdeveloped areas.

Regional co-operation. The Development Plan also proposed that there should be greater interprovincial co-operation in the supply of materials and products, in technology, and in the form of economic alliances. This in part was an attempt to rectify the shortages and wastage that had arisen under the former system whereby most of the significant materials and products (such as coal, rolled steel, cement, and timber) had been allocated by the central government, thus weakening horizontal connections between provinces.

Co-operation in material supply embraced the sharing by regions of state-allocated materials; the disposal by regions of output that exceeded planned targets; and the use of locally generated foreign exchange to purchase imports. In 1982, for instance, 2 million of the 7 million tons of coal sent from Shanxi Province were exchanged for timber, plate glass, cement, and other products in short supply. Technological co-operation included technology transfer; consulting and advisory services; and direct assistance by people with particular skills. Economic alliances, not confined to particular sectors, regions or ownership, took several forms including compensation trade and co-operative production: the Shanghai Sewing Machine Company, for example, signed compensation contracts with six inland manufacturers to which it transferred more advanced technology.

Territorial development and consolidation. As indicated already, planners in China had been absorbing ideas from the broad stream of international literature concerned with inequality, space, and polarized growth and their implications for regional planning, and were experimenting with new ways of formulating and achieving long-term goals. The 1982 Development Plan listed seven tasks, including the preparation of long-term economic regional plans for the Changjiang River Delta focused on Shanghai, and for the coal and heavy chemical producing area centred on Shanxi Province: both were undertaken by the Development Research Centre (with which two of the authors are affiliated).

Seventh Five Year Plan: 1986 to 1990

The Seventh Five Year Plan, approved in April 1986, introduced a new tripartite regional classification by subdividing the inland into Central and Western Regions (Figure 1.1). Along with this came the concept of the Coastal Region acting as a 'growth pole' which, through linkage and multiplier effects, would send development impulses inland, thus building up a step-by-step growth momentum in accordance with productivity differentials and comparative advantage (Woo, 1996: 283).

Development of the Coastal Region was to be accelerated during the Plan period and through into the 1990s: it was to be technologically advanced, attractive to foreign investment, and export orientated. The Central Region would have key energy projects, and produce raw and partly processed materials and foodstuffs, while the Western Region would be further developed by processing its mineral and animal resources. Stress was laid on the need to maximize the comparative advantages of the three regions and to develop the horizontal connections between them.

Other issues that had spatial implications were also canvassed. The enterprises established in the former Third-Line region to produce defence *matériel* were expected to make goods for civilian use. Around all large municipalities regional economic networks of various kinds and characteristics were to be gradually established. Considerable stress was to be laid on the economic and cultural advancement of the minority regions and on positive measures to improve the backward status of the old revolutionary bases, the border regions, and areas of poverty. Small and medium-size towns were to be fostered as well as cities having good transport links to large municipalities. Territorial planning and development needed to exploit water, land, mineral, and forest resources effectively and carefully, referring specifically to 'key projects to harness the big rivers' and the utilization of 'the resources of the mountainous regions, particularly those in the south, in a comprehensive way'.

Eighth Five Year Plan: 1991 to 1995

The 'Outline of the Eighth Five Year Plan and the Ten Years Development Program of the National Economy and Social Development', authorized in March 1991, was promulgated during the austerity programme that followed double-digit inflation in 1989–90 and a slowdown in the economy. Thus, the regional planning objectives more or less continued those of the Sixth and Seventh Plans, although the alleviation of poverty was given greater prominence.

The first four sections in the 'Layout of Regional Economic Development and Policies' reiterated much that had been said before about the coastal, inland, ethnic minority, and poor regions. The fifth discussed regional economic co-operation and alliances, the sixth was devoted to urban and rural planning and construction, and the seventh considered territorial development and environmental protection.

To alleviate poverty, priority was to be given to locally generated, self-sustaining forms of development. Experience had shown that active programmes emphasizing poverty alleviation were more successful than passive ones based on subsidies and loans. Thus, the more developed regions were encouraged to strengthen their bilateral assistance programmes with poorer parts of the country through contractual arrangements (such as supplying cloth to Shanghai garment makers), joint development projects, the establishment of co-operative enterprises, and the provision of financial, material, and human support.

The territorial development policies contained in the Sixth and Seventh Plans were bolstered by the addition of a new environmental protection programme, including the construction and management of a monitoring system and the accelerated planning of key national nature conservation zones. Particular attention was to be paid to pollution control and to the reduction in the production and use of ozone-depleting substances.

Assessment

Regional development after 1978 became a mixture of planning goals overlain with pragmatic solutions to particular economic and political problems as and when they arose. Thus, the special roles given to the three designated Regions of China based on natural endowments and comparative advantage soon became blurred. The preferential arrangements initially accorded the coastal provinces became more widely diffused, with or without central government approval, as the decentralization of financial and administrative decision making strengthened the capacity of local governments to pursue initiatives while weakening Beijing's control over them. In the mid-1980s the inland areas 'engaged in economic protectionism to press for better terms of trade with the coastal areas' while Coastal Region authorities 'used the privileges, concessions, and autonomy granted in accordance with the graduated regional development strategy to expand existing activities with unchanged production techniques, for rent-seeking purposes; not to upgrade products and enhance efficiency' (Woo, 1996: 284).

Deng Xiaoping's advocacy in 1991–92 of 'seizing opportunity and quickening economy' promoted by economic liberalization and even greater opening up to the outside world spelled the demise of the coast-to-inland diffusion concept. From the outset this idea of growth impulses trickling down flew in the face of experience when similar concepts had been used to try to solve 'real-world' problems in other countries (Darwent, 1969; Linge, 1988). In effect, it was replaced by the view that the switch to a socialist market economy would itself lead to a more equitable kind of spatial development through the free play of market forces.

In May 1992, the Open Door policy was extended to the hinterland with more than thirty cities being given preferential policies similar to those of Shenzhen and Zhuhai. This was expected to reduce the income disparities. Instead, the advantages enjoyed by the Coastal Region in the 1980s were reinforced and fuelled in the 1990s by 'the relatively more rapid growth of per labour investment; by an improvement in labour quality; and more importantly by the perpetuation of policies favouring foreign-involved economic activities, non state-owned enterprises, and light industries' (Woo, 1996: 296). As a result, income disparities between the coastal and inland areas, and more especially those in the far west, actually widened.

The Ninth Five Year Plan

The regional planning issues canvassed in the Ninth Five Year Plan (1996–2000), adopted on 17 March 1996, have to be seen in the

context of the related 'Long Term Target for the Year 2010' document which set out two main goals: to double the GNP reached in
2000 and to hold the population below 1,400 million. Among the
principles underlying the Plan was the need to 'gradually narrow
the gap between regions', to 'pay greater attention to supporting
the development of inland areas', and gradually intensify efforts 'to
carry out policies which can help slow this widening trend' (*Xinhua
News Agency*, 18 March 1996). In effect, the bias shown towards
the coastal areas in the Seventh Five Year Plan, along with the
notion of growth impulses being transmitted thence to the inland,
was replaced by a bias towards more direct and affirmative action
to bolster the Central and Western Regions.

The Ninth Plan includes a lengthy section spelling out the need
to co-ordinate regional economic development, to establish seven
economic zones with their own characteristics, and to rationalize
national economic distribution as an important condition for
gradually narrowing development gaps.

While observing the principles of unified planning, taking local conditions
into consideration, giving play to superiority and sharing out the work and
cooperating with one another for a coordinated development, we should
handle correctly relations between national and regional economic development; relations between establishing the regional economy and arous-
ing the enthusiasm of various provinces, regions and municipalities; and
inter-region relations. Various localities should, under the guidance of
national planning and industrial policy, identify their own development
priority and industrial superiority to avoid overlapping of industrial structure, so as to push economic development of various localities to a higher
level. Besides, we should actively promote mutual supplementation,
rational exchanges and economic association among various regions
(*Xinhua News Agency*, 18 March 1996).

The Seven Zones

Of particular interest was the proposal for seven economic zones
to take shape gradually—regardless of provincial, regional, and
municipal boundaries—'in accordance with the law of market
economy, intrinsic economic association, and special geographical
and natural features; with existing economic distribution, central
cities, and major traffic lines as a foundation'. The idea of cutting
across administrative boundaries to form major economic regions
which take account of geographical and economic realities so that
they can be developed in a co-ordinated way, has been noted as a

desirable goal in various planning documents since the early 1980s. Intuitively, it makes good sense in terms of achieving greater efficiency, avoiding duplication of infrastructure, protecting the environment, and upgrading the use of human and material resources. Regions with coherent and workable long-term development strategies are more likely to attract investors, particularly from overseas, who are being courted by an ever-increasing array of cross-border growth triangles and circles in the Asian region.

Politically, however, any proposal to carve out regions from the present administrative arrangements seems to be wishful thinking. Indeed there is no map that gives even a notional indication of official thinking about the possible boundaries of these seven economic zones, and the description published in the 1996 planning documents merely hints at which parts of some provinces might be included in a particular zone. Thus, as noted in Chapter 6, the Liaodong and Shandong Peninsulas are included in the Plan's description of the 'Bohai Sphere Zone', but the chances of Liaoning and Shandong Provinces surrendering even partial control of such economically significant and relatively prosperous portions of their territories seem very slight indeed.

The reality is that any such regions would have to be groupings of complete provinces. Even this would be an achievement as there are neighbouring administrative areas (like Beijing and Tianjin Municipalities) that have, until recently, shown little interest in cross-border co-operation. By international standards, the proposed zones would be very large: even the area covered by Beijing and Tianjin Municipalities and Hebei Province—the core portion only of the Bohai Sphere Zone—is five times greater than the Netherlands and has ten times the population.

Inland and Impoverished Regions

Ways of boosting development in the Central and Western Regions were listed at some length in the Ninth Plan but without adding much to the list of initiatives that had already been announced, or to the projects already in hand. The catalogue included: implementing favourable investment policies to encourage resource extraction; providing from government sources most of the investment funds needed for trans-regional infrastructure; readjusting the distribution of localities with processing industries; guiding resource-related and labour-intensive industries to resettle there; rationalizing the prices of resource-related products to enhance self-development capabilities; implementing a regulated central government financial transfer payment system and gradually raising financial support; guiding more foreign investors there; and raising the percentage of state policy-related loans going to central and west China which should get 'over 60 per cent' of loans provided by international financial organizations and foreign governments. The Plan also pleaded for greater efforts to assist impoverished regions as well as those occupied by minorities, by facilitating construction projects in Xizang AR, the Three Gorges reservoir area, and other poor localities. Investment in the Central and Western Regions by east coast enterprises should be encouraged, and the government should 'organize the shift of labour forces from the central and western regions to the eastern coastal region'.

The long-term outlook for these regions is discussed in Chapter 9. Suffice it to say here that some of the inland provinces protested during 1996 that there had been much talk but little action to formulate a long-term development plan, although the State Council's agreement to enlarge Chongqing City (now, with 30 million inhabitants, the largest city in China) and upgrading it to municipality status may help to boost inland areas. Indeed, the authorities hope that this upgrade will not only stabilize and develop this part of Sichuan Province, which is being greatly affected by the Three Gorges Project (see Chapter 5), but also a much wider area including Qinghai and Gansu Provinces. They were also told in June 1996 that most of the soft loans received by China from international financial agencies and two-thirds of the State Development Bank loans would be used in inland areas, and that earnings from minerals could be used to pay off some of their foreign debts.

Major Economic Policies Affecting Regional Development

Fiscal Policies

The centralized control of finance during the first two decades after 1949 meant that lower levels of government were little more than accounting units with no power to use budgetary policy as a lever to influence development. The gradual decentralization of financial authority, beginning in the early 1970s, had led by the mid-1980s to a very complex system whereby the division of tax revenues between the provinces and the central government was determined on a case-by-case basis, with some areas receiving more favourable treatment than others. In addition, a menu of preferential policies was used to attract foreign investment into the SEZs and numerous micro-regions, such as the Pudong area in Shanghai, coastal open cities, border area open cities, ETDZs, high-tech industrial development parks, and bonded zones. Tax, investment, and other conditions not only differed between the various types of zone but also between local administrations, which had considerable power to change or waive such imposts.

These arrangements, in line with the principle of 'efficiency as the top priority', had a significant impact on the spatial economy of China because, until the mid-1990s, most of these special zones were concentrated in the Coastal Region. Thus, while they encouraged the entry of foreign investment, technology, and entrepreneurial skills that stimulated the national economy, they also had the less desirable effect of widening the disparity between the coastal and inland regions.

The decentralization of fiscal power introduced since 1979 created four problems. First, the central government's revenue in the share of GDP decreased from 34.4 per cent in 1978 to 15.4 per cent in 1993 and to 10.8 per cent in 1995, thus greatly reducing its capacity to guide social and economic development. The root cause of this decline has been the worsening performance of the state enterprises to which no early solution seems likely. Second, it accentuated the problem of 'dual subordination' where the responsibility of organizational units was both to their line ministry superiors and also to the same level of the local government; the latter could use the flexibility of China's tax administration to reduce their tax effort and therefore the share of their resources paid to the central government. Third, the variety of non-unified preferential arrangements and the power of local governments to alter them not only engendered an environment of unfair competition but also cut central government revenue. Fourth, the funds derived from charges and revenue from undertakings available for 'extra' (or 'outside') budget use by local authorities and enterprises have been mounting, and by the end of 1996 were nearly equal to those 'within' budget.

Central government expenditures have steadily declined from 16 per cent of GNP in 1978 to 7.8 per cent in 1986, 5.7 per cent in 1993, and 3.5 per cent in 1995 (Chan, 1996a). This is despite new guidelines early in 1994 clarifying not only which revenue streams are to be wholly retained by the central government on the one hand and the provincial governments on the other, but also the funding responsibilities of each (one explicit task retained by central government being the co-ordination of regional development). Revenue from value-added, resource, and securities exchange taxes is shared between the two levels of government and used in a 'central to local revenue return and transfer payment system' to support the development of economically underdeveloped areas and the renovation of old industrial bases.

The key to provincial acceptance of these revised arrangements, which over time will reduce their share of total revenue, will be a clear demonstration that the central government is improving overall efficiency and effectively promoting regional economic development which, in turn, will require improvements to the legal system and clarification of the responsibilities of each department. Yet the dual system can only work if the local authorities pass on all the tax revenue collected on behalf of the central government: reportedly, only 60 per cent of the funds due in 1996 were surrendered (as against 70 per cent in 1995).

The central to local revenue return and transfer payment system aims to adjust both the distribution and the regional structure of revenue flows, with transfer payments being one important way of supporting underdeveloped regions. Yet such payments could reduce the stimulus to achieve local vitality and growth potential or to make better use of existing resources, including labour. The Ninth Five Year Plan has recognized this by suggesting that local enterprises be encouraged, the geographical distribution of some processing industries be rearranged and, as a possibly more effective and economical solution, labour be shifted to the Coastal Region.

Investment Policies

Regional development is, of course, greatly influenced by investment arrangements and policies. Prior to 1979, all projects authorized by the State Planning Commission were financed centrally: now most investment-approval powers are in the hands of provincial governments and enterprises. This has led to concerns that local governments have been wasting development funds by investing in similar and repetitive projects rather than on tasks like unifying small, scattered state enterprises into larger firms to achieve economies of scale (Chan, 1996b).

Discrimination between regions is also occurring because of the reduction in direct financial appropriations for fixed investments and the increased reliance on bank loans. Key projects of national significance still rely to some extent on central financing, but the majority of investments will depend on fund-raising by local governments and enterprises. Whereas the less developed areas will need considerable support in the form of loans from international agencies and foreign governments, regions commanding greater authority and having a warmer investment climate are in a better position to attract finance from market sources.

Goals of Regional Planning in China

The Development Research Centre sees regional planning as having three objectives. First, to enable economic targets, such as certain rates of GNP or GDP growth and their supply and demand-side components, to be achieved; second, to facilitate such social objectives as alleviating poverty, redistributing income, expanding employment opportunities, boosting local economies, improving health and education, and preventing crime; and third, to attain environmental goals leading to sustainable development. These objectives are not always compatible and therefore one of the tasks facing planners is to try to resolve or minimize the tensions that arise. In China, as in other countries, sectoral strategies can conflict with spatial ones; the drive for efficiency can result in geographical inequalities in social welfare; and environmental considerations may affect the way a region's physical and human resources can be appropriately utilized. The general pursuit of national goals can penalize particular communities, households, and individuals. Thus, the policy of reducing the number of car factories may assist enterprise reform and lead to greater efficiency and better technology but, simultaneously, adversely affect inland towns losing them. The closure of dozens of polluting woollen and paper-mills along the

Changjiang and Huang He (Yellow) rivers may be environmentally desirable but be economically devastating for the workers and their households.

The central government has to focus mainly on two crucial issues. One is the co-ordination of provincial, municipal, and inter-regional policies within the national context; the other is the preparation of a national development plan which takes proper account of administrative, functional, and natural regions as well as arrangements straddling such boundaries. In practice, even co-ordinating the ideas of central government ministries remains a problem, with the impression sometimes being given that one hand does not know what the other is doing.

China has been searching for a methodological framework in which national and regional development can be co-ordinated. Experience has indicated that some decentralization of power is important in mobilizing local initiative, and this points to the need to evolve some kind of hierarchical planning system. This raises two kinds of problems. First, decentralization empowers provincial governments to frustrate or even ignore national strategies that run counter to their more parochial interests. It also strengthens their propensity to compete rather than co-operate with other provinces, so leading to wasteful duplication of infrastructure and less efficient use of human and material resources.

Second, regions in China have long been viewed as part of an hierarchical *administrative* framework, but the concept of an administrative region does not sit easily with the realities of a modern industrial society where the factors of production and the operations of enterprises interact across sub-national political boundaries. This issue has particular relevance here because some of the provinces are larger and more populous than many nearby nation states: Qinghai Province, for example, has an area of 720,000 km^2 as against Japan's 378,000 km^2, while the population of Sichuan Province (113 million) is almost double that of Thailand (58 million).

Spatial planning in China, as elsewhere, has to be dynamic. It must keep pace with the rate at which change is occurring in the economy as a whole as well as accommodate the frequent shifts in the central government's priorities. These not only stem from internal considerations—such as the need to keep an appropriate balance between sectoral and spatial goals—but also changing political circumstances, like the emergence of agreements with neighbouring countries to develop the Tumen River area in the north-east (see Chapter 7) and the Mekong Valley in the south-west. Any long-term regional plans for the Bohai Sea Rim have to allow for the possibility of its becoming associated with a North-East Asia Co-operation Zone, just as those for the south-east of the country must consider the implications of its becoming more involved economically in a South China Sea Basin Co-operation Zone (see Chapter 4). Planners must accommodate the speed at which enterprises—and even industry segments—can be shifted into and out of China, depending on extraneous circumstances like the value of the Japanese yen. In short, the more that China opens to the world, the more the organization of its space will be tempered by influences which no one country can control.

During the 1950s, Chinese regional economists depended on the Soviet Union for their ideas and they continued to use these for a further two decades. Then, after 1979 too many of the new ideas that flooded in from the rest of the world were taken up uncritically, even though China's economic and social system was still evolving and its situation still differs greatly from that in developed countries. To be successful, regional theories and practices have to take account of the realities of the conditions in China, yet current planning is still based on imported ideas. A framework based on indigenous needs is essential to raise the seeds and buds of creative local concepts about regional planning that take more account of the welfare of people rather than blindly chasing growth, especially if this, as discussed in Chapter 1, is based on unsustainable development.

3 Linking the Regions: A Continuing Challenge

RONG CHAO-HE, LI WEN-YAN, GODFREY LINGE, AND DEAN FORBES

China's space economy consists of a set of loosely articulated functional macro-regions. Overlaid on these is a series of linkages, most notably the very large north–south flows of coal, oil, and grain; the east–west flows of raw materials and manufactures (including imports and exports); and the movement, especially of people, between rural and urban areas. The overland cross-border trading links that have been emerging since the mid-1980s have also begun—as yet only in a small way—to reorientate the spatial organization of this country. Improvements in communications have led to greater spatial interaction, while the development of air travel has enabled more of its citizens to experience the diversity and complexity of their country.

The inadequacy of the national transport system remains, however, the major barrier to greater regional integration. During the 1980s, when inter-city freight demand was increasing by 8 per cent a year (and passenger demand by 12 per cent), annual investment in this sector amounted to only 1.3 per cent of GNP. The railway system, long the backbone of the overland network, can barely cope with the huge quantity of coal and other freight that needs to be hauled around the country let alone passengers, even though it remains the only practical form of transport for most people. Considerable efforts have been made to upgrade the railways: by the end of 1995, 31 per cent of the system had double tracking compared with 16 per cent in 1980; 18 per cent was electrified, up from a mere 3 per cent; and diesel operations were possible on 45 per cent of the 54,600-km system (Figure 3.1). None the less, the extent to which further regional integration is possible will depend not only on significant increases in overall transport capacity, but also on a greater deregulation of pricing structures (such as those applying to rail fares and road tolls) which have been

Figure 3.1: Railways in operation, 1997. In addition to the ten actual border crossing places shown, international railway freight can be checked through customs procedures at Shanghai, Wuhan, and Zhengzhou.

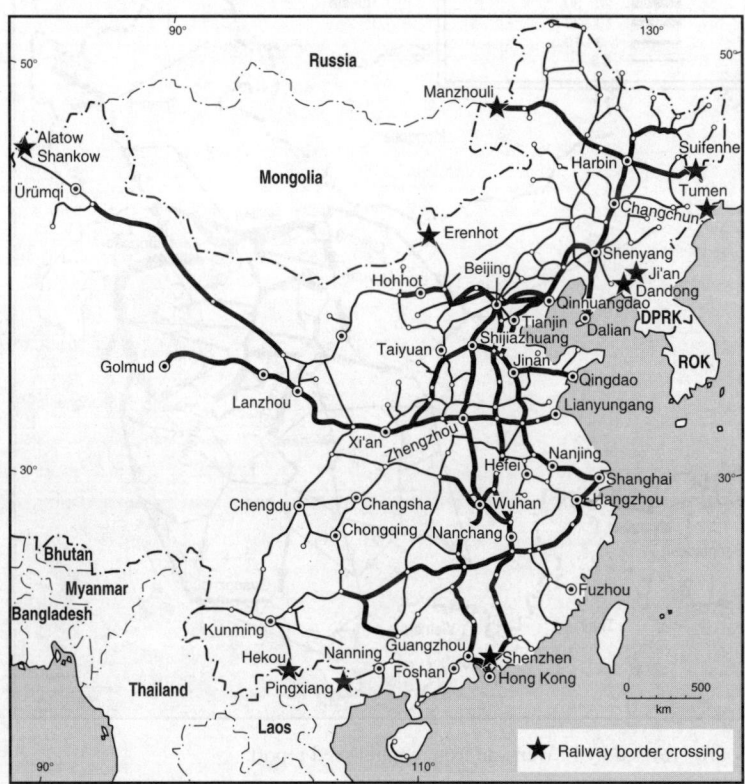

Source: based on Editorial Group, 1995, 102–3.

described as a mystery to Chinese and foreigners alike (Zhou, 1993: 92).

Energy Flows

China's energy-rich areas are distant from the main consuming regions. Since coal accounts for 74 per cent of the energy used in China—a pattern likely to persist into the foreseeable future—over half (670 of the 1,370 million tons mined in 1996) has to be railed

Figure 3.2: Coal flows, 1990.

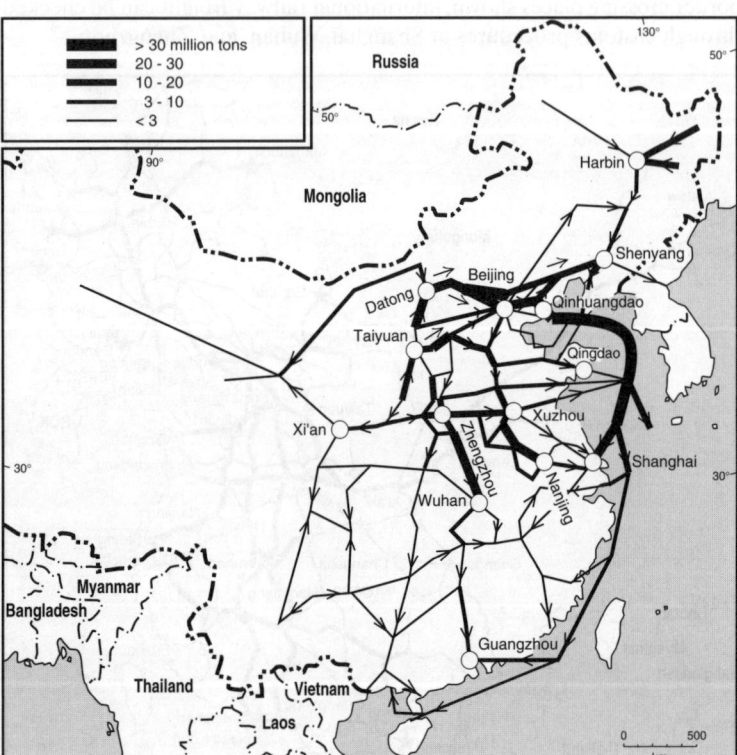

Source: revised by Li Wen-yan from unpublished report.

from the north and north-west to the rest of the country (Figure 3.2). Coal alone accounts for two-fifths of the overall railway ton/km freight task, while on the trunk routes from Beijing to Shanghai, Guangzhou, and Shenyang and from Lanzhou to Lianyungang it takes up 45 to 60 per cent of total capacity (Yan, 1994: 161). As China is expanding its output by about 40 million tons a year and plans to raise exports to about 50 million tons annually by 2000, the construction of purpose-built coal lines has become an urgent necessity.

Installed power topped 230,000 MW in March 1996 and is expected to rise to 290,000 MW by 2000 and 650,000 MW by 2010, but the need for more power and an expanded distribution network is clear. Per capita, installed capacity is a mere 0.154 kW and annual consumption is only 700 kWh (about a quarter of the world average). These averages hide large disparities: consumption per capita ranges from less than 400 kWh in Anhui and Guizhou Provinces to 1,900 kWh in Beijing Municipality and 2,400 kWh in Shanghai Municipality, while more than 100 million people in rural areas lack any power supply (Department of Resources Conservation & Comprehensive Utilization, 1994: 68). Power failures are thus common, and the shortage rate across the country averages about 20 per cent (Barret, 1994; Department of Resources Conservation & Comprehensive Utilization, 1994: 43).

Electricity generation more than tripled between 1980 and 1995 when it reached 1,000,000 million kWh, 80 per cent from thermal stations (Li, 1995b: 605). Four of the multi-province power grids have capacities above 20,000 MW: that serving the north-west is somewhat smaller (Figure 3.3). All are under the control of the central Ministry of Power Industry and co-operate to cope with demand fluctuations and supply interruptions caused, for example, by drought. In addition, there are eight independent provincial power grids with capacities above 2,000 MW—the two largest (8,000 MW) serving Guangdong and Shandong Provinces—which also assist each other. Thus, Guangdong is safeguarding its future supplies by committing US$4,000 million to three projects in Yunnan Province, in return for which it will receive agreed amounts of electricity for twenty years. Proposals to bring most of these grids into a national system operated by a new centrally owned power company have been resisted by several provinces (Clayton and Foo Choy Peng, 1996).

Despite growing concerns about pollution from thermal stations—Guangdong Province in mid-1995 put a moratorium on new coal, oil, and gas power stations in the Zhujiang (Pearl) River Delta—two-thirds of the new power plants coming into operation before 2010 will be of this kind. There are also ambitious plans to construct more large hydro-projects, among them the Three Gorges scheme currently underway on the middle reaches of the Changjiang (Yangtze) River—partly paid for by a levy on electricity charges—which will start generating in 2003 but not reach its planned installed capacity of 18.2 GW until 2009.

Oil production totalled 158 million tons in 1996, but China has been a net importer of oil products since 1994. The traditional oil-fields in the eastern provinces pump about 90 per cent of the

Figure 3.3: Regional power grids and future power flows.

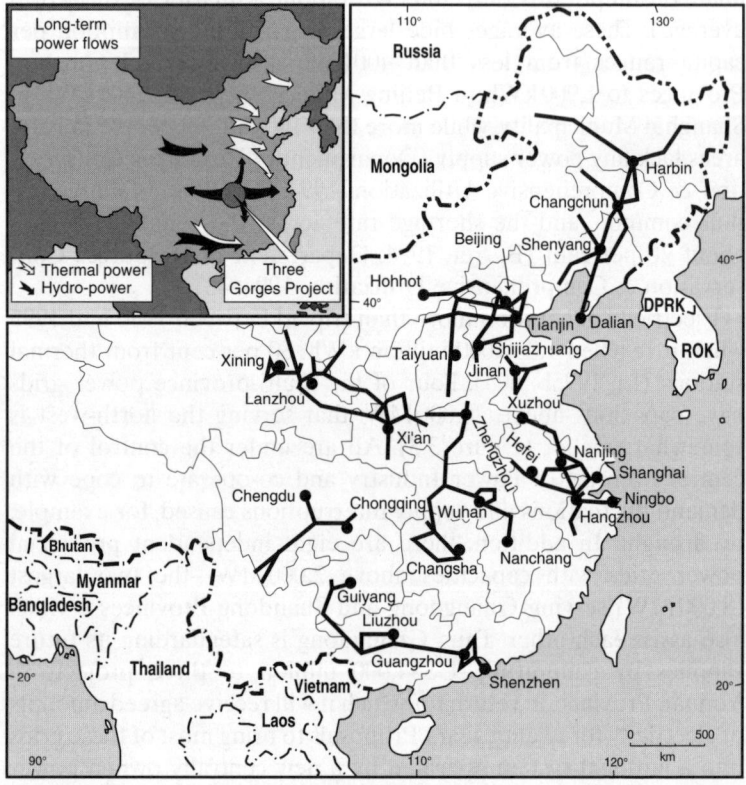

Sources: based on authors' research; Clayton and Foo Choy Peng, 1996.

onshore oil but produce no more now than in the late 1980s and, to prevent yields declining, have to use expensive secondary recovery techniques. Offshore territory was opened to foreign exploration in 1982 but the results have proved disappointing. None the less, boosted by supplies that began to flow from the Liuhui II-1 field (south-east of Hong Kong) in March 1996, the country's nineteen offshore fields produced 14 million tons that year (*Xinhua News Agency*, 11 December 1996). Most hope, however, is being pinned on intensifying oil and gas exploration and increasing refinery capacity (already 8.5 million tons) in the Tarim, Junggar, and Turpan–Hami basins in Xinjiang Uygur AR. In the 1980s Chinese geologists assessed reserves in the Tarim Basin at 13,000–28,000 million tons, but the failure of foreign oil companies to make significant discoveries since they began exploring there in 1993 has cast doubts on whether it can become 'the next Saudi Arabia' (Yatsko, 1996: 68).

Oil refining capacity will have to rise by a third by 2000, mostly by expanding existing refineries (especially those in the south-east at Zhenhai, Maoming, and Meizhou Bay), and by foreign companies establishing new joint ventures. Traditionally, southern markets like Shanghai, Fujian, and Guangdong bought their oil products from the north-eastern refineries, but the 36 per cent increase in oil and oil-product prices in May 1994 and the simultaneous introduction of fixed market and retail prices made this operation unprofitable for distributors because of high transport costs. With southern refineries relying more on imported crude, those in the north-east periodically have to cut production. National pricing policies have significant differential impacts on provincial economies. Higher energy prices transfer wealth from regions lacking significant energy resources to those possessing them, and the overall impact of increased fuel costs is greater in inland areas where the state sector is more important (Barret, 1994).

Freight Flows

Apart from coal, the other main freight flows are of grain and iron and steel (each 8 per cent of the railway ton/km task). About 75 million tons of grain are railed annually from the main growing areas in the north-east and Changjiang Valley to the eastern seaboard and the south and south-west of the country (Chen et al., 1993). Rail congestion helps to distort the market: in March 1995 feed grain, selling for US$134 per ton in Jilin Province where it was grown, cost pig farmers US$214 in Sichuan Province. At this time, imported grain landed for US$154 per ton at east coast ports could not be dispatched inland because of a lack of rail wagons (*Reuter Australasian Briefing*, 25 and 30 March 1995).

Most long-distance freight is carried on a few backbone links, especially those from Beijing to Shenyang, Shanghai, Guangzhou, and Baotou and between Harbin and Dalian, which make up only 13 per cent of the total network but handle 44 per cent of the ton/km task. Average freight-flow densities on these lines reach as much as 69 million tons—about 3.5 times that on the railway system as a whole.

Freight movements by inland waterways are mainly confined to coastal areas, with particular use being made of the Changjiang, Zhujiang, and Huang He (Yellow) rivers, and the Grand Canal between Xuzhou and Hangzhou. Together these account for 37 per cent of the domestic water-borne freight and 24 per cent of the total ton/km achieved. The estuary ports of Shanghai and Guangzhou serve as transhipment points for the Changjiang and Zhujiang river traffic. Southerly flows along the coast—dominated by coal, crude oil, ores, and grain—far exceed those, mainly of general cargo, sent north. In 1995 some 84 million tons of coal (about a quarter of all interprovincial coal movements) were shipped out of Qinhuangdao (48 million tons), Tianjin (17 million tons), Shijiusuo, Qingdao, and Lianyungang to Shanghai, Ningbo, and other southern ports. By 2000 such movements are expected to reach 130 million tons (Yan, 1994: 69).

The nation's ports have about forty purpose-built container berths able to handle 4 million twenty-foot equivalent units (TEUs) a year (with another 2 million being handled across multi-purpose or general cargo berths), but even the leaders—Shanghai, Qingdao, and Tianjin—are not yet in the same league as other Asian ports like Hong Kong, Singapore, Kobe, and Pusan. Until 1994 most of the containers moved coastwise were carried aboard mixed passenger/cargo vessels but there was then a marked increase in fully containerized shipping services. About 800,000 TEUs were shipped coastwise in 1996 (compared with 5.2 million on international services).

Interprovincial Freight Flows

Several regional linkage patterns can be identified. First, there are those among the provinces in the north-east, those in the Bohai Sea region, and those in the Changjiang Delta area (Figure 3.4), groups that form the economic cores of north-east, north, and east China. Second, Guangdong Province is a traffic hub with fast-growing connections between the Zhujiang River Delta and Fujian, Hunan, and Guizhou Provinces and Guangxi Zhuang AR. Third, interprovincial traffic within both south-west and north-west China is rela-

Figure 3.4: (a) Primary two-way freight links between main administrative areas based on annual railway data for the late 1980s, inclusive of coal and other bulk goods.

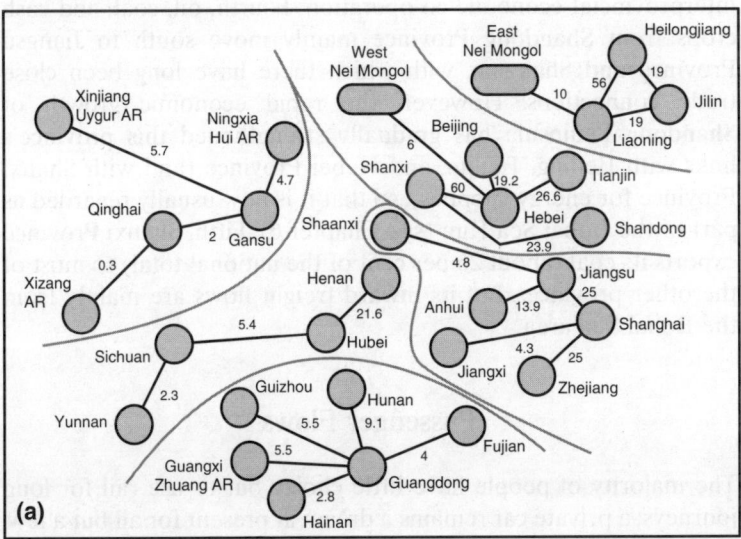

Source: Zhang et al., 1992: 294.

Figure 3.4: (b) Main product flows within and between regions.

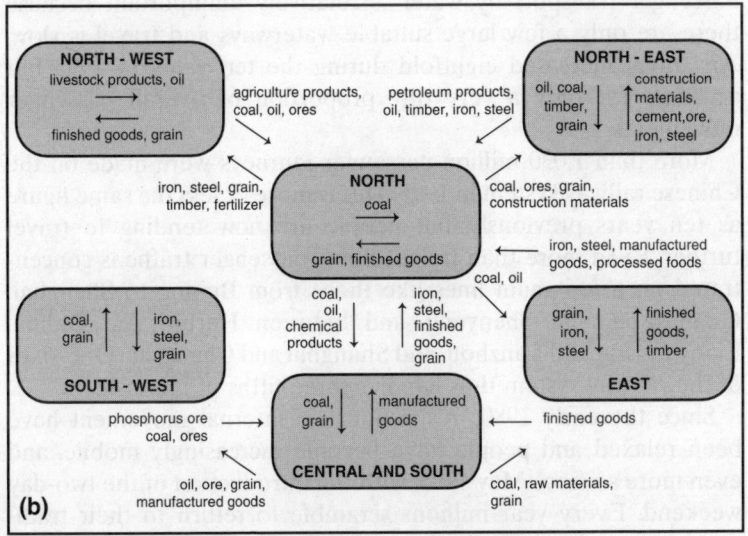

Source: compiled by Rong Chao-he from unpublished data.

tively sparse, reflecting the weak linkages in these thinly populated, often rugged, peripheral areas. These are likely to strengthen
in the near future following proposals in both regions to promote
interprovincial economic co-operation. Fourth, oil, coal, and cash
crops from Shandong Province mainly move south to Jiangsu
Province and Shanghai, with which there have long been close
trade connections. However, the rapid economic growth of
Shandong Peninsula has gradually strengthened this province's
links with Beijing, Tianjin, and Hebei Province (and with Shanxi
Province for energy supplies), so that it is now usually regarded as
part of the Bohai Sea Rim (see Chapter 6). Fifth, Shanxi Province
exports its coal (about 26 per cent of the national total) to most of
the other provinces, but its inward freight flows are mainly from
the Bohai Sea area.

Passenger Flows

The majority of people have little choice but to use rail for long
journeys; a private car remains a dream at present for all but a few.
The vehicles that gridlock city streets are chiefly taxis or belong to
enterprises, government departments, and the People's Liberation
Army (PLA). Outside urban areas buses are now being used for
increasingly lengthy journeys and in rural areas not served by rail.
Passenger transport by water is relatively unimportant because
there are only a few large suitable waterways and travel is slow.
Air travel increased eightfold during the ten years to 1995 but
accounts for only a very tiny proportion of overall passenger
movements.

More than 1,030 million passenger journeys were made on the
Chinese railway system in 1995. This is more or less the same figure
as ten years previously, but people are now tending to travel
further. Even more than freight flows, passenger traffic is concentrated on a few main lines like those from Beijing to Shanghai,
Guangzhou, and Shenyang, and between Harbin and Dalian,
Lianyungang and Lanzhou, and Shanghai and Changsha. One-sixth
of the railway system thus handles three-fifths of the task.

Since the early 1980s restrictions on internal movement have
been relaxed and people have become increasingly mobile, and
even more so since May 1996, with the introduction of the two-day
weekend. Every year millions scramble to return to their tradi-

tional homes through the Spring Festival in February–March, with the railways alone carrying 108 million people during the 40-day surge in 1996: no fewer than 3.4 million travelled on the busiest day even though the whole system has only 2.2 million seats and berths.

Inter-city bus services developed from fairly informal beginnings in the mid-1980s until now, with regular, reliable, and frequent services, they have become a more serious—and, as railway fares rise, cheaper—option for medium-distance journeys between adjoining provinces, a role traditionally performed by the railways.

Communication and Information Flows

Though greatly improved since 1978, China's telecommunication system remains among the least developed in Asia. In 1995 there were 3.7 telephones per 100 people nationwide, but rising to 15.0 in urban areas generally and 28.0 in coastal cities like Haikou, Guangzhou, and Beijing (*People's Daily*, 22 June 1995: 1). China recognizes that it is still well behind world standards and has set a target of 8 telephones per 100 people overall by 2000 and 30–40 per 100 in provincial capitals and coastal cities. Cellular phones numbered 0.06 per 100 people in 1996, a density above that in Pakistan (0.01) and Indonesia (0.03), but well below that in the Philippines (0.2) and Thailand (0.7), although the 5 million users in 1996 are expected to triple by 2000. Long-distance telephone capacity has grown from 22,000 lines in 1980 to 616,000 in 1995 and facsimile machines are now widely used (She and Yu, 1993).

The expansion of the fibre-optic network was made a national priority in the early 1990s, and by mid-1994 45,800 km of cable were in place (Figure 3.5), with the PLA assisting the Ministry of Posts and Telecommunications (MPT) to roll out some 8,000 km annually to create a system of twenty-two national trunk lines connecting all provincial capitals. The MPT has indicated that a further sixteen national trunk lines will be installed by 2000. In addition, most provinces have deployed some fibre-optic cabling in their inter-city networks and some seventy places have used it for their intra-city communications. China is rolling out about twice as much fibre-optic cabling each year as the United States, in part because it is not encumbered with an existing copper and coaxial network and therefore can move directly from open-wire (where it exists) to

Figure 3.5: Fibre-optic trunk routes, 1997.

Source: authors' research.

fibre. A major project already in hand is a 7,500-km underwater fibre-optic cable being laid around the coast to link twenty-seven coastal cities from Dandong in the north to Fangcheng in the southwest (Figure 3.5) (Yuasa, 1996). An Asia–Europe fibre-optic cable is being built with the Xi'an–Lanzhou–Ürümqi section coming into operation late in 1994 (*People's Daily*, 11 August 1994), and in July 1996 agreement was reached for China to build a 3,900-km Shanghai–Pingxiang link to Singapore via four other countries (*Xinhua News Agency*, 4 July 1995).

Formerly, the MPT supervised the entire telecommunications industry, but this monopoly ended in December 1993 when the State Council approved a second network operator, United

Telecommunications Corporation Ltd (Unicom), jointly owned by the Ministries of Electronic Industry, Railways, and Electric Power and such major businesses as the China International Trust and Investment Corporation (CITIC) (Zhang and Wang, 1995: 89). By early 1997, however, this new entity had made little progress mainly because it was denied access to MPT's network until the State Council intervened in September 1996. It now faces an uphill battle for market share as it has only 15,000 subscribers in Guangzhou, for example, as against MPT's 400,000 (Sender, 1997: 75).

Since 1983, satellites have been used for transmitting national, educational, and provincial television programmes within China. The use of standard Mandarin for national news and other broadcasts is gradually helping to break down some of the long-standing language, ethnic, and other barriers. The 1991 launch of Hong Kong-based StarTV, which broadcasts across East and South Asia, brought international television to China, although in 1993 access to it and other foreign broadcasters was controlled by restrictions on the sale and use of satellite receiving dishes. Since then rival broadcasters have been competing to secure a foothold in the burgeoning Chinese market for free-to-air and pay-TV. Yet another development has been the introduction of the electronic mail network (Internet) which became available in most major cities during the mid-1990s and quickly found favour not only with official, academic, and business users but also with the owners of personal computers, sales of which took off after 1991 and totalled over 1.5 million in 1996 (*Market Daily*, 14 January 1997). Internet users numbered 200,000 at the end of 1996 (*Market Daily*, 16 January 1997).

Financial Flows

A national financial network is emerging (Wang and Li, 1995: 72–81; Wong, 1995; Yang, 1995), thus helping to facilitate the greater capital flows that have accompanied the strengthening regional economic linkages. By early 1995 eleven nationwide or regional share-issuing commercial banks (such as the Bank of Communications, and the Guangdong Development Bank) were operating, although only 40 of their network of 150 branches were located away from the coastal zone (Liu Weiling, 1995). There are also numerous rural and municipal credit unions.

A significant contribution to the inter-regional movement of capital is made by the remittances of millions of peasants temporarily working in the coastal cities. By far the largest net transfers through the post office system (amounting to US$263 million in 1995 alone) are to Sichuan Province, with all the south-eastern provinces stretching from Hebei to Guangxi Zhuang AR receiving net inward transfers except Guangdong (the largest outflow) and Hainan. Since some of the poorer rural counties derive more money from this source than from local taxes or the profits of their collectively owned enterprises, these remittances have become an important stimulus for local development (*People's Daily*, 5 March 1995).

Gateways

In 1978 only 51 ports, airports, and road and railway border crossings were permitted to handle international freight and passenger traffic; by 1995 such authorized 'gateways' numbered 229 to 124 sea and river ports, 50 airports, and 40 road and 15 railway border crossings (Press House, 1996: 337). Most seaports along the east coast handle foreign trade, although the bulk of this traffic passes through Dalian, Tianjin, Qingdao, Shanghai, Guangzhou, and their satellite ports. Several inland river ports, mainly along the Changjiang, Xi, Heilong, and Songhua rivers, also handle international cargoes. Some of the newly authorized road and rail border crossings have long been used as informal trading places; others have been reopened after being closed for several years for political reasons; and others again reflect the trade and investment relationships that have been developing with countries like Myanmar, Laos, and Thailand. As a case in point, in February 1996 the railway crossings on the Sino-Vietnamese border at Pingxiang–Dong Dang and Hekou–Lao Cai, shut when relations soured in 1979, were reopened to allow through-running from Beijing to Hanoi and better access for the Chinese businesses which have started to invest in Vietnam (Murata, 1996: 22). In the north-west, the Lianyungang–Lanzhou–Ürümqi line was extended westwards late in 1992 to connect up with railways in neighbouring Kazakhstan, and Hunchun in the north-east was linked by rail early in 1997 with coastal ports in Russia and the Democratic People's Republic of Korea (see Chapter 7).

Much of the international air passenger traffic passes through the gateways of Beijing, Shanghai, and Guangzhou before moving to and from other parts of the country by train or by the thirty or so regional airlines which have started operations during the last decade. Gradually other cities are developing direct international flight connections, such as Harbin with Urkutsk, Dalian with Seoul and Tokyo, Kunming with Rangoon and Bangkok, and Qingdao with Osaka and Seoul. During 1996, over 51 million tourists entered China, of whom nine-tenths were Chinese from Hong Kong, Macau, Taiwan, and other South-East Asian countries. Early in 1996 the Federal Express Corporation was granted permission to operate an all-freight air service between China and the United States.

Inter-regional Economic Integration

Although transport and communication links within and between regions have been improving, many obstacles still hinder the flows of people and goods. Apart from the clogged railway system, several other key transport problems impair the overall efficiency of the system (Rong, 1993a,b). The main seaports have insufficient handling capacity and too few deep-water berths to meet the growing demand; inadequate warehouse and storage space causes delays and necessitates multiple handling; inter-modal transfer of containers is restrained by the lack of facilities; and transport planning is poorly co-ordinated both between modes and between the various levels of government.

The main transport problem, as stressed already, is the serious shortage of railway capacity, largely because of the priority given to coal, building materials, and other bulk freight. Space for non-priority freight has to be booked weeks in advance and there is no certainty as to when consignments will reach their destination, thus tying up capital in stock-in-transit and making 'just-in-time' manufacturing strategies impossible. About one-third of the hubs in the network are saturated; the number of serious 'bottle-necks' has doubled since the early 1980s; and the lack of places where trains can pass further constrains operations.

In general, roads are poorly maintained, with vehicular traffic having to share narrow pavements with pedestrians, bicycles, donkey carts, and tractors (Rong, 1993a: 314–20). Although some

90 per cent of the 1.2 million km of roads are described as 'paved', only about 4 per cent can handle even 2,000 vehicles daily. A national highway system is being developed, and those stretches of multi-lane expressway between major centres already open—2,140 km by the end of 1995 (*People's Daily*, 23 January 1996)—or under construction will eventually form part of four key routes (see later). Several have been financed through 'build, operate, transfer' (BOT) arrangements by which foreign companies finance construction and then retain toll-booth revenues for a set period before handing over the project to the domestic partner. The most publicized example is the 123-km Shenzhen–Guangzhou six-lane expressway built at a cost of US$1,200 million by Hopewell Holdings Ltd as part of a system which includes a 4.6-km bridge across the Zhujiang River connecting with another similar link from Guangzhou to Zhuhai near Macau (Stevens, 1994). Opened in July 1994, this cut travelling time between the Hong Kong border and Guangzhou from five hours to one. Revenue comes from tolls and the development, under a forty-year lease, of shopping centres three storeys high underneath each of the ten feeder road access points. Even though these tolls are low by international standards, they have discouraged many truck drivers (Becker, 1995) so that the expressway attracted only two-thirds of the traffic expected. Other explanations given are the large number of accidents and the inability of much of the ageing truck fleet to keep above the 60 kph minimum speed usually required.

Evidence about the impact of these new expressways seems mixed even though they reduce travelling times considerably. Thus, the 144-km Taiyuan–Shijiazhuang highway opened in June 1996 allows through-running to Tianjin, cutting on-road time between Shanxi's provincial capital and its nearest port from two days to twelve hours (Cheung, 1996b). In some cases people appear to have been reluctant to change their habits. Shandong provincial traffic authorities, for example, found that the 347-km Jinan–Qingdao expressway did not lead to the expected shift from railways to buses (*Reuter Australasian Briefing*, 8 December 1995). A contrasting claim is that traffic volumes on the 375-km Shenyang–Dalian expressway increased from 15,000 vehicles a day when it opened in August 1990 to 25,000 vehicles by the end of 1994, giving rise to the hope that the investment of US$258 million might be recouped in ten rather than twenty years as originally envisaged. Furthermore, by introducing easy access to modern

transport, this expressway provided opportunities 'for formerly isolated towns where rural factories were previously restricted to
making bricks and tiles' to operate 'enterprises in co-operation
with partners in big cities' (*Xinhua News Agency*, 28 September
1994).

The limited use of highways also reflects the absence of a national road haulage system. Most carriers are local operators with
limited resources. Even so, multinational companies involved
in joint venture manufacturing operations—Johnson & Johnson,
Unilever, and United Biscuits among others—are now turning to
road transport for a growing proportion of their long-distance
freight needs (Anon., 1996a). Direct costs are higher than rail, but
they are more than compensated for by the greater flexibility,
reduced damage, and faster and more certain delivery times. Yet
problems about using roads for interprovincial deliveries remain:
in many inland areas the number of semi-official tolls and police
and customs checks is growing, as is the incidence of highway
robbery (Becker, 1995). Another obstacle is that most Chinese
cities require vehicles with out-of-town plates to buy special
permits.

Tackling the Problems

The plethora of transport problems is not helping the development
of a cohesive and nationally orientated spatial economy. Indeed,
firms trying to sell throughout the country still see it as 'a collection of markets' (Bradbury, 1996), a situation that will change only
slowly during the next couple of decades. The same basic transport
tasks will remain: coal will continue to be the main energy source
and, along with grain and fuel oil, will dominate north–south freight
movements. Increasing quantities of minerals, timber, and pastoral
products will have to be moved from inland areas to the coastal
zone, with manufactured products moving in the opposite direction. Increasing quantities of imports and exports will need to be
channelled to and from seaports, inland river ports, and border
crossings.

Despite all the construction activity in hand or about to begin,
the supply is unlikely to catch up with the growth in demand for
transport in the near term. To keep the national economy growing
at an annual rate of about 9 per cent, one estimate has suggested

that each year rail freight capacity will have to increase by 60 million tons, port handling capacity by 54 million tons, and air passenger facilities by 5.5 million people (*Zhongguo Xinwen She News Agency*, 25 June 1993). Efforts are being made to ameliorate some of the problems by curbing additional demand and increasing capacity, but the transport sector has to bid against other sectors for local and imported investment funds.

Railways

Railway construction projects already in hand—such as doubling the length of electrified track to 20,000 km by 2000—will reduce congestion on some routes. In the north–south direction, the 2,368-km Beijing–Kowloon railway will eventually handle 50 million tons of coal annually, thus easing the pressure on the Beijing to Shanghai and Guangzhou routes. East–west movement has already been greatly improved by the double-tracking of the 1,622-km Lanzhou–Ürümqi line, and the construction of the 498-km link from Baoji (Shaanxi Province) to Zhongwei (Ningxia Hui AR). In the north-east the Dalian–Harbin line is being electrified and that from Harbin to Manzhouli on the border with Russia is being double-tracked.

More specifically to help improve coal transport, the 635-km dedicated line from the 'coal capital' Datong to Qinhuangdao (China's leading coal port) has been upgraded to carry 100 million tons annually, and another 630-km line will be completed in about 2015 to shift 60 million tons of coal annually from Xinxiang (Henan Province) to Shijiusuo (Shandong Province). Due for completion in 2003 is a 599-km railway from Shenfu on the recently discovered Shenmu–Fugu field in Shaanxi Province to a new seaport being built at Huanghua (Hebei Province), and there are also proposals to make Shaanxi coal more accessible to the Shanghai and Sichuan regions.

The problem of financing these proposals remains. From 1980 through 1994, railway construction used US$4,000 million in loans from foreign governments and international financial organizations. The Ministry of Railways, recognizing in 1992 that it could no longer continue to depend on central government funds and institutional loans, added a levy to regular freight rates for a Railway Development Fund. This provided 63 per cent of the 1993 investment outlay of US$2,800 million—four times the amount spent during the previous five years put together (*Reuter Australasian Briefing*, 20 March 1995)—with a further 29 per cent being provided as loans from domestic banks. This Fund will be a major source for the US$40,000 million needed by 2000 to build 8,100 km of new lines, upgrade others, and buy rolling stock. A US$420-million railway bond issue was floated to help meet the US$4,100-million railway work programme proposed for 1997 (compared with outlays of US$3,900 million in 1996). As another initiative, the Ministry of Railways has entered into joint ventures with local governments, one of the first being the 357-km Sanshui–Maoming line in Guangdong Province.

So far, foreign direct investment in railways has been minimal, with the 252-km Jinhua–Wenzhou line—jointly owned by Hong Kong interests (25 per cent), the Ministry of Railways (30 per cent), and the Zhejiang Provincial Railway Corp. (40 per cent) being the only such venture (*China Daily*, 6 September 1996). Cautiously, however, the Ministry has been paving the way towards some foreign involvement in the railway system, with the Dalian, Nanning, and Fuzhou areas being selected for experimental shareholding reforms, along with the Datong–Qinhuangdao and Guangzhou–Shenzhen lines. The latter, the 147-km Guangshen Railway Company, was given considerable autonomy to set schedules and fares, and floated on the Hong Kong Exchange in December 1995 (Lai, 1996: 8).

Private investment in railways dedicated to specific uses like coal haulage or operating entirely within the boundaries of one province may create fewer political problems, but some observers see strong arguments for retaining central control of the whole system to avoid the difficulties involved in operating trains that enter, exit, and re-enter listed, unlisted, and centrally controlled sections of track. Elsewhere, private investors are attracted to railway ventures mainly because of the income that can be generated from commercial and residential property developments around stations and other nodes along the route but, to follow suit, China will need to clarify pricing arrangements, land use, ownership, and other complex legal issues. Such difficulties would be exacerbated by provinces competing for lucrative, but sometimes illusory, property development rights alongside the tracks (Ngai, 1995).

Enlarging and modernizing the railway system will at best be only a partial answer to the transport problem, much of which stems from the priority given to coal. To try to minimize further increases in this traffic, new fields in the eastern part of China— including those located in eastern Nei Mongol AR, eastern Heilongjiang, south-western Shandong, and northern Anhui Provinces—are being assessed and exploited. Large power stations are being built or are under consideration in the main coal-producing areas so that electricity rather than coal can be distributed (see Figure 3.3 inset). In Shanxi Province, for instance, the Yangcheng power station has five thermal units under construction, and the Phase 2 expansion of Shentou power station, which will draw coal from the opencast coal-mine at Pingshuo, is being evaluated (Cheung, 1996b). Considerable effort, too, is being put into improving the efficiency of energy production and reducing pollution through clean-coal technology. As another partial solution, a 102-km pipeline, the first of its kind in China, carries 2 million tons of coal and water mixture a year to the Taiyuan Steel and Iron Co. plant in Shanxi Province. Application of a policy to locate more of the energy-intensive plants, such as those producing aluminium and ferro-alloys, close to energy sources is illustrated by the further expansion of the Shanxi Aluminium Plant at Hejin.

Power

Work on four more nuclear power stations—the Lianyungang and Guangdong Ling'ao plants, and the Qinshan Phase 2 nuclear plant and Phase 3 heavy water reactor—is due to begin before 2000. These will produce 6,600 MW and, along with the existing plants at Qinshan in eastern Zhejiang Province and at Daya Bay near Hong Kong, will bring China's total nuclear capacity to 9,000 MW (*Reuter Australasian Briefing*, 2 February 1996). The state plan envisages installed total nuclear capacity reaching 20,000 MW by 2020.

Roads

Some of the stretches of highway being opened will eventually form part of a national system—envisaged in the Ninth Five Year Plan—centring on four key routes, two running north–south and two east–west (see Figure 3.6). These trunk roads will be linked to local economic nodes by feeder highways and expressways, largely financed and managed by provincial and local governments (Crothall, 1996). How much of the 3,500 km of expressways

Figure 3.6: Key highways, ports, and waterways forming the basic structure of China's transport system.

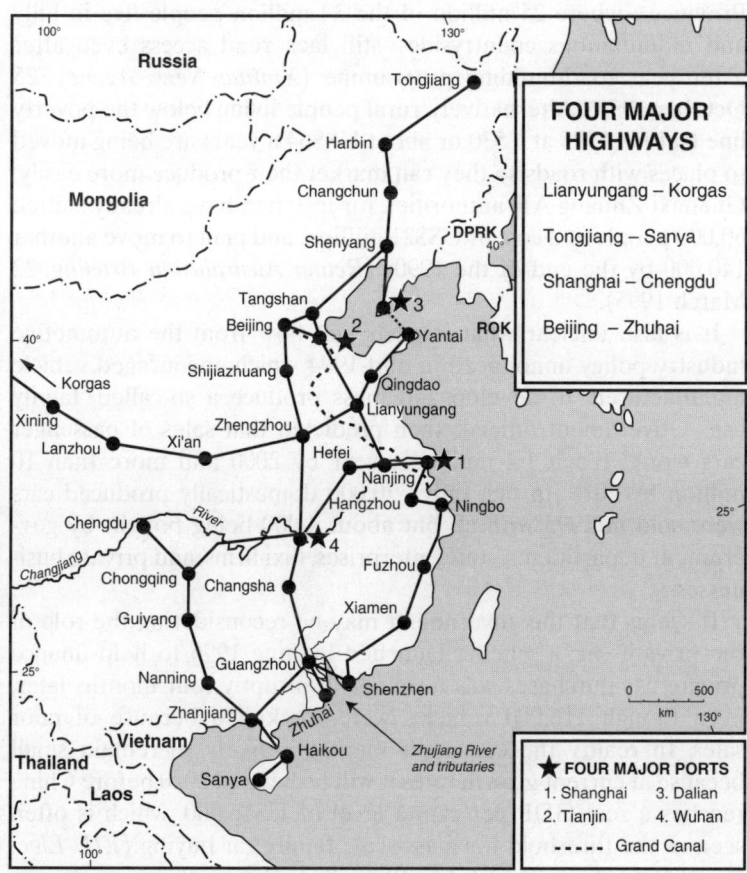

FOUR MAJOR HIGHWAYS

Lianyungang – Korgas

Tongjiang – Sanya

Shanghai – Chengdu

Beijing – Zhuhai

★ **FOUR MAJOR PORTS**
1. Shanghai   3. Dalian
2. Tianjin   4. Wuhan
----- Grand Canal

Source: after Crothall, 1996.

planned for construction by 2000 actually appears on the ground depends very much on the availability of overseas investment and how best it should be allocated (*People's Daily*, 24 January 1996). The benefits of additional high-quality expressways have to be weighed against the outlays needed to slow the mounting costs of urban traffic congestion and the further deterioration of urban public transport services.

Decisions have to be made, too, about the priorities for funding roads other than highways. Thus, road construction forms part of the nationwide campaign to reduce rural poverty and stimulate agricultural production, yet a fifth of the villages in Shaanxi Province—where 25 million of the 34 million people live in hilly and mountainous countryside—still lack road access even after a ten-year road-building programme (*Xinhua News Agency*, 25 October 1995). Alternatively, rural people living below the poverty line (set for 1995 at Y530 or about US$64 a year) are being moved to places with roads so they can market their produce more easily; Guangxi Zhuang AR authorities, for instance, have already shifted 60,000 people at a cost of US$21 million, and plan to move another 140,000 by the end of the 1990s (*Reuter Australasian Briefing*, 22 March 1995).

It is also unclear what impacts will flow from the automotive industry policy announced in mid-1994 which encouraged vehicle manufacturers to develop and mass produce a so-called 'family car'. Government officials then predicted that sales of passenger cars would reach 1.2 million a year by 2000 and more than 10 million by 2010. In fact only 370,000 domestically produced cars were sold in 1995 with all but about 4,000 being bought by government departments, state enterprises, taxi firms, and private businesses.

It seems that the government may be reconsidering the role of the private car: a scheme launched in June 1996 to help finance private car purchases was terminated abruptly four months later, even though 116,000 vehicles were stockpiled because of poor sales. In reality the consumer market is likely to remain small because at current growth rates it will be beyond 2020 before China reaches a real GDP per capita level of US$6,000, which is often seen as the threshold for mass-scale family car buying (*EIU Electronic Publishing*, 21 October 1996). Speculation about numbers is idle, however, because much will depend on how the central government manipulates such levers as credit and interest rates, on the level of taxes and fees imposed by local authorities, and on the availability of the logistical support facilities like service stations— largely lacking in the mid-1990s—necessary to keep vehicles on the road.

Ports and Waterways

An ambitious programme to build new sea and river ports, and upgrade existing ones, will help to relieve chronic waterfront con-

gestion. Four large-scale deep-water international ports are proposed or are under construction at Dayao Bay in Dalian (Liaoning Province), Beilun in Ningbo (Zhejiang Province), Yantian
in Shenzhen (Guangdong Province), and Meizhou Bay (Fujian
Province). The latter has no large river depositing silt into the bay
whereas Guangzhou Harbour will have to be constantly dredged
to enable 50,000-ton vessels to enter and leave, thereby raising
handling capacity from 70 million tons in 1994 to 100 millions tons
by 2015.

The lack of a co-ordinated port operating strategy involving all
the authorities and tiers of government has, however, long been a
concern of Chinese transport economists (Shen, 1990: 107). The
resulting problems are illustrated by the situation at Ningbo, 140
nautical miles south of Shanghai across Hangzhou Bay (Anon.,
1995). This became the country's largest iron ore handling facility
when Shanghai's Baoshan Iron and Steel Works needed a second
port and is now also striving to become an international container
port and a transit centre for goods consigned to places along the
Changjiang River. Yet Shanghai, by far the largest container port
in China, wants to develop facilities within the Municipality rather
than 'lose' cargo to Ningbo in Zhejiang Province. Such divergent
ambitions, it is argued, merit central government intervention to
initiate an overall development plan for Shanghai and Ningbo,
nearby ports like Zhoushan, Nantong, and Zhapu, and—as discussed in Chapter 5—for those along the Changjiang River.

China's 110,000-km network of rivers, lakes, and canals has been
described as 'a vast resource waiting to be revitalized'. By 2000
work will be underway on numerous projects, such as improvements to the 800-km waterway from Nanning to Guangzhou so that
it can handle 1,000-ton vessels. One of the most ambitious projects
is a US$557 million programme (supported by the World Bank to
the tune of US$210 million) designed to take seagoing vessels deep
into landlocked areas (Land, 1995). This work, to be undertaken
mainly in Zhejiang and Hunan Provinces and Guangxi Zhuang
AR, will rehabilitate six major waterways to raise shipping capacity from 100 to 1,000 d.w.t.; reopen sections closed when dams
were built without locks for ships; widen and deepen stretches so
that they can take larger and more efficient vessels, thus helping to
nurture the economy of inland areas and transferring more freight
to a less polluting mode of transport (*Xinhua News Agency*, 22 June
1995).

Air Links

The growth of nationwide business operations and rising living standards are expected to increase air passenger traffic by over 10 per cent annually until well into the next century, thus creating a demand not only for more airports, aircraft, and navigation equipment but also for pilots, air traffic controllers, and maintenance technicians, all of whom are in short supply. Nine new airports were opened in 1994 and another twenty were built or significantly upgraded during 1995 (*South China Morning Business Post*, 22 April 1995: 5). Industry analysts point to the need for some 500 airports by 2005, compared with about 139 in civilian use in 1996 (only 81 of which can accommodate Boeing 737, or larger, aircraft). The main impediment to expansion is the lack of funds.

Although the rules were changed in 1994 to allow foreign companies to put money into airport construction, uncertainty surrounding the status of Zhuhai airport—which was opened in 1995 to domestic traffic only and not, as anticipated, to international flights—has made foreign investors more wary. This problem in Guangdong Province is repeated elsewhere in China because of the conflicting aims of local governments, which see airports as a good source of tax revenue, and provincial authorities, which are concerned about the cost-effectiveness of local facilities less than about 30 km apart unless they play a complementary role to larger hub airports.

Freight Handling

Attention is also being paid to provision and upgrading of commodity handling facilities and the logistics of multi-modal operations. Thus, in July 1992, Nippon Express Co. Ltd (the world's largest general transport company) joined with Chinese interests to engage in freight forwarding and warehousing services which it hopes to extend throughout China. Many large corporations are setting up warehouses and entire logistic chains in China that they are using to tranship cargo to other Asian ports until the domestic market here can absorb their goods.

Use of containers will increase and lead to both competition and co-operation between transport modes. Following the lead of Zhengzhou in Henan Province, container depots will spread through inland places as enterprises there become better informed about the savings that containerization can bring, especially by reducing the incidence of theft and damage.

A Longer-term View

The main framework of China's spatial economy for at least the first half of the twenty-first century will be the major transport-orientated corridors now being formed or further consolidated. Leading them will be the economic belt along the coast, the Changjiang Valley, and the Lianyungang–Lanzhou, Beijing–Guangzhou, and Beijing–Hong Kong railway corridors. They will be joined by others. After 2000, a train ferry linking Liaoning with Shandong will probably be operating across the Bohai Sea, thus allowing freight traffic (in particular) to move north and south without passing through the congested Beijing–Tianjin–Tangshan area, saving both time and about 1,000 km distance. The possibility of building a bridge or tunnel across the Bohai Sea between Dalian and Yantai has also been researched. Even if only one of these schemes eventuates it will radically change the organization of the transport system along the eastern seaboard.

There are proposals, too, for linking Japan by tunnel with the Korean Peninsula and China, or connecting Japan by bridge or tunnel via Sakhalin Island to Russia and thence to China. The possibility of linking Hunchun with the Trans-Siberian Railway at Borzya is being considered as part of the Tumen River cross-border project that is beginning to take shape in Jilin Province (see Chapter 7). In the south-west, interest focuses on developing the Mekong River as a passageway to the sea although, in the meantime, Kunming (Yunnan Province) was connected early in 1997 by an 899-km railway to Nanning and thence to the upgraded port of Fangcheng in Guangxi Zhuang AR. The feasibility of upgrading or building road and rail links from Kunming into Thailand and Myanmar is being examined.

Yet another proposal is for an Euro-Asia Continental Bridge— a railway, road, and communications corridor running from the eastern seaboard of China (and hence accessible to Japan, the Republic of Korea, and Taiwan) across China and countries on its western border to the Netherlands. This would not only link the major economies of Asia and Europe but would also give them access to the rich natural resources in between. Provinces alongside this corridor, including Jiangsu, Shandong, Henan, Shaanxi, and Gansu, and Xinjiang Uygur AR, are already considering how best to draw benefit from it.

China's first high-speed trains are likely to go into service before 2020, with several international consortia already making feasibility studies. The first will connect Beijing and Shanghai. Some have argued that China cannot afford investments of this kind and that the high fares needed to cover costs would be beyond the reach of most people; others point out that they are necessary in densely populated parts of the country as part of the drive towards a modern, efficient transport system.

Greater competition between long-distance rail and road transport will lead to better use of existing infrastructure: the railways, for example, will double-stack containers on parts of the system where tunnels or low bridges are not a problem, and there will be better integration of long-haul road services with local door-to-door collection and delivery arrangements. Pricing structures will become more competitive and bring market forces to bear on traditional ways of handling merchandise. Direct shipping and air services between mainland China and Taiwan will challenge Hong Kong's role as the transhipment centre for international cargoes, and boost the tonnages passing through ports in Fujian and Guangdong Provinces and, perhaps a little later, other ports along the eastern seaboard.

China's energy situation is greatly influenced by limited oil resources and the dominance of coal. It is predicted that 450 million tons of coal will be moved from the Shanxi–Shaanxi–West Nei Mongol producing areas to the rest of the country in 2000 rising to 750 million tons in 2020. The full-cost pricing of coal, often of poor quality and produced in remote township and private mines, and a greater willingness to consider alternative sources of energy such as imported oil, could change the geography of the energy industry and thus, in particular, the transport task involved and the direction of flows.

For example, the traditional movement of coal and oil from the west and north to the east and south may be replaced to some extent by imported oil being piped from the coast towards the west and north. Other changes may come about if Russia and China go ahead with the proposal to construct a 4,000-km pipeline (at a cost of US$6,000 million) to transport 20 million tons of oil and 26,000 million m^3 of gas annually from Siberia to China (*ITAR-TASS*

News Agency, 7 June 1996). Russia has also indicated a willingness to sell its southern neighbour 15,000 to 20,000 million kWh of power annually from the Irkutsk region of Siberia. If funds became available, there is potential, too, to make more use of resources within China itself such as by further developing hydro-power in the south-western provinces, and the Liupanshui coal deposit in Guizhou Province (the largest reserves south of the Changjiang River) which, if fully developed, could replace Shanxi Province as the main coal supplier to the southern part of the country (*Jingji Cankao Bao*, 15 May 1996: 2).

Another issue is whether the growth of energy consumption can be held below the rate of growth of the national economy. Some observers think this may be possible if structural change continues to favour production processes and sectors that consume less energy. On the demand side, an important uncertainty is the rate at which urban and rural consumers will shift to more energy-intensive modes of transport (e.g. private cars) and types of household appliances (e.g. water heaters and air conditioners). Further, there is growing concern in China about environmental pollution and the need to reduce the use of dirty coal (only 22 per cent of the annual output is washed), particularly in urban areas.

The danger is that central ministries and local governments will make decisions about these kinds of issues from their own separate perspectives and without considering the likely impacts, individually and collectively, on the structure and operation of the various modes of transport.

4   The South-East: The Cutting Edge of China's Economic Reform

Noel Tracy

The period since economic reform began in 1979 has seen a substantial shift in the strategic balance of China's economy. This has been caused primarily by the rise to economic and industrial prominence of the South-East embracing Guangdong, Fujian, and Hainan Provinces (Figure 4.1). At the outset of the reform process, the South-East, with over 8 per cent of China's population, contributed only 7 per cent of GDP, or about half that of the Changjiang (Yangtze) Delta (see Chapter 5), while the industrial output was less than Shanghai Municipality alone and little more than one-third of the Changjiang Delta region. By 1993, the position had changed dramatically: the South-East's share of GDP had almost doubled to 13.4 per cent while Guangdong, with 9 per cent of GDP, had become the leading economic province and the second most important industrial province after Jiangsu. Furthermore, the South-East was responsible for 12.9 per cent of agricultural output—a figure that had risen steadily, if not spectacularly, during the previous decade. Substantial improvements in productivity must have occurred given the region's reorientation to industry and the resulting loss of arable land, and the changes in the structure of the workforce.

This, however, was only part of the transformation. More startling was the region's leading role in China's Open Door strategy, its influence being even greater in this respect than its growing contribution to the domestic economy. By 1992, the South-East was contributing 27 per cent (22 per cent by Guangdong Province alone) of China's exports. The region's international trade surplus was double that of China as a whole, suggesting that even in a good year the rest of China had a trade deficit in excess of US$4,500 million (*Statistical Yearbook of Guangdong* [*SYG*], 1993: 95; *Fujian's Statistical Yearbook* [*FSY*], 1993: 359). More recent figures indicate that Guangdong's dominance in foreign trade is accelerating: its share of China's total international trade reached 44 per

Figure 4.1: Main physical features of the South-East, showing also the boundaries of the regions and sub-regions discussed in the text.

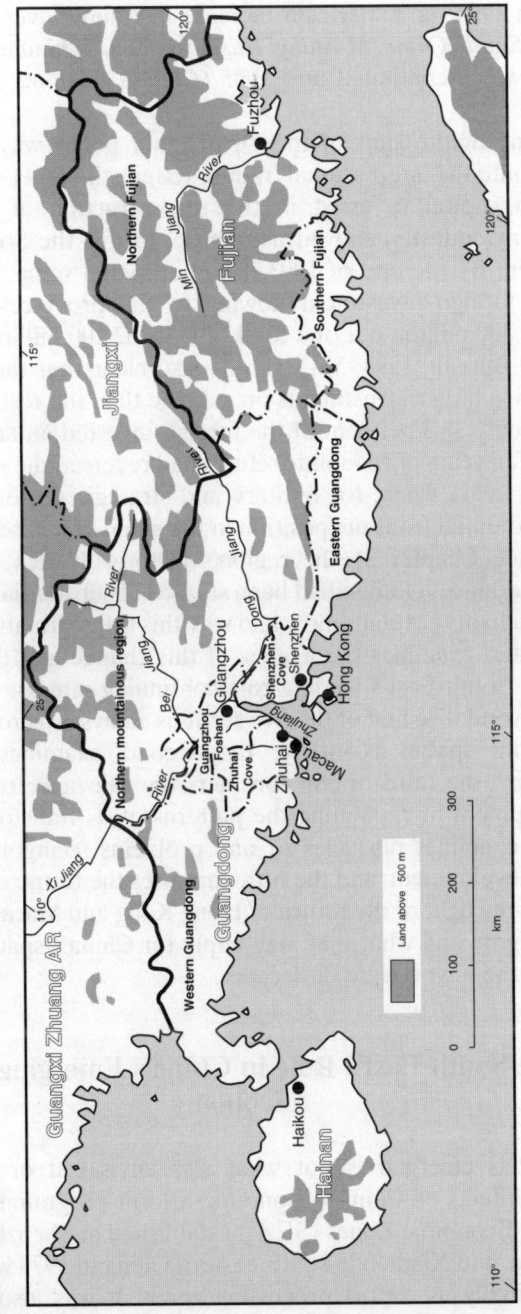

cent in 1994—a 70 per cent increase in volume over the previous year (*South China Morning Business Post*, 5 January 1995: 6), a trend which continued into 1995 (*China's Customs Statistics*, (3), 1995).

If one of the aims of the Open Door policy was to integrate China into the international trading system, the other was to attract foreign capital to assist in the reconstruction of the nation's economy, industry, and infrastructure. In this the South-East has excelled. By the end of 1993 it had attracted some 51.8 per cent of all foreign investment flowing to the provinces since 1979, US$77,800 million out of a total of US$152,200 million (State Statistical Bureau, 1994: 531). It was also clear that the region was attracting larger investments on average than the rest of China for it had only 38.3 per cent of the foreign-invested enterprises.

Fifteen years of economic reform had reversed the neglect of the Maoist years when, for military and strategic reasons related to their potential frontline position in the event of any seaborne invasion (see Chapter 2), the region's historically rich provinces of Guangdong and Fujian had been starved of substantial investment.

This chapter explains how and why this transformation has taken place, and examines the agency of this change and the prospects for the South-East's leading role continuing into the next decade and beyond. The first of the five sections analyses its role in China's emerging spatial economy; the second examines its spatial economy; the third briefly considers the relevance of theories of development in explaining the patterns of its transformation; the fourth examines obstacles to, and problems facing, its continued rapid development; and the fifth appraises the future of the South-East in the light of the return of Hong Kong and Macau to Chinese sovereignty and what that may imply for China's spatial economy during the next couple of decades.

The South-East's Role in China's Emerging Spatial Economy

What has emerged is not what was envisaged or planned by the architects of China's economic reform programme. The four Special Economic Zones (SEZs) established at Shenzhen, Zhuhai, Shantou, and Xiamen in south-eastern China in 1979 were thought of originally as export processing zones. It was also considered

likely that foreign capital would use them as such, thus quarant-
ining smaller and more entrepreneurial capital, whereas multinational capital could be attracted into joint ventures (JVs) with the
large state firms with a view to reorganization and technology
transfer. Foreign capital could thereby be contained within the
central plan.

This did not eventuate. Before 1985, the SEZs were kept going
by domestic investment and registered an overall trade deficit
(Chan, 1985) while multinational capital remained largely aloof,
except for investments in offshore oil exploration in collaboration
with central government ministries (Chan, 1993; Zhang and Tracy,
1994). The crucial date for the South-East was not 1979 but 1985
when, because of the very limited success of the previous strategy,
the whole of the Zhujiang (Pearl) River Delta region and the triangle delineated by Xiamen, Quanzhou, and Zhangzhou in southern Fujian Province were opened to foreign capital (Linge and
Forbes, 1990b: 14–26). Since then the rise of the South-East has
proved unstoppable. Ever-increasing volumes of foreign capital
have flowed in while Guangdong Province's own producers have
become increasingly export orientated: by the early 1990s, some 60
per cent of its substantially increased industrial output was being
sold outside the province, half to export markets and half to the
rest of China (Wang Xue-ming, 1992: 24; *SYG*, 1993: 185).

The explanation for this rapid transformation lies in the synergy
created between the emerging social forces in the South-East and
Overseas Chinese entrepreneurs from Hong Kong, Taiwan, and
South-East Asia and beyond, who flooded into the region, but particularly into the Zhujiang River Delta after 1985. In Hong Kong
and Taiwan, increasing labour costs coupled with rising land prices
and rents meant that labour-intensive manufacturing was no longer
sustainable. This was coupled with another crisis arising from their
very success as export-orientated economies: they needed profitable new outlets for their growing capital. The opening of the
Zhujiang River Delta and southern Fujian Province provided solutions to both these difficulties. Labour-intensive industries could be
moved out of Hong Kong and Taiwan to sources of cheaper labour
where such activities could also be expanded. The Overseas
Chinese have subsequently dominated investment flows into the
region, contributing at least 80 per cent of the very substantial
sums invested there—more than US$32,000 million of the total
US$38,800 million foreign direct investment (FDI) during the

1979–92 period (*SYG*, 1993: 364; *FSY*, 1993: 346, 349; Tracy, 1994: 2–4).

The initial reform period had seen the flowering of township and village enterprises (TVEs) following the abandonment of the commune system in the countryside, which freed the rural economy from the dictates of the central plan. These industries had grown rapidly by soaking up latent consumer demand for a greater variety of food and consumer products, and resulted in rapidly rising living standards in both country and city in the early 1980s. By the middle of the decade, however, the momentum of this type of development had begun to decline (Lardy, 1992). The arrival of the Overseas Chinese in the South-East gave TVEs fresh momentum as they provided new opportunities for JV partners and subcontractors to orientate themselves towards export openings in which the Overseas Chinese had the marketing expertise and outlets (Overholt, 1993). A new partnership was born which has grown from strength to strength.

This did not just mean shifting labour-intensive Hong Kong and Taiwanese industries to China: it also involved the exponential growth of a whole component of world capitalism. In 1985, manufacturing industry in Hong Kong occupied just over 950,000 workers, but by 1993 it employed barely 500,000. At this time, Hong Kong industrialists employed a conservatively estimated 3 million workers in the Zhujiang River Delta alone (Baldinger, 1992: 14; Yamaguchi, 1993: 6). Hong Kong entrepreneurs had increased their manufacturing capacity at least fourfold and, as the trade figures showed, had won international markets for their increased production. The situation for Taiwanese entrepreneurs was similar but not as spectacular as they were moving from a larger industrial base. Nevertheless, Taiwanese industry employs as many people in China as in Taiwan itself.

In 1980, 51 per cent of Guangdong Province's miserly US$2,550 million international trade, consisting mostly of foodstuffs for local consumption, went to Hong Kong, with some 96 per cent of it being controlled by state trading corporations. By 1993, 85 per cent of the international trade, which had increased thirteenfold to US$35,262 million, passed through Hong Kong or Macau, while the share of central government and provincial trade corporations had fallen to 37 per cent.

Hong Kong marketing channels were clearly the means of launching Guangdong-produced goods on to world markets. The number of import/export enterprises there grew rapidly from little more than 14,000 in the early 1980s to more than 89,000 in 1992 (Baldinger, 1992: 14; *South China Morning Business Post*, 2 July 1994: 2). Hong Kong also has a major entrepôt role for southern Fujian Province, particularly because of the prohibitions on direct trade with Taiwan. Hong Kong estimates also suggest that a further 55,000 wholly Chinese-owned firms in Guangdong Province alone are producing export goods for Hong Kong companies (Overholt, 1993: 189–91). Without doubt, the South-East's export orientation depends substantially on the Overseas Chinese connection.

The South-East, clearly led by Guangdong Province, is the principal exporting region, contributing 44 per cent of China's total exports, over 40 per cent of its exports of manufactured goods, and 65 per cent of all exports by foreign-invested enterprises in 1994 (*SYG*, 1993: 95, 351; *FSY*, 1993: 359; *South China Morning Business Post*, 5 January 1995: 6). Thus, its role in China's spatial economy is to lead the way in export-orientated industrialization and in attaining international competitiveness. This is the strategy which produced the 'four little dragons'—South Korea, Taiwan, Hong Kong, and Singapore—and the similarities between the South-East and these countries at the outset of their climb to international prominence are striking. Like them, being deficient in raw materials, importing capacity has to be provided by export revenue, therefore ruling out an industrialization strategy based on domestic markets. Its comparative advantages are its position in East Asia—the fastest growing region of the world economy—and the ready availability of reserves of relatively cheap labour, while its competitive advantage lies in its ability to link up with the already proven entrepreneurial talents of the Overseas Chinese from Hong Kong, Taiwan, and South-East Asia.

Another crucial role of the South-East is the way it has reduced the importance of the state sector, the restructuring of which has long been at the forefront of China's reform programme, though so far with little success (Chapter 1). The problem is being overcome in the South-East by the growth of the private sector, both local and foreign, which is responsible for an ever-increasing share of the regional economy. As Table 4.1 shows, the ownership structure in the South-East is now quite distinct from that in China as a whole, with the possible exception of Shanghai, and in 1994 accounted for 36 per cent of the total national industrial output

Table 4.1: Gross output value of industry by form of ownership, South-East region, 1993 (per cent)

Area	State	Collective		Other[a]
		urban	village	
Total South-East	40.3	14.6	11.6	33.5
Provinces				
Guangdong	38.4	15.9	12.2	33.4
Fujian	44.5	10.3	9.9	35.4
Hainan	77.5	3.9	2.0	16.7
Total China	57.6	12.7	9.5	10.2

[a] Overwhelmingly private, including foreign-invested enterprises.
Source: *Statistical Survey of China*, 1994: 76.

from the private sector (*Statistical Survey of China* [*SSC*], 1995: 76).

The South-East has also taken the leading role in privatizing the state sector, including several important provincial government instrumentalities such as shipyards, power stations, and toll roads. Quanzhou City in Fujian Province is also famous throughout China for having completely abolished the state sector. All forty-one state companies in the municipality were privatized in 1992 as a result of a JV between one of the city's most famous returned sons, Oie Hong-leong, and the city government, with management rights being ceded to the former. Oie is the son of Indonesian tycoon, Eka Tjipta Widjaja, the founder of the Sinar Mas group, the third largest conglomerate in Indonesia. Control of the group's China operations, however, rest with Oie's publicly listed Hong Kong company, China Strategic Investments (Corporate International, 1994: 55). The government of Fuzhou, the Fujian provincial capital, announced that half the state-owned industries in the city's administrative division had become engaged in JVs with foreign capital by the end of 1993 (*BBC, Summary of World Broadcasts, Far East Economic Weekly Series* [*BBC*], 27 April 1994).

The South-East has thus firmly established itself as the leading region in the economic reform process and therefore in the nation's new spatial economy. It leads the way in raising living standards, in restructuring the economy, in building the private sector, in attracting foreign capital, and in reorientating the Chinese economy towards export markets. It is also the means by which the Overseas Chinese business community has been mobilized to provide the capital and entrepreneurship needed to carry the 'Guangdong model' further into China.

The Spatial Economy of the South-East

The Zhujiang River Delta

At the centre of the South-East's spatial economy is the Zhujiang River Delta—the dynamo with an output dwarfing that of the rest of the region (Figure 4.2). In 1992, this Delta sub-region, with little more than 18 per cent of the population, contributed some 46 per cent of regional GDP and 63 per cent of industrial output, its share of which was still rising. It also contained 57 per cent of the South-East's foreign capital—almost US$22,000 million out of US$38,800 million—and contributed 57 per cent of its exports (Tracy, 1994: 10–14).

The Zhujiang River Delta itself, however, can no longer be seen as a single undifferentiated sub-region. In 1978, it was dominated by the provincial capital, Guangzhou, which contained 67 per cent of the Delta's urban population and produced almost 63 per cent of its industrial output. The only other significant centre in what was still essentially an agricultural area was nearby Foshan (Xu and Li, 1990). The biggest changes have been the rise of other urban places and the growing role of rural-based industry. By 1992, the Guangzhou administrative region (including its outlying towns and villages and the new development zone at Panyu) was contributing barely 30 per cent to the Delta's industrial output, Foshan more than 20 per cent, and the two new production centres around the Shenzhen and Zhuhai SEZs almost as much as Guangzhou and Foshan combined. Essentially, the core-periphery polarization of the Delta had become a thing of the past, and a more balanced spatial economy had emerged with at least three distinct centres.

The first, the old core area around Guangzhou in the north, remains of great importance as it contains 48 per cent of the Delta's population of 18.8 million and generates about half its GDP and industrial output. As it has absorbed only about a third of the Delta's foreign capital and produces only a similar proportion of

Figure 4.2: Main economic features of the South-East.

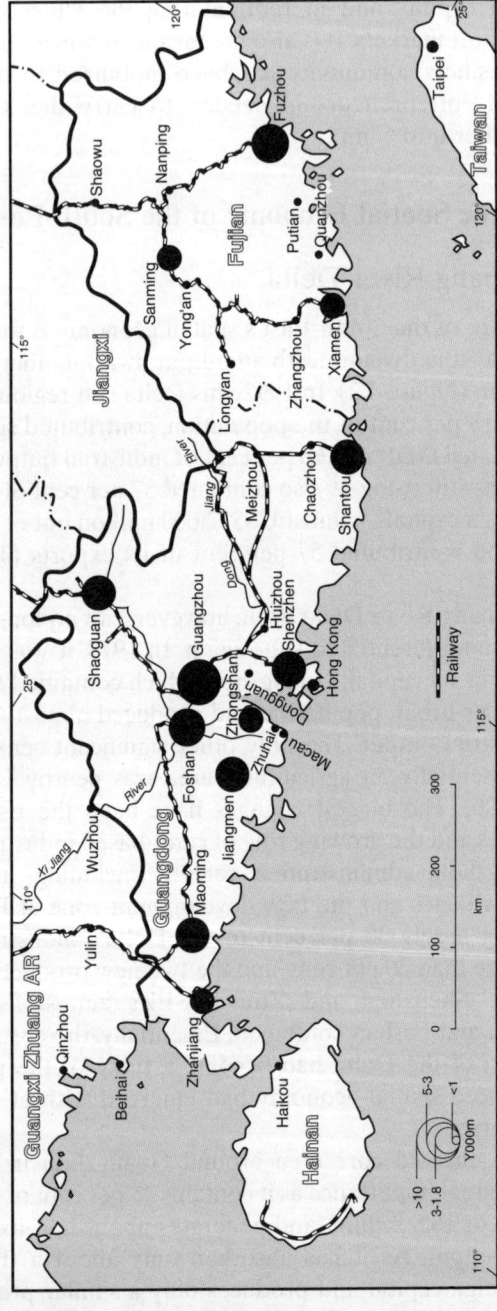

Sources: production data based on Li and Lu, 1995: 533; railways based on Editorial Group, 1995: 104–9.

its exports, it clearly remains more orientated to the domestic market than the two emerging centres in the south.

The second, lying just north of Hong Kong, contains the administrative districts centred on the Shenzhen SEZ and the cities of Dongguan and Huizhou. It has a quarter of the Delta's population (about 4.5 million), produces about 30 per cent of its GDP and more than a quarter of its industrial output. Its real strength is that it contains almost half the Delta's entire stock of foreign capital and is responsible for 48 per cent of its exports.

The third, much less developed than the others, is situated just north of Macau and contains the administrative districts centred on the Zhuhai SEZ and the cities of Zhongshan and Jiangmen. Although having a slightly bigger population than the Shenzhen centre, it contributes only 20 per cent of GDP and 23 per cent of industrial output to the Delta, has less than 20 per cent of its foreign capital, and is responsible for less than 20 per cent of exports. However, its recent rapid growth suggests that it is shaping up to become more significant.

Perhaps the most interesting aspect of this new spatial arrangement of the Delta's economy is the very strong correlation between the shares of foreign capital and of exports, as shown in Table 4.2.

The three centres are also beginning to specialize in different industrial activities (Table 4.3). The old Guangzhou–Foshan core centre still remains the principal base for metal fabrication and machinery, while the area spreading out from Shenzhen has become the focus for the new electronics industry established only since the reform process began. The province's second industrial activity, textiles, clothing, and leather, is well established in both the old Guangzhou–Foshan centre and in the newer south-west area near Macau, especially in the cities of Jiangmen and Zhongshan.

Southern Fujian

While the Delta clearly dominates the economy of the South-East, there are other sub-regions which in a different environment might well be considered dynamic economies in their own right. The most important is southern Fujian Province, delineated by the triangle formed by the cities of Xiamen, Quanzhou, and Zhangzhou, which has attracted over two-thirds of the foreign capital flowing to this province. It is mainly responsible for Fujian's substantial

Table 4.2: Guangdong Province: basic statistics by region, 1992 (per cent)

Areas	Population[a]	GDP[b]	Industry gross output[c]	Exports[d]	Foreign capital investment[e]
Zhujiang River Delta					
Guangzhou	9.5	21.4	22.9	13.3	16.2
Foshan	4.5	10.0	15.4	9.6	8.4
sub-total	14.0	31.4	38.3	22.9	24.6
Shenzhen	1.2	11.9	13.3	26.0	21.8
Dongguan	2.1	3.5	3.5	5.1	7.8
Huizhou	3.7	3.5	3.4	3.0	5.9
sub-total	7.0	18.9	20.2	34.1	35.5
Zhuhai	0.8	3.9	4.7	4.6	6.2
Zhongshan	1.8	3.0	4.2	3.5	3.0
Jiangmen	5.6	6.0	8.4	5.1	4.7
sub-total	8.2	12.9	17.3	13.2	13.9
Total Delta region	29.2	63.2	75.8	70.2	74.0
Eastern region	20.1	9.6	6.5	11.5	10.3
Northern region	21.1	9.3	5.5	2.1	4.0
Western region	29.6	17.9	12.2	5.5	7.4
Guangdong Province	100.0	100.0	100.0	89.1[f]	95.7[f]

[a] Total population: 64,361,000 (year-end 1992), excludes military.
[b] Gross Domestic Product: Y239,000 million.
[c] Gross Output Value of Industry: Y276,000 million.
[d] Exports: US$18,400 million.
[e] Direct foreign investment US$29,670 million.
[f] Excludes contributions of provincial level institutions and projects.

Source: Statistical Yearbook of Guangdong, various years.

international trade surplus, which approached US$2,000 million in 1992 and exceeded US$3,000 million in 1993, making it China's third largest foreign currency earner after Guangdong Province and Shanghai Municipality (*FSY*, 1993: 359; *BBC*, 17 August 1994).

Table 4.3: Gross industrial output, leading industrial groups, Guangdong Province, 1992

Rank	Industry	Output (Y000m.)	Per cent	Centre
1	Metal fabrication and machinery	45.2	16.3	Guangzhou, Foshan
2	Textiles, clothing, leather	43.4	15.7	Guangzhou, Foshan
3	Chemicals (inc. petrol refining)	34.6	12.5	Guangzhou, Maoming
4	Food and beverages	34.4	12.4	Guangzhou, Foshan
5	Electronics, communications	30.4	22.0	Shenzhen, Huizhou
6	Electrical machinery, equipment	25.7	9.3	Guangzhou, Foshan
7	Building materials	12.7	4.6	Foshan
8	Plastic products	11.7	4.2	Foshan, Shantou
9	Paper, printing	9.2	3.3	Guangzhou
10	Cultural, educational products	8.6	3.1	Guangzhou
	Other	21.0	7.6	
Total		276.9	100.0	

Source: *Statistical Yearbook of Guangdong*, 1993: 185, 190–3.

In Xiamen SEZ, foreign-invested enterprises were responsible for 67 per cent of industrial production and more than 80 per cent of manufactured exports in 1993. It had attracted over 2,500 such enterprises by 1994—less than half the number in the Quanzhou district about 100 km to the north—but is attempting to become a centre for the electronics industry. In contrast, Quanzhou (along with its outlying cities of Shishi and Jinjiang) is still concentrating on labour-intensive clothing and footwear processes so that the average investment is lower. Officials in all three cities emphasize the essentially enclave nature of the local economy, noting that few of its manufactured goods have been sold on the domestic market in China because the region is isolated by natural barriers and poor transport links (personal interviews with Xiamen Foreign Investment Executive Committee and Quanzhou Overseas Chinese Investment Service, June 1994). Exporting and a generally outward-looking orientation remain therefore the only feasible path to development and increased living standards.

Eastern Guangdong

Centred on the cities of Shantou and Chaozhou, eastern Guangdong has also emerged as an important contributor to the South-East's relationship with the Overseas Chinese and to the region's international trade orientation. It had attracted more than US$6,000 million in foreign capital by the end of 1993, some 12 per cent of the regional total (*SYG*, 1994: 327), and was also responsible for 9.4 per cent of regional exports in 1992, valued at more than US$2,000 million. Yet, even though it has almost 13 million people or more than one-fifth of the provincial population, it generated only 9.5 per cent of its GDP—a reflection of the backward rural hinterland. The most significant industries are chemicals and plastics, although the textiles, clothing, and leather industries have recently become increasingly important and have begun to attract significant foreign capital to the cities of Chaozhou and Jieyang.

Like southern Fujian, eastern Guangdong remains relatively isolated by natural obstacles and poor transport links not only to other parts of China but also to the rest of the province. This isolation is compounded by linguistic differences, with the local population speaking Teo-chiu, a dialect distinctly different from the Cantonese spoken by most people in Guangzhou Province. Seeking to improve communication links, the provincial government has built a new 459-km, double-track, electrified railway from Guangzhou to Shantou via a northern route through Meizhou, while the new 123-km six-lane Shenzhen–Guangzhou expressway opened in July 1994 has reduced travelling time from five hours to one.

These three regions have largely achieved their positions through their links with particular groups of Overseas Chinese. The Zhujiang River Delta is the Cantonese heartland, southern Fujian is the ancestral home of the Hokkien, while the Chaozhou–Shantou area is the homeland of the Teo-chiu. These are by far the three largest ethnic components of the Chinese diaspora in South-East Asia. The majority of Taiwanese are also of Hokkien ancestry, while Hong Kong—for all its cosmopolitan flavour—is essentially a Cantonese city. The key to success for all three would seem to be their ability to link up with important strands of the Overseas Chinese diaspora, whose connections and knowledge of local customs give them an unassailable advantage in establishing business contacts.

Other Regions

The South-East also contains four other regions, three of which are perhaps notable for having been much less successful in attracting foreign capital and in their weak export orientation.

Northern Fujian. Centred on Fuzhou the provincial capital, this area is somewhat distinct from the rest of the South-East in that its people (with a few exceptions, notably the Malaysian tycoons, the Kuoks, and the Sino-Indonesian Liem family) have not been emigrants and therefore do not have the extensive links to sections of the diaspora enjoyed by the rest of the region. This, coupled with linguistic differences, seems a sufficient explanation for its failure to attract foreign capital to modernize and restructure the economy to anything like the same degree as the southern part of this province or Guangdong Province. Moreover, its economic backwardness is highlighted by the leading position of the relatively small amounts of foreign capital that it has attracted. Despite having only 1,146 foreign-invested enterprises operating at the end of 1993, these contributed 48 per cent of Fuzhou's industrial output and over 80 per cent of its exports. However, Fuzhou's US$73 million-worth of exports in 1993 made up less than 15 per cent of the Fujian Province total, and were regionally insignificant (*BBC*, 27 April 1994). A longer-term comparative advantage for Fuzhou might be its close proximity to Taipei, but this requires resolution of the China–Taiwan issue.

Guangdong northern mountainous region. This is generally considered the poorest and most backward area in the South-East. It does, however, contain the bulk of the province's limited coal deposits which support mines at Shaoguan (the main industrial centre) and Meizhou. Although relatively small, foreign capital is not insignificant here. At the end of 1993, US$3,136 million had been invested in 2,972 foreign enterprises—somewhat more than the number attracted to Fuzhou. It seems to have two potential advantages. First, the mountainous topography means that its fast-flowing rivers may be harnessable for much needed hydroelectric power, both for local use and to supply the Zhujiang River Delta.

Second, the area around Meizhou was the source of many of the nineteenth-century Hakka migrants, many of whom have become prominent in business overseas, and may decide to invest in their ancestral homeland, particularly now it has improved communication links, as the Guangzhou–Shantou railway makes Meizhou accessible from both directions.

Western Guangdong. This area is different again from the rest of the South-East in that its economy is more affected by national politics and policy inputs because the South China Naval Command of the People's Liberation Army Navy (PLAN) is based at Zhanjiang. The South China Fleet, which has about one-third of the PLAN's ships and responsibility for patrolling the South China Sea, is scheduled for expansion and upgrading to blue-water capacity, with at least one aircraft carrier (Goodman and Feng, 1993: 18–19). Because of this and the strategic importance placed by Beijing on its territorial claims to the potentially oil-rich Spratley Islands, the infrastructure of this area is likely to be significantly upgraded in the immediate future. Already, much of the economy of the principal city, Zhanjiang, is given over to servicing the military, and also has a direct link to Beijing via the 'Third-Line' railway.

Further east, Maoming has the country's second largest petroleum refinery (with an annual capacity of 6.5 million tons), while Zhaoqing is an important centre of labour-intensive export-orientated manufacturing. Agriculture still occupies the rest of the region, providing over half its GDP—the highest proportion in Guangdong Province (*SYG*, 1993).

Hainan Province. Hainan Island is in a rather different category from the rest of the South-East. Although industrial development is planned for a special zone around the new port at Yangpu in the north-east, which it is hoped will become a transit zone for processing and manufacturing goods for distribution throughout South-East Asia (Huus 1994a: 48), its future lies mainly in the development of tourism. This sub-tropical island was seen as China's answer to Bali and Phuket and a potential attraction for the tourist dollar. Previously part of Guangdong Province, it was designated the fifth SEZ and granted provincial status in 1988. Since then it has attracted substantial foreign capital, more than US$8,000 million by the end of 1993 (State Statistical Bureau, 1994:

531). Yet, at the same time, it has gained an unenviable reputation for lawlessness and corruption (Huus, 1994a,b,c). While foreign investment has been brisk it has been dwarfed by investment from the mainland, mainly by provincial and municipal governments and wealthy officials hoping to make a quick fortune out of real estate speculation. However, new regulations on bank lending for such speculative projects introduced at the beginning of 1994 burst the real estate bubble of the early 1990s.

Tourism in 1994 was still dominated by visitors from the mainland, who accounted for more than 80 per cent of the 2.8 million arrivals in 1993; Hong Kong has provided the only significant numbers of international visitors. Hainan Province has been held back from becoming an international tourist destination by the poverty of the island's infrastructure, the paucity of first-class hotels, and the sleaziness of much of the service sector in Haikou, the capital. Until a new airport was opened in 1995, the principal resort area at Sanya on the southern tip of the island could only be reached by a 365-km drive on substandard roads. Surface communications with the mainland and Hong Kong are no better, but a new port being developed at Yangpu and the construction of a new north–south highway should lead to significant improvements. Few international operators have so far committed themselves, although the Shangri-La and Hilton Hotels and Club Med have taken options (Cheung, 1993; Huus, 1994a).

Despite its 'boom town' reputation and substantial growth rates, Hainan Province has yet to show dividends for the investment located there. With 7 million people, it contributed little more than 0.7 per cent of China's GDP in 1993 (*SSC* 1995: 10–11) although, because of the general air of lawlessness, this may have resulted from deliberate understatement.

The South-East and Development Theory

Two broad rival categories of development theory have been dominant in recent years: those based on the concept of increasing core-periphery polarization and those which see capitalism, economic and social development, and internationalization gradually being diffused throughout the world. Unfortunately the development of the South-East does not clarify this: rather it provides considerable evidence for both theses.

There can be little doubt that the old core-periphery dichotomy between Guangzhou and the rest of the Zhujiang River Delta has broken down, to be replaced by a much more decentralized economy, and a pattern of urbanization in which the areas growing out from Shenzhen and Zhuhai may be seen as important new core areas in their own right. Likewise, the eastern region of Guangdong Province has gained greater autonomy from the provincial capital because of its ability to develop an industrial base and attract its own sources of foreign capital. Equally, or perhaps more so, in Fujian Province the south has become more important both industrially and in terms of international trade than the provincial capital Fuzhou, again as a result of its ability to link up with an important strand of Overseas Chinese capital. Hainan has also broken most of its dependency links with Guangdong. At the regional level, the South-East has clearly severed whatever links of economic dependency it had on Beijing. Before 1979, Beijing had contributed more than 80 per cent of the South-East's investment capital, but by the 1990s this had been reduced to little more than 2 per cent as a result of its rapid economic growth and vitality, its ability to draw on its own sources of foreign capital, and its access to the capital markets of Hong Kong (Goldstein, 1993).

However, the outcome is not so clear. It could equally be argued that the degree of decentralization reached is merely a reflection of the whole region's becoming the periphery of Hong Kong, which has clearly brought it into the world economy, since the vast majority of its trade flows through Hong Kong and its marketing channels. Hong Kong has been the conduit by which people in Taiwan have been able to bypass their government's restrictions and participate very actively in the reindustrialization of China, and has also been the source of most of the massive flows of foreign capital into the South-East and the staging post for the best part of the rest. Culturally, Hong Kong has also become the principal source of news, ideas, attitudes, and fashions, at least in the Zhujiang River Delta where Hong Kong TV transmissions can almost universally be received. It could be further argued that the role model of the Hong Kong entrepreneur—the independent self-made business person—has been as effective in changing attitudes and expectations as has the flow of capital.

Undoubtedly, the role Hong Kong has been able to play in mobilizing capital for the massive reindustrialization of China since 1985 and in marketing Chinese-made goods globally, has significantly strengthened its position in the international capitalist economy, both as trader and financier. Arguably, this role has also clearly established it as the financial capital of the entire Chinese world.

Yet, even so, there can be little doubt that the structure of the economy of the South-East is now much more balanced and the resources and the future potential of the various components of the spatial economy are more evenly spread than they were before 1979. This is despite the fact that income differentials within the region are, for the moment, widening. Foreign capital and links to the international economy and the changes and opportunities that come with them are beginning to penetrate into even the most backward areas.

The effects of these changes are also being felt well beyond the region. Labour shortages created by rapid industrialization have drawn millions of members of previously underemployed peasant families to the Zhujiang River Delta in search of work. These account for the massive increase of more than 10 million in Guangdong's workforce since 1985 (*SYG*, 1993: 129). This means that one of the effects of the South-East's renaissance is to draw more backward provinces—in particular Hunan, Jiangxi, and parts of Sichuan—into its orbit but it is also further evidence of diffusion of the effects. Remittances from the migrant workers are a significant source of rural income in the inland provinces, thereby creating a demand for goods made by the TVEs (Chapter 3).

Problems Facing the South-East

Despite its immense economic success, rising living standards, and strategic importance in China's outward orientation, the South-East is not without its problems. These fall essentially into three categories: regional identity, infrastructure, and environment.

Lack of Regional Integration

One of the most surprising things about the South-East is that the economy is less an integrated whole than a series of separate parts which have very little interaction. Trade between the spatial components is extremely limited, in part because prior to 1979 horizontal links between provinces were discouraged. As has been explained in Chapter 2, they were encouraged to seek self-sufficiency, with any links to the rest of the economy being mediated by Beijing through its various purchasing and trading arms. Even after 1979 the lack of overland transport and communication links has continued to impede trade. Moreover, coastal shipping does not facilitate internal commerce, and is almost as difficult and costly for most localities as trading internationally or with more distant provinces. Thus coastal areas like southern Fujian Province find it much easier to seek out international markets than domestic ones, particularly as the distribution channels of both Hong Kong and the Hokkienese are available to assist the people there. Likewise for eastern Guangdong Province, cut off from the markets of the Zhujiang River Delta, exporting was easier than intra-regional trade.

Essentially what holds the region together are not so much its internal linkages as the external ones to Hong Kong and the Overseas Chinese who have provided most of its industrial investment and new ideas, as well as its marketing channels into global markets. Without these external linkages it would be hard to envisage this as a coherent region rather than a series of unconnected areas arbitrarily grouped together by location, and for historical reasons that are no longer valid.

Inadequate Infrastructure

Infrastructure remains a huge problem. The shortage of adequate and reliable power has been an everyday headache for industrialists and households alike, as have transport constraints. Until the opening of the Shenzhen–Guangzhou expressway, it was as quick to travel from Hong Kong to Guangzhou by river-boat as by rail, road, or air, the last because of the difficulties of getting from the airport to the city. Likewise to travel the bare 100 km from Xiamen to Quanzhou in Fujian Province took more than three hours. Given the volume of the Zhujiang River Delta's industrial output, the railway north to Beijing (only a single track in each direction) was woefully inadequate but this difficulty has in part been overcome by the opening of the new 2,368-km Beijing–Shenzhen railway in September 1996.

While the last decade has seen massive investment in infrastructure—ports, docks, container terminals, airports, roads, railways, and power installations—such has been the rate of economic growth and lack of co-ordination that what seemed at the planning stage to be potential improvements are outdated almost before they are completed. Increased resources, greater planning, and new foreign capital will all be needed if the inadequate infrastructure is not to remain one of the greatest obstacles to continued development and improved living conditions.

Within the Zhujiang River Delta, transport routes are beginning to improve. The Shenzhen–Guangzhou expressway is a 'build, operate, transfer' (BOT) arrangement between Guangdong Province and Hopewell Holdings Ltd. A ring road around Guangzhou is under construction as is another 110-km expressway between Guangzhou and Zhuhai, with a side road to Jiangmen. Connections between the eastern and western sides of the Delta are to be improved by two bridges across the estuary, one linking Taiping and Nansha (half-way between Hong Kong and Guangzhou), and the other joining Shekou and Zhuhai, thereby linking the two SEZs. These bridges will also connect the two expressways so that the transport network of the Delta region will be transformed before the end of the decade.

The most profound impact of the inadequate infrastructure is in the rapid environmental degradation of some parts of the region. Paradoxically, what has served Guangdong so well—the decentralization to the localities of decision making about industrial and commercial development—has led to extensive pollution problems. The inadequate power supplies have encouraged enterprising townships to construct their own facilities (in many cases assembling them cheaply using antiquated technology), thus leading to a proliferation of inefficient, polluting plants. The preference at all administrative levels for coal-powered installations—because they are cheaper and quicker to build—has led to an almost continuous pall of polluted air hanging over much of the Delta. The spread of such plants also means that those localities which are concerned about pollution are fighting a losing battle. As a result, more than half the rainfall in Guangdong Province is now acidic, causing damage to buildings, crops, trees, plants, and animals (*South China Morning Post*, 27 August 1994: 6).

Fujian Province has not faced these same problems, partly because its industrialization has been less rapid, but also because it has had the good sense to foresee them. Up to 60 per cent of Fujian's power has been generated by hydro-schemes using the province's fast-flowing rivers, and several more hydro, thermal, and tidal schemes are projected for completion before 2000 (*South

China Morning Business Post, 22 June 1995: 5). The differences are quite dramatic: in Xiamen skies are blue and the air visibly cleaner. This is not just due to the absence of dirty power plants: the city authorities have also restricted industrial development to the suburbs and discouraged polluting activities, a policy that had its roots in the partially successful attempt to make Xiamen a centre for electronics production. Help from Singapore's Jurong Town Corporation has also been enlisted for Xiamen's urban planning and the proposal to preserve its historic port area (personal interviews with Xiamen Foreign Investment Executive Committee, June 1994).

Other regional environmental problems concern the air quality in the older-established cities, where the increased volume of traffic on the inadequate road systems causes congestion and slow-moving vehicles. Carbon monoxide levels have increased to such an extent that traffic police are being badly affected, whilst respiratory complaints among the general population are increasing. These can only get worse as China seems quite determined to expand its car industry despite clear evidence that its cities will be unable to cope with increased traffic volumes (Chapter 1). Discharge of untreated sewage and industrial waste into rivers is another mounting problem.

On the credit side, the mountainous nature of much of the South-East means that more than half the land area is still forested, and the water in all but the lower reaches of many of the rivers remains fit to drink. The establishment of Environmental Protection Agencies by Guangdong and Fujian Provinces and new legislation also suggest that these authorities are beginning to take the problem seriously.

If environmental degradation is to be reversed, certain policy changes are required. Provincial control over power generation must first be re-established either directly or by enforceable regulation. In Guangdong, it has now been recognized that coal-powered electricity generation needs to be substantially reduced (see Chapter 3). Seeking a solution from hydroelectricity, even if only a partial one, in the northern mountainous region of Guangdong, and persuading Guangxi Zhuang AR of the desirability of a major river-based scheme on the Xijiang and its tributaries to meet their future needs, are also essential. Another possible partial answer is to fuel future plants with natural gas instead of coal and to convert existing ones as the pipeline network is extended.

Changing to natural gas, of which there are substantial reserves in the nearby South China Sea fields, would not undermine existing industries as Guangdong Province has few natural resources though, again, the problem is the lack of pipelines. The other alternative, and the one already decided upon by the provincial government, is to construct a second nuclear plant at Ling'ao thus adding to the existing installation at Daya Bay, near Hong Kong.

Yet a further problem created by both industrialization and pollution concerns the agricultural future of the Zhujiang River Delta. Much arable land in one of the most fertile areas in China, capable of bearing three crops a year, has been taken out of farming and converted to industrial use, and what is left is also increasingly affected by acid rain and other air and water-borne pollutants. At the same time, production on the much less fertile land in other parts of the region will have to be increased to make up the shortfall—particularly of grain. Quite probably in the not too distant future the region will have to start importing grain from overseas since it is unlikely that other parts of China will be able to make up the shortfall: fortunately, income from exports will be available to pay for it.

Future Prospects for the South-East

The next decade, assuming no convulsions emanate from power struggles in Beijing, is likely to be dominated by three processes: first, the absorption of Hong Kong and Macau back into China; second, the sustainability of the 'Guangdong model' in the light of problems emerging in 1995; and, third, the continuing integration of the South-East with the rest of the South China Sea Basin economy—essentially South-East Asia and Taiwan.

Hong Kong and Macau

The return of Hong Kong and Macau to China in 1997 and 1999, respectively, can only increase the economic primacy of the South-East. The formal addition of the tertiary sectors of Hong Kong and Macau to the industrial capacity of Guangdong and Fujian Provinces will add to the integrating tendencies within the region, even though immigration and customs barriers are likely to be in place between the new Special Administrative Regions and Guangdong for some time. Hong Kong's role as the major source of capital, both in its own right and as the mobilizer of capital from the entire diaspora, for mainland China's continued development is unlikely to be challenged. While Western companies left Hong Kong in anticipation of 1997, Overseas Chinese corporations have been moving in with a different expectation.

The idea that Shanghai will be able to compete with Hong Kong for the title of China's financial capital is essentially wishful thinking. International financial centres are not created by political will, however much the Beijing authorities may wish it, but by a critical mass of expertise, experience, credibility, and institutions built up over a long period. Hong Kong has these and Shanghai does not, and the latter will have to serve a long apprenticeship before it can hope to compete. Already Hong Kong is certainly the world's fifth, and possibly fourth, most important financial centre and capital market after New York, London, Tokyo, and Frankfurt, whereas Shanghai does not even rate in this league. Using Hong Kong's financial markets, surpluses generated in the South-East will be recyclable into the rest of China, thus strengthening the position and primacy of this region.

The Sustainability of the Guangdong Model

By the end of 1995, it had become clear that the continuing ascendancy of the South-East, and particularly Guangdong, could no longer be taken for granted. In 1995 for the first time, Guangdong's rate of economic growth and increase in foreign capital flows slipped behind those for China as a whole, and this trend continued in 1996. This slowdown in Guangdong needs, however, to be put in perspective. The province continues to generate 40 per cent of China's exports and to attract more than US$10,000 million in foreign investment annually, more than a quarter of China's total: it is its relative rather than absolute position which is in jeopardy. The result, however, of this slowdown is that Guangdong's influence in, and on, the rest of China is beginning to decline.

There are several reasons for this. The growing degree of Guangdong's export orientation has been such that its share of domestic markets outside the South-East have declined substantially from their high points in the early 1990s. At the same time, changes to China's foreign trade regime, particularly the loss of the provincial governments' right to retain foreign exchange earnings for their own purposes, have made exporting much less attractive while also reducing both the provincial and local governments' ability to provide export incentives to domestic producers. The result is that the foreign trade sector of the economy, the engine of growth, is now very firmly in the hands of Hong Kong and to a lesser extent Taiwanese entrepreneurs: in 1996 more than 75 per cent of the province's exports originated in foreign-invested companies or their subcontractors (*Guangdong Socioeconomic Statistics Monthly*, (12), 1996). While this is less serious than it might have been were it not for Hong Kong's return to China in 1997, it none the less makes Guangdong a much less attractive model for other parts of China than has hitherto been the case. The slowdown in the rate of economic growth also means that Guangdong's ability to absorb any new waves of migrant labour has been reduced, raising questions within China about its ability to retain its status as the Mecca of the new economic prosperity into the next century.

While much of the pessimism and scepticism about Guangdong's achievements, particularly in official circles in Beijing and Shang-hai, is overblown, evidenced by the province's ability to continue to generate US$60,000 million in exports and attract US$10,000 million in new foreign investment even in the 'bad years' of 1995 and 1996, there can be little doubt that its period of meteoric rise is probably over and consolidation of its position is more the order of the day. What is also clear is that Guangdong's future prosperity, and with it the whole of the South-East's, is now even more firmly tied to Hong Kong and the latter's ability to provide both the investment capital for future growth and the mar-keting channels to put the region's industrial products into world markets.

A phenomenon of the past decade has been the rapid integra-tion of the South China Sea Basin economy. Trade and investment flows between the two ends of this economy—Hong Kong, Taiwan, and mainland China on one side and the Association of South-East Asian Nations (ASEAN) plus Indochina on the other—have increased rapidly. Exchanges within the Basin in 1992 accounted for 37 per cent of the region's trade, up from 20 per cent in 1980, and by the 1990s accounted for a greater proportion than that with North America and Japan combined (Table 4.4). The value of ASEAN's trade with Hong Kong, Taiwan, and China increased

Table 4.4: Trade of the South China Sea Basin[a], 1980 to 1992 (US$000 million)

Trade with:	1980	Per cent	1985	Per cent	1992	Per cent
US/Canada	36	17	50	19	124	16
Japan	48	23	59	22	129	16
Intra-Basin	43	20	75	31	290	37
Other	84	40	82	31	241	31
Total	211	100	266	100	784	100

[a] ASEAN countries (Brunei, Indonesia, Malaysia, the Philippines, Singapore, Thailand and Vietnam), Hong Kong, Taiwan, and People's Republic of China (the latter included in full because of the very large proportion of its trade passing through Hong Kong—two-thirds in the early 1990s).

Source: International Monetary Fund, various years.

more than sixfold between 1980 and 1992, twice as fast as with any other region. The South China Sea Basin itself was also the principal source of foreign investment for virtually every country in South-East Asia, this particularly being the case in China, Vietnam, and the Malaysian state of Johore, where regional sources contributed more than all the external ones combined (International Trade News, 16 May 1994: 1; Baum, 1994; Vatikiotis, 1994). With China's insatiable demand for imports and its ability to pay for them with export earnings, intra-regional trade is likely to grow in the coming decade and with it continuing regional economic integration. In this, the links of the Overseas Chinese are the crucial glue binding the South China Sea Basin together.

The South-East's role will therefore remain what it has been since 1985: to bring the business community of the region—the Overseas Chinese—into the project to transform China and at the same time to take this country out into the region and beyond. The South-East is likely to continue to base its development strategy on the production of light industrial goods and the satisfaction of consumer demand at home and abroad. At the same time the demand for more sophisticated tertiary activities to service both industry and consumers is certain to grow so that such enterprises from Hong Kong and new locally based ones will play a more important role in the regional economy. However, if the quality of life within the South-East region is to match the industrial dynamism there, some of the bottom-up approach to development will have to be modified. The living environment is likely to be a major issue for the coming decade and beyond: fortunately, it is also one of the few regions in China with resources enough to contemplate doing anything substantial about it.

5 The Head and Tail of the Dragon: Shanghai and its Economic Hinterland

SHE ZHIXIANG, XU GUAN, AND GODFREY LINGE

The image has emerged of Shanghai as the head of a dragon with the riverside zone along the Changjiang (Yangtze) Valley as its body and tail, in all covering some 330,000 km^2 and supporting a population of more than 300 million. Part of it, the 99,000-km^2 Delta economic area consisting of Shanghai Municipality and much of Jiangsu and Zhejiang Provinces, is identified in the Ninth Five Year Plan as one of the seven economic zones to be developed in China without regard to administrative boundaries (Figure 5.1). The Plan sees the advantages as 'its river-sea link, well-developed agriculture, solid industrial foundation and relatively high technological level', and notes the opportunities being created by the development of the Pudong area in east Shanghai, as well as the construction of the Three Gorges project. Upstream, three other economic co-ordination regions are developing—around Nanjing in the lower reaches, Wuhan in the middle, and Chongqing in the upper reaches.

The Changjiang Valley, stretching 2,400 km into the western interior, has become the leading foreign investment belt, attracting 30 per cent of the flow entering China in 1995 as against a mere 5 per cent in 1991. Its annual exports have reached US$30,000 million or more than one-fifth of the national total. This change in fortunes occurred for a variety of reasons but was boosted by a strategy put in place in 1992–93 to co-ordinate and facilitate development among the string of large and medium-size cities along the Changjiang River, which is navigable 1,460 km upstream from Nanjing to Yichang in Hubei Province. The stated aim is to build an export-orientated economic structure based on enterprise groups and regional and international co-operative arrangements (*Xinhua News Agency*, 18 July 1996).

This chapter focuses on the recent revival of Shanghai as a major commercial centre and its ambitious goals for the future, the industrialization of the Delta area adjacent to it, and the articulation of

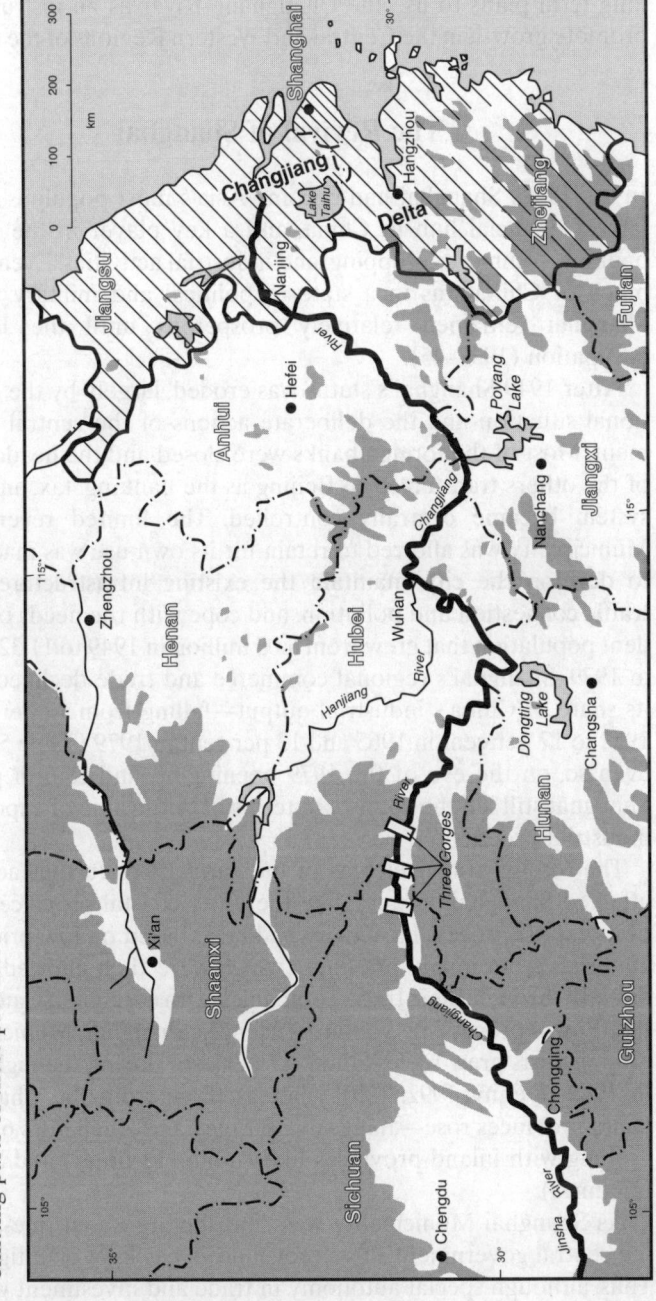

Figure 5.1: Main physical features of the Changjiang River–Shanghai region. Here the whole of Jiangsu and Zhejiang Provinces have been included as part of the Changjiang Delta but sometimes a stricter definition is used (as in Figure 5.3) omitting parts of these provinces.

long-term plans to use the Changjiang River as an instrument to promote growth in the Central and Western Regions of the country.

The Revival of Shanghai

In the 1930s Shanghai had become Asia's most populous city, the largest financial hub in China, and a key player in the region's banking, commerce, shipping, and industrial activities. Even though much of China was in a state of political and military turmoil, Shanghai remained relatively prosperous until the Japanese occupation (1937–45).

After 1949 Shanghai's status was eroded, largely by the international situation and the deliberate actions of the central government. Most of the foreign banks were closed and the headquarters of the others transferred to Beijing as the banking, tax, and credit system became centrally controlled. The limited revenue the Municipality was allowed to retain for its own use was inadequate to develop the city, maintain the existing infrastructure, tackle traffic congestion and pollution, and cope with the needs of a resident population that grew from 5.03 million in 1949 to 11.32 million in 1979. Shanghai's regional commerce and trade declined, as did its share of China's industrial output—falling from 19 per cent in 1952 to 17 per cent in 1965 and 13 per cent in 1979 (Table 5.1), but, even so, on the eve of the 1979 opening-up and reform policies, Shanghai still led the country in terms of both value of exports and industrial production.

The foreign trade reforms of the early 1980s further adversely affected Shanghai because, like the other coastal provinces, much of its export processing activity had been based on low-priced raw materials from inland provinces which were then allowed to deal directly through their trade companies with foreigners, and set up their own processing ventures. Hence, Shanghai Municipality's total exports grew by less than 8.7 per cent during the eight years to 1988 (Denny, 1992: 199), whereas those from the Changjiang Delta provinces rose—Jiangsu's 2.8 times, and Zhejiang's 6.7 times —along with inland provinces like Anhui (12 times) and Sichuan (23 times).

As Shanghai Municipality was contributing about one-third of the central government's fiscal revenue, it was kept on a tight rein. Thus, although special autonomy in trade and investment was also given to Shanghai, Beijing, and Tianjin Municipalities in 1979,

Table 5.1: Percentage of China's gross industrial output by Changjiang Valley administrative areas, 1952 to 1995[a]

Administrative area	1952	1957	1965	1974	1979	1984	1991	1995
Shanghai Mun.	19.0	16.3	16.9	15.4	12.9	10.6	6.9	5.6
Jiangsu Province	7.6	5.9	5.2	6.8	8.4	9.7	11.2	12.9
Zhejiang Province	3.2	3.1	2.7	2.3	3.3	4.7	6.4	8.8
Total Delta region	29.8	25.3	24.8	24.5	24.6	25.0	24.5	27.3
Other provinces[b]	8.6	9.3	8.2	8.4	11.7	12.7	11.4	12.0
Changjiang Valley	38.4	34.6	33.0	32.9	36.3	37.7	35.9	39.3

[a] After 1984, village-run enterprises were transferred from agricultural to industrial output statistics.
[b] Anhui, Hubei, Hunan, and Jiangxi Provinces.
Sources: Pannell, 1988: 22; State Statistical Bureau, 1992, 1996a.

Fujian and Guangdong Provinces were granted additional privileges. Importantly, for a five-year period Guangdong's annual fiscal transfer to the central government was set at a relatively modest fixed annual amount, with any additional revenue being retained for local developmental purposes, whilst through much of the 1980s Shanghai Municipality had to remit about three-quarters of the revenue raised locally—a much greater impost than on any other region in the country (Ho, 1993: 12.15; Sung et al., 1995: 18).

There were other important differences. Guangdong used its powers innovatively, allowing its local governments to compete entrepreneurially for foreign direct investment (FDI). In contrast, Shanghai not only centralized decision making but also pursued high-tech industries appropriate for its built-up areas while paying less attention to labour-intensive, export-orientated processing activities that might have revitalized its more rural hinterland (Sung et al., 1995: 26). For all these reasons overseas investors tended to bypass Shanghai: during the 1979–89 period, for example, it received only 8 per cent of the realized FDI flowing into China, whereas Guangdong Province attracted 42 per cent (Nyaw Mee-kau, 1993: 16.13).

To some extent Shanghai was caught in a vicious circle. The obligations to the central government left it without the means to upgrade decaying infrastructure or tackle the chaotic mixture of land-uses, traffic congestion, air and water pollution, decaying housing, and even the shortages of drinking water, as they tried to cope with a burgeoning population, expected to grow from 11.8 million in 1982 to 13 million in 2000, that was sprawling beyond the so-called City Proper into the surrounding areas under municipal control (Hyslop, 1990). In short, it was difficult for the Municipality to implement the structural and spatial adjustments needed to attract FDI, export competitively, and progress economically. By the mid-1980s Shanghai had forfeited its position as China's leading industrial producer (in terms of gross output value) and by 1990 had been relegated to fifth place.

Fortunes Change

The greater emphasis placed on coastal development following the 1987–88 Party Congress (Fincher, 1990: 43–4) triggered moves to restore the city's fortunes. Important, too, was the rising political influence of the Shanghai leadership. The central government now backed the development of this city and its hinterland by granting priority access to various kinds of state investments and loans, and arranging favourable policies to attract foreign capital (Lam, 1995). A wider political agenda may have been involved. While China's paramount leader Deng Xiaoping was making his now-famous visit to south China early in 1992, suggestions were being made that the central government wanted to spearhead economic reform in Shanghai as a counterweight to Guangdong so that the reformist south did not race too far ahead of the rest of the country (*Reuter Australasian Briefing*, 3 February 1992). This seemed easier said than done. Observers pointed out that 'unlike the south, where whole towns devoted to export industry have been built to order by foreign business, Shanghai is saddled with a lumbering industrial sector that is mired in debt and seems immune to reform' (Quinn, 1992).

A significant step occurred in 1991 when additional foreign-owned banks were permitted to establish branches in Shanghai, joining the four foreign and overseas Chinese banks that had been allowed to operate there after 1949, considerably deepening the developing financial network. This opening of the local financial markets to the outside world was crucial to the fund-raising needed to develop Pudong, a farming area east of the Huangpu River (Dai and Li, 1992). This proposal—first suggested in the 1920s and revived by Shanghai Municipality in 1986—was adopted as a central government initiative in April 1990, and formally endorsed by the Party Congress in October 1992. Deng Xiaoping proclaimed during his 1992 Shanghai visit that the development of Pudong (discussed later) was not only important in its own right but also because it would invigorate the Municipality, help it regain a role as an international economic, financial, and trade centre, and act as an engine to stimulate development in the Changjiang Delta and Basin areas. His call for people to 'emancipate their mind and take bolder and quicker steps' further boosted the massive programme that the municipal government had in hand to build and improve infrastructure and to attract business investment, especially from overseas. In Shanghai alone, an estimated 7 million m^2 of commercial, retail and residential space were built each year from 1990 through 1995 (*Business Times*, 26 May 1995).

Some major projects were already in train, including two high-level bridges over the Huangpu River, an inner city ring road, a subway line, and the renovation of the waterfront Bund (Figure 5.2). Problems like traffic congestion, air and water pollution, substandard housing, dilapidated public utilities, and the mix of inappropriate land uses in the existing built-up area of Shanghai were among those tackled with renewed vigour. Programmes were set in motion to shift old factories, government offices, and residents to new industrial and housing estates in the suburbs so as to make room for financial and other service activities in and around the central business district. By mid-1994 300,000 people had thus been relocated and 200 new industrial nodes created (*Xinhua News Agency*, 1 June 1994).

Financing these projects became somewhat easier after November 1993 when the Third Plenum of the Fourteenth Central Committee reduced the tax revenue payable to the central government by the Municipality from around 67 per cent to 60 per cent (Kohut, 1993). Shanghai reckoned to pay 40 per cent of the infrastructure projects from its own coffers, 20 per cent through bond and share issues, and the remainder through loans from foreign banks and agencies. Overseas finance was particularly important for major

Figure 5.2: Layout of Shanghai Municipality and the Pudong New Area.

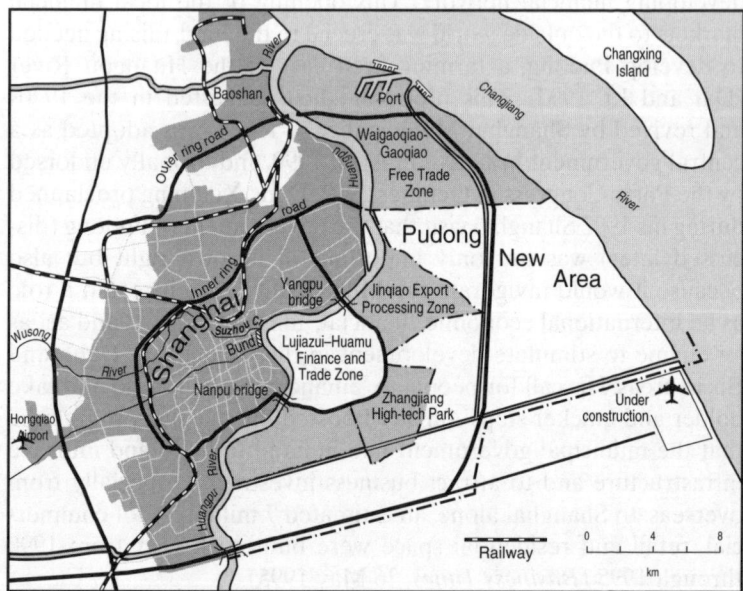

Source: based on Shanghai Pudong New Area Administration, 1993.

projects like the subway, which drew funds from Germany, France, and the United States. In 1994 alone Shanghai used special foreign preferential discount-interest and foreign loans to the tune of US$210 million, as well as multilateral and bilateral international aid totalling US$26 million (*Xinhua News Agency*, 11 February 1995). By the mid-1990s the World Bank had lent US$2,000 million to the city, half of it for transport and environmental schemes. Among these was a project to clean up the infamous Suzhou Creek by diverting 5 million m^3 of treated dirty water (over half Shanghai's total sewage) to the Changjiang River, and another to shift the city's drinking water intakes to less polluted sources (Jiang, 1994; Earnshaw, 1996).

Yet even the completion of the 48-km Inner Ring Road late in 1994 and the opening of a north–south 16-km mass transit subway in April 1995 only partially solved Shanghai's traffic problems, with the planners arguing that a further 300 km of rail line and many more viaducts were needed (*South China Morning Post*, 3 May

1995). Furthermore, despite the supplementation of the existing tunnels and ferry services by the two new bridges across the Huangpu River, parts of Pudong remained inaccessible. In particular, enterprises and workers have shown a marked reluctance to relocate to the Lujiazui financial and commercial district being developed across the river opposite the Bund.

Another pressing problem was the need to rehouse residents of some of the older parts of Shanghai, where per capita living space was only 4 to 7 m^2 and even basic sanitary facilities were missing, as well as people affected by infrastructure projects. The overall aim is to raise the residential space for 70 per cent of the urban population to at least $10\,m^2$ per person by 2000, up from $8\,m^2$ in 1995. However, it is claimed that a third of the replacement housing built during 1994 lacked utilities and only 14 per cent of the 100 million m^2 under construction in 1995 was expected to have access to gas, water, and power in the short term (Chen, 1995a). Much of this housing, it seems, was built in unsuitable areas and the US$120 million needed to provide these services is not available.

Several solutions to these housing problems are being tried. Fees and levies have been reduced to encourage local and foreign developers to replace substandard housing with inexpensive apartments, and the Municipality has also become a leader in China in selling public housing. By mid-1996 over 600,000 families had bought their homes, accounting for about half the city's stock of public residential accommodation. Lowering the purchase tax, raising rents, and restructuring the house allocation system are among the measures introduced to stimulate the market. Banks in Shanghai have become more competitive and now offer a variety of mortgage schemes.

Enterprise Ownership and Employment

A chronic and continuing difficulty is the dominant position of state-owned enterprises (SOEs) in Shanghai's economy, a problem that has been exacerbated by the increasing competition from Sino-foreign joint ventures (JVs) and township and village enterprises (TVEs) with lower overheads and fewer retired workers to support. While the number has shrunk since the late-1980s, the remaining 16,000 SOEs still account for 70 per cent of the Municipality's GDP and employ about 5 million people or around 80 per cent of its workforce.

The Shanghai government was instructed in 1994 to experiment with ways of improving the efficiency of a hundred or so selected state enterprises—for instance by reducing their social responsibilities—to set an example to other cities (*South China Morning Post*, 28 November 1994). Two years later President Jiang Zemin again pressured the Shanghai administration to implement controversial measures aimed at turning inefficient loss-making enterprises (officially estimated as one-third of the total) into lean and profitable businesses while ensuring that job losses were kept within politically acceptable limits (Foo Choy Peng, 1996). Some have been bankrupted or broken up into smaller independent units; converted into limited companies or partnerships; bought by the employees; or moved to cheaper sites. Other strategies include the transfer of property rights to some enterprises so they can transform run-down sites into supermarkets, hotels, and other profitable businesses (E. Chan, 1996), and the sale of valuable inner city sites by textile ventures which then relocate production to other parts of China where labour and material costs are lower (*Reuter Australasian Briefing*, 7 August 1996). Shanghai's Economic System Reform Commission estimated that these stronger measures would require 600,000 people to change jobs by the end of 1997 and 1 million by 2000. The workforce in the textile industry alone is being reduced by 120,000 to 250,000 (already down from 550,000 in 1990), and in the instrument making industry by 80,000 to 120,000. It is hoped that out of this restructuring will emerge four or five corporate giants by 2000, each with annual sales of US$12,000 million. Conglomerates like the Baoshan Steel Group, the Shanghai Petrochemical Company, and the Automobile Industry Corporation are being groomed to take their place among the world's leading 500 firms.

In effect, Shanghai has been experimenting with grassroot solutions to the China-wide problems appearing during the transition from a state-run economy, where everyone was allocated a job, to the socialist market economy, where efficiency and profitability are paramount. The Municipality has also been trying out ways of assisting the workers made redundant by setting up employment agencies; running retraining courses; encouraging SOEs to establish service sector subsidiaries; and extending embryo pension, unemployment, and medical benefit schemes that have traditionally been the responsibility of, and increasing burden on, state enterprises (*South China Morning Post*, 25 August 1996). Another solution has been to arrange for labourers to take up work on contract projects abroad or as crew on ships.

Claims that many laid-off people do not want labouring or service sector jobs highlight the role of the 'floating' population—believed to number about 2.5 million—living in the Municipality. About 500,000 have official permits, mostly to work on construction projects, but others are working illegally with their employers risking a fine. As is commonplace elsewhere, migrant workers are accused of taking the jobs of local people as they are prepared to work two shifts, seven days a week for about Y1,000 (US$120) a month. Official responses are that migrants do difficult and hazardous jobs that no one else wants (in fact the only ones they are permitted to do under regulations introduced early in 1995).

At the end of 1995 there were some 6,000 foreign-funded industrial enterprises in Shanghai creating one-fifth of the Municipality's gross industrial output. The manufacturing sector continued to attract about two-thirds of the FDI entering Shanghai, much of it associated with prominent multinational companies (MNCs). Indeed, by the end of 1994, 190 of the world's leading 500 manufacturing enterprises had invested US$1,980 million there, 126 of them during the previous three years (*Shanghai Star*, 21 March and 13 June 1995; Cao Yong, 1995). Of these, 92 (with an average investment of US$11.3 million) were Japanese (e.g. Mitsubishi Elevator and Ricoh Fax Machine); 42 (US$20 million) were American (e.g. Johnson & Johnson, and Xerox); and 15 (US$49 million) were German (e.g. Volkswagen and BASF Dyestuffs). As these examples indicate, much of this investment was in the Municipality's six priority 'pillar' industries—motor vehicles, iron and steel, telecommunications and information equipment, power generating equipment, petrochemicals and fine chemical processing, and household electrical appliances—which in 1995 accounted for 46 per cent of the value of the Municipality's gross industrial product. Improvements to infrastructure have made suburban industrial zones increasingly attractive to overseas-funded investors with some (like DuPont and BASF) locating in high-tech parks (*Xinhua News Agency*, 30 April 1996).

Future Development

The goals set out in a development plan through to 2010 are robust (Chen, 1995b). Between 1996 and 2000 the GDP is expected to increase by 10 to 12 per cent annually, and the six existing pillar industries are targeted to account for more than half the industrial output. Already, however, competition is stiffening as other places are promoting similar industrial portfolios, so the plan is for Shanghai to put more emphasis on activities like shipbuilding and environmental protection equipment, as well as new 'strategic' industries such as biomedicine, micro-electronics, and high-tech substitutes for traditional materials in such fields as construction and electronics (Liu, 1996). As labour costs are rising and the Municipality has few natural resources, the manufacturing of capital and technology-intensive export items, like complete plant and equipment, are high on its list of priorities. Total overseas trade is targeted to reach US$38,000 million (with exports valued at US$20,000 million, half consisting of electrical goods and machinery), roughly double the 1995 results when exports were valued at US$11,557 and imports at US$7,479 million. With one-third of its local industrial enterprises operating at a loss, in part because of stiffening competition on the domestic market, Shanghai has established distribution agencies and franchise outlets nationwide with the aim of selling 40 per cent of locally made industrial products in other parts of China and 40 per cent abroad (*Xinhua News Agency*, 1 September 1996). Some 200 Shanghai-owned ventures are operating in the Changjiang Delta and Valley alone with, for example, Shanghai No. 1 Department Store having branches in Hefei and Chongqing.

During the second phase from 2000 to 2010, GDP is expected to grow by 10 per cent annually to reach US$241,000 million, with finance and insurance accounting for 20 per cent and domestic trade for 16 per cent. Tertiary activities are seen as the lead sector in 2010, contributing 60 per cent of GDP (up from 45 per cent in 2000) and employing 30 to 40 per cent of the workforce. Pillar and high-tech industries will contribute over 60 per cent of the Municipality's industrial output value.

A physical plan to shape Shanghai into an international metropolis during the next two decades was released in mid-1996 (Chen, 1996a). The blueprint divides Shanghai into four sections: the central urbanized area, three medium-size cities, six county towns each accommodating 200,000, and 220 small towns in the suburbs. The core area of 600 km², encircled by a 98-km ring road that includes part of Pudong, will have a population of 8 million. The emphasis here will be on service industries focused around a central business district embracing the Bund and the Lujiazui areas, and four commercial centres.

The three medium-size cities in the Baoshan, Jiading, and Minhang districts will contain Shanghai's main industrial zones and food processing activities based on local produce: these will have a combined area of $300\,km^2$ and a population of 3 million. Circulation will be facilitated by the construction of an outer ring road and a suburban ring road to connect all the county towns plus eleven new subway lines and ten light rail lines totalling $400\,km$. The plan also envisages that the area of the Municipality will have been increased to $6,340\,km^2$ (compared with the current figure of 5,910 km^2) when it will have an estimated 17 million inhabitants, including a floating population of 3 million.

In January 1996 Premier Li Peng announced plans to turn Shanghai into an international shipping hub in co-operation with Jiangsu and Zhejiang Provinces. His statement was probably also designed to stop the squabbling between ports in the Delta region (see Chapter 3) and to serve as a warning to rivals like Taiwan and Singapore that Shanghai intends to become a regional port of call by 2010 and an international shipping centre capable of accommodating the largest container carriers by 2020. Even though Shanghai was China's leading container port, handling 1.8 million twenty-foot equivalent units (TEUs) in 1996, mostly along the Huangpu River, much needs to be done if this goal is to be achieved. A 20-km sandbar, formed because the Changjiang River widens, slows and deposits silt at Shanghai, prevents the passage of vessels with draughts of over $7\,m$ and laden with more than 1,600 TEUs. Shanghai Municipality and Jiangsu Province are collaborating to deepen port access from $7\,m$ to $12.5\,m$ at a cost of US\$1,200 million, but most of the port activities will eventually be relocated to Waigaoqiao (containers), Luojing near the Changjiang River mouth (coal and bulk), and a proposed new deep-water port at Hangzhou Bay (general cargo).

The Opening-up of Pudong

The development of Pudong—a 522-km^2 triangular area located between the Huangpu and Changjiang rivers—is being energetically subsidized by the central government in support of the strategy of 'facing the world, facing the 21st century and facing modernization' (Shanghai Pudong New Area Administration, 1993: 3–5). Indeed, it has become such a prestigious symbol, 'an emblem of new Shanghai in the 21st century', that any sign of faltering or failure would have immense political ramifications. When approval was given in April 1990 for work on Pudong New Area to begin, it already had a population of 1.1 million, largely concentrated along the east bank of the Huangpu River in a narrow 38-km^2 urbanized strip with large iron and steel, petrochemical, glass making, and shipbuilding enterprises interspersed between innumerable small factories and workshops. The rest consisted of paddy fields and vegetable plots amidst long-established villages. From the outset it was recognized that before further development could take place in this area—accessible only by ferry and two narrow road tunnels—an inner ring road bypassing the congested inner city and two bridges across the Huangpu River had to be completed.

Shanghai Municipality, assisted by central government grants and overseas loans, invested US$9,000 million in Pudong during the 1990–95 period, about half of it in key projects designed to kick-start this area and mould it into an organic part of the existing city. The Nanpu and Yangpu bridges, opened in 1991 and 1993, respectively, were among key transport, energy, communications, and other infrastructure put in place. Overseas investors showed little interest until September 1990 when Mayor Zhu Rongji announced details of incentives, including those for setting up foreign bank branches. In effect these brought Pudong into line with the five special economic zones (SEZs) in the south-east of the country but with additional concessions to apply to a proposed free trade zone, the first in China (Cheung, 1990a,b).

Much of the initial effort has been concentrated on four key relatively independent zones (Figure 5.2).

The Lujiazui–Huamu Finance and Trade Zone opposite the Bund is being developed as a centre of finance, trade, real estate, and other modern service activities. Some fifty high-rise financial and trade buildings had been completed by the end of 1996, with others under construction. The Shanghai offices of the People's Bank of China and other major Chinese banks have already moved there from across the Huangpu River and by 2000 will have been joined by all the city's commodity, foreign currency, stock, and other markets (Higgins, 1996). Many foreign financial institutions are already registered in, and pay their taxes to, Pudong to take advantage of a concessional 15 per cent tax rate even if they continue to operate from their main offices in the older part of Shanghai. This also explains why several branch banks that had been allowed to continue operating after 1949 are registered by the Bank of China as having reopened in Pudong in 1991.

Waigaoqiao–Gaoqiao in the north is focused around port, cargo handling and transhipment facilities, a power station, sewage works, shipbuilding and repairing yards, petrochemical plants, and a multi-functional comprehensive free trade zone (at 5.5 km^2 the largest bonded area in China). This, the first of the thirteen such bonded areas to be approved throughout the country, became operational in 1992 and by the end of 1995 had attracted 2,200 enterprises, including several large MNCs like General Electric, Monsanto, and Mitsubishi. The shipyard will be the biggest in the country with a capacity to launch six 150,000-ton vessels a year. Waigaoqiao can accommodate 50,000-ton vessels and is expected to be handling 600,000 TEU containers by 2000 and 800,000 by 2010.

Jinqiao Export Processing Zone had attracted 302 ventures, including 46 MNCs, by the end of May 1996 with a total investment of US$4,250 million.

Zhangjiang High-Tech Park opened for business later but has already attracted several MNCs, such as Roche Pharmaceuticals Ltd (a US$45 million Sino-Swiss JV), Medtronic from the US, and Nycomed from Norway.

Pudong authorities claim that over 4,000 foreign firms had invested US$10,900 million there by late 1996, 85 per cent with investments of less than US$5 million. Among them were 60 MNCs with an average investment of US$44 million in 100 projects. A further 3,900 enterprises representing an investment of US$3,370 million had been established by central government departments and other provinces.

Such figures have to be treated with some caution, however, because it is unclear whether all these contracts—covering every-thing from factories to golf courses—have led to functioning ventures. Moreover, some of the so-called foreign funding is in fact mainland Chinese capital recycled through Hong Kong to gain tax and other privileges granted to foreign investors. A more useful indicator of progress is that Pudong's GDP in 1995 was close to

US$5,000 million, a 170 per cent increase in real terms since 1990. Of the total output value of US$13,000 million in 1995, 76 per cent was contributed by SOEs which provide the main impetus behind Pudong's rapid economic growth (*Shanghai Star*, 24 May 1996).

The second phase of infrastructural construction is in hand with US$36,000 million—four times the 1990–95 outlay—budgeted for projects to be completed by 2000. Among these are the first runway of the Pudong International Airport scheduled to come into operation in 1999; the first 13.6-km stage of a 26.5-km subway that will link this new airport with the existing Hongqiao Airport; a 375-km underwater pipeline from the Pinghu offshore oil and gas field to Pudong; a fibre-optic telecommunications system; and extensions to Waigaoqiao Port.

Problems

Pudong has problems, though some may soon be overcome. The reluctance of local and foreign financial and commercial businesses to shift across the Huangpu River to the Lujiazui area has lessened following the 15 per cent decline in office rents during 1996 when high-rise space flooded the market. The official vacancy rate for residential and office accommodation in Pudong in mid-1996 was 30 per cent, but property consultants put the figure nearer 80 per cent (*South China Morning Post*, 11 September 1996). Developers may postpone projects because, even though sales of land for commercial development in Pudong were halted in mid-1996, property analysts believe that it will be several years before the existing glut of accommodation will be absorbed. A further problem is that, of the 115 km^2 of land approved for sale in Pudong since 1990, 37 km^2 of it bought for 400 projects remain idle because of shortage of funds (O'Neill, 1996b; *South China Morning Post*, 14 August 1996).

Rising unemployment and falling domestic sales of Shanghai-made goods may also have been factors influencing municipal authorities to be more enthusiastic about luring investment to other parts of the city than Pudong. For example, apart from the industrial investment mentioned earlier, overseas business is now being encouraged into modern agriculture, intensive industry, and urbanization projects in Shanghai's suburbs (*China Daily*, 8 August 1996).

Potential investors are also looking further afield. The high cost of land, labour problems, lack of access, and various other overheads such as the cost of accommodation for expatriate staff have made Pudong one of the most expensive industrial zones in China. Neighbouring provinces are actively bidding for business claiming that the same incentives are available at places like Suzhou and Wuxi. They point to leases at Suzhou being available for between US\$20 and US\$35 per m^2 whereas those in Pudong cost US\$120 to US\$200 per m^2. Thus Sharp, which has an air conditioner plant in Pudong, chose Wuxi as the location for its liquid-crystal panel factory, and the Shinmei Electric Co., which makes switches in Shanghai, opened its second factory in Taicang (Ryuji Sato, 1995).

Pudong's future prosperity depends to no small extent on central government policy decisions. It was, for instance, given special consideration when, from 1 April 1996 (later deferred for some projects to 31 December 1997), a 17 per cent value-added tax was introduced on imported capital goods (made more onerous because it is charged on the total amount after the 25 to 40 per cent customs duty has been added). A special transitional arrangement was made for Pudong—as well as for the Shenzhen, Zhuhai, Shantou, Xiamen, and Hainan SEZs, and Suzhou Industrial Park (discussed later)—granting an annual quota to allow Sino-foreign JVs and Chinese enterprises there to import capital goods free of duty until 2000. Pudong's 1996 quota of US\$1,000 million shrinks each year by 20 per cent until it graduates from the scheme. As this arrangement did not apply to wholly owned foreign enterprises and embraced only the Chinese partner in JVs, some MNCs—especially those aimed at producing competitively priced goods for export—reconsidered their investment plans as they reckoned that this tax change would push up project costs by 35 to 40 per cent (Seidlitz and Murphy, 1996).

Changjiang Delta

For many decades, Shanghai remained the focus of industrial and commercial activity in the Delta region (defined in Figure 5.1). In 1979 it accounted for 52 per cent of this region's total industrial output value, although accommodating only 13.6 per cent of its population (Table 5.1). There were moves in 1982 to create a Shanghai Economic Region embracing most of the larger cities within about 75 km of the Municipality's boundary (Fung et al., 1992: 124), but the opening to foreign investment in April 1984 of Lianyungang and Nantong cities in Jiangsu Province and Ningbo and Wenzhou cities in Zhejiang Province spurred competition rather than co-operation as each was anxious to promote its own Economic and Technological Development Zone (ETDZ). These were expected to play the dual role of 'windows' opening to the outside world and 'radiators' spreading economic development while building up an export-orientated economy but, importantly, they also provided a way of concentrating the construction of infra-structure necessary to attract investment, especially from overseas (Kueh, 1987: 456). Competition was further widened in February 1985 when the whole of the Delta region was opened to foreign investors.

In 1981, 50 per cent of the Delta's gross output value came from industry in Shanghai Municipality, 26 per cent from industry in the two provinces, and 24 per cent from agriculture. In 1994 the respective percentages were 17, 71, and 12. This quite remarkable change reflects in large measure the rise of TVEs in Jiangsu and Zhejiang Provinces, as in other parts of China, from 1984 to 1988 and again after 1990. The reasons include reforms that enabled these enter-prises to obtain capital goods and sell products in urban markets, changes to banking which allowed TVEs better access to start-up finance, and the growing need by local governments for extra-budgetary revenue of which TVEs were a prime source. Impor-tantly, too, the increase in rural living standards following decol-lectivization in the late 1970s and early 1980s 'created a huge market for home appliances and construction materials, as peas-ants demanded amenities previously reserved for urban residents' (Zweig, 1992: 419).

Unlike Shanghai which was dominated by the indebted state sector, the remainder of the Delta was freer to raise capital for TVEs which had no social obligations to fulfil, fewer regulations to obey, and a plentiful pool of migrant labour to choose from. In 1995 township enterprises accounted for 68 per cent of the gross indus-trial output value scored by Zhejiang Province, and for 55 per cent of that recorded in Jiangsu Province where 920,000 such busi-nesses were operating (*Xinhua News Agency*, 17 June 1996). The importance of these township enterprises is further highlighted by noting that the value of their output in the two provinces taken together was more than double that of *all* industrial enterprises operating in Shanghai Municipality. Even there, township and other private enterprises contributed 35.9 per cent of the 1995 gross industrial output value, not far behind the 37.5 per cent from the SOEs and considerably ahead of the 26.6 per cent from foreign-funded firms.

Growth Corridors

Two major growth corridors anchored in Shanghai are developing along major highways opened or under construction. One running north-west to Nanjing and the other south to the port of Ningbo are drawing the region together. The ten hours it took to travel the 386-km road from Shanghai to Nanjing was slashed to three in September 1986 when a 247-km four-lane expressway opened via Suzhou, Wuxi, Changzhou, and Zhenjiang. This, in turn, connects with the expressway linking Nanjing with Hefei.

These and other infrastructural improvements did not escape the notice of foreign investors, many of which located their JVs in the main cities along the emerging Shanghai–Nanjing corridor. At first, small to medium-size producers viewed China largely as an export platform and their investments there as a way of reducing costs and, in the case of Japanese firms, cushioning the impact of the rising yen. In the mid-1990s the growing realization that the Delta was also one of the wealthier parts of China and a fast-growing domestic market heightened the interest of major manufacturers like Sony Corp. and Mitsubishi Motors from Japan, and Philips and Ericsson from Europe.

Some investments are on a significant scale. At Nanjing, BASF has entered a 50:50 JV arrangement with Sinopec Yangzi Petrochemical Corp. to invest US$4,000 million in a 2.5 million-ton-per-year petrochemical complex making some thirty-four products. Trading companies, too, saw opportunities: 50 of the 120 subsidiaries owned by the conglomerate Marubeni Corp. in China are in the Changjiang Delta. Foreign investors are also being attracted to agricultural projects in the Delta, which is one of China's most important grain producing areas: Nantong City (Jiangsu Province), for example, has an export-orientated agricultural development zone with JVs operating aquaculture, food processing, and export industries.

The 317-km expressway from Shanghai south to Ningbo via Hangzhou was opened in 1997 and plans are being made for another between Hangzhou and Nanjing, projects that will tie this region more firmly into the core parts of the Delta. Much of the investment here is associated with developments at Ningbo's Beilun deep-water port together with its large-scale oil, coal, ore, and container handling facilities, and petrochemical, power generation, shipbuilding, and steel complexes being built or proposed along a 120-km-long coastal zone.

There are literally dozens of development zones of various kinds and sponsored at several administrative levels in the Delta region but one in Jiangsu is of particular interest because of its status politically. Suzhou Industrial Park (SIP) is being developed, following an agreement between China and Singapore signed in February 1994, by a 65:35 JV between a Singapore-led consortium and a Chinese consortium (*Straits Times*, 17 September 1996). Described as 'a new model of Sino–Singapore co-operation', the vision is of a 70-km^2 greenfield site forty minutes by highway from Shanghai being transformed by 2010 at a cost of US$20,000 million into a city of 1 million—a mini-Singapore incorporating many of its industrial, commercial, and residential planning concepts.

The political leaders of both countries have taken a personal interest in this project, regarded as Singapore's flagship in China. This explains why the SIP was one of only seven zones in the country to be assigned a duty-free quota (of US$600 million for 1996) when an import tax on capital goods was imposed on 1 April 1996 (*Business Times*, 26 October 1996). By mid-1996 pledged investments, mainly from the US (19), Singapore (16), and Japan (8), totalled US$1,700 million (*Straits Times*, 17 September 1996). Publicly, at least, Shanghai has welcomed the Suzhou project and the possibility of its becoming the source for just-in-time component deliveries.

Changjiang Valley Development Strategy

A uniform planning strategy for the whole 1,890-km riverside zone stretching from the Three Gorges project in the west to Pudong on the coast would be difficult because of the considerable differences in the levels of economic and social development. Yet co-ordination is necessary if sustainable development is to be achieved and waste is to be avoided when planning and constructing large projects. It is important, too, that development plans be formulated for main tributaries like the Jinsha and Hanjiang rivers and those forming the Lake Dongting and Lake Poyang systems (Figure 5.1).

The Three Gorges scheme and the Beijing–Kowloon railway have been seen as two of the most important engines of growth for the middle and upper reaches of the Changjiang, as were key industrial developments such as sedan car production at Wuhan and nonferrous metals at Panzhihua (*Ching Chi Tao Pao*, 24 January 1994: 27). The 1,460-km stretch from Nanjing west to Yichang is comparatively well endowed with water, agricultural, and mineral resources. Several of the dozen or so key river ports have been declared open cities (like Huangshi, Wuhan, and Yichang in Hubei Province) helping them to attract foreign investment and loans (Figure 5.3).

The opening in September 1996 of the Beijing–Kowloon railway, running 1,130 km through Hubei and Jiangxi Provinces, is generating a very significant development impulse for urban and rural areas. The seven major industrial bases promoted by Jiangxi Province alongside this line have two-thirds of its overseas-funded enterprises (*Xinhua News Agency*, 21 and 28 October 1996). Indeed, the Jiangxi government's 1995 work report made clear its intention to seize the opportunities arising from the push to develop the Changjiang Valley and the completion of the Beijing–Kowloon line by making Nanchang, Jiujiang, and Jingdezhen the core bases in its Changjiang River and Poyang Lake Economic Zones (*Jiangxi Ribao*, 13 February 1996: 1–3).

Wuhan, the capital of Hubei Province and 1,125 km upstream from Shanghai, is developing into one of the country's most significant inland industrial, distribution, and cargo handling centres, and is the headquarters of the China Changjiang National Shipping Co., the country's largest operator of inland waterway vessels (Fossey, 1996). In the short-term Wuhan has been boosted by port and industrial activity generated by the Three Gorges project (with the new Wuhan–Yichang expressway halving the journey to the construction site), but sees its longer-term role as a key financial, technology, information, skills, and transport link between western and eastern China. Hence container facilities are being expanded to consolidate cargo moving between the less developed areas upstream and the international and hub ports in the Delta, with shippers being encouraged to stuff containers there rather than send cargoes downstream in bulk. This change is already occurring

Figure 5.3: The Changjiang riverside development zone showing the income per capita in cities, 1994.

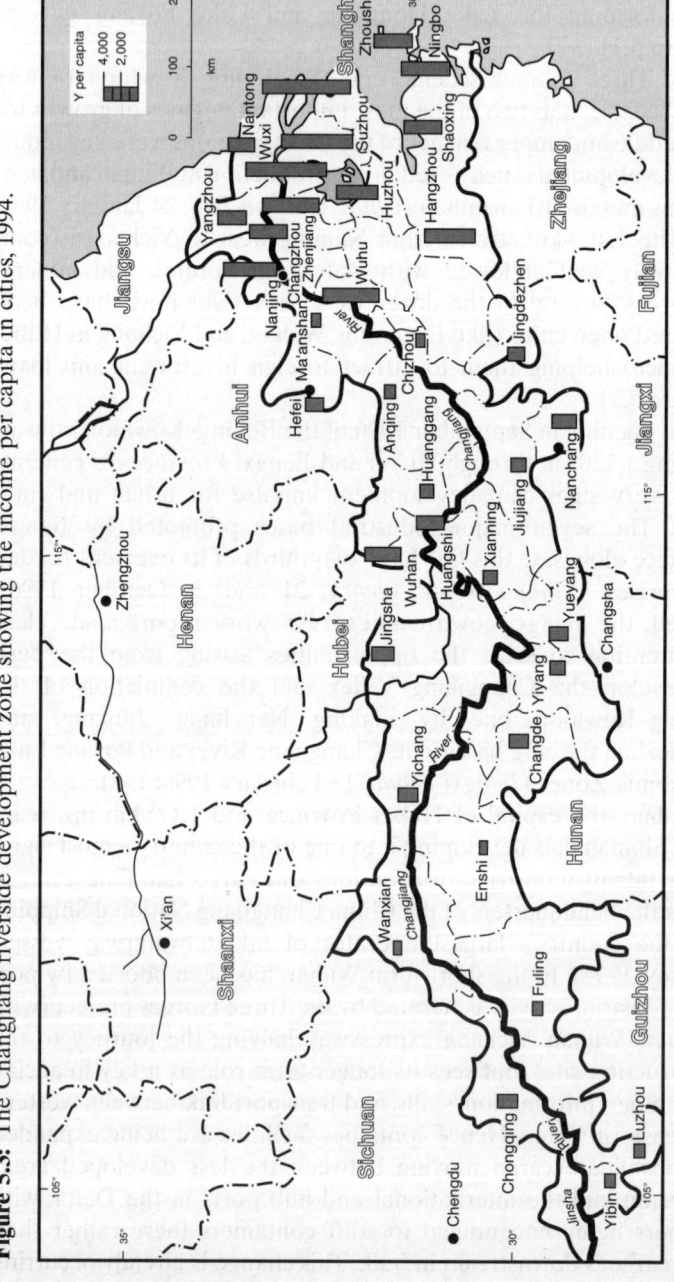

Source: based on data from State Statistical Bureau, 1995b.

as manufacturing and assembly activities along the Changjiang augment or even replace more traditional agricultural and extractive industries. The Wuhan Economic Development Zone, set up in 1993, had attracted fifty-six foreign-funded enterprises by mid-1995 including Citroën, Pilkington, and Hyundai, and the city has set its sights on producing 10 million tons of steel, 500,000 cars and 500,000 km of fibre-optic cable annually (*China Business Weekly*, 13 October 1996).

Three Gorges Project

Construction of the Three Gorges hydroelectric and flood mitigation project between Yichang and Wanxian commenced in December 1994 and is targeted for completion in 2009. The considerable controversy it has aroused within China and abroad is well documented. Apart from its possible adverse environmental impacts, there has been much concern about the well-being of the 1.1 million or more people being evacuated from towns and villages inundated by the 632-km^2 reservoir. On paper, the project will reduce the damage and loss of life caused by flooding along the central and lower parts of the Changjiang River, will add 18,200 MW capacity thus reducing the need to burn coal, and will enable 10,000-ton vessels to ply between Wuhan and Chongqing. In addition the associated road, bridge, airport, telecommunications, and other infrastructure will contribute to development further west.

Upper Reaches

At the National People's Congress in March 1997, Chongqing was elevated to become China's fourth self-administered municipality—the first new one since Tianjin regained municipality status in 1967—with its administrative powers extended across three neighbouring counties, parts of which will be flooded by the Three Gorges reservoir. It has in effect been designated as the bridgehead for the opening up of a wide expanse of central and western China. Sometimes described as the 'industrial metropolis of the southwest' and already one of the largest cities in China, the boundary extension will more than double this city's population to 30 million. Some see the new status as a 'sweetener' because Chongqing, once the capital of wartime China under the Kuomintang, was generally opposed to the dam project, starved of investment during the

1980s, and felt itself in the shadow of the Sichuan capital Chengdu, even though the latter is not so attractive to investors because of its less convenient transport links (Becker, 1996).

Challenges
Environment and Pollution

Throughout its length the Changjiang River Valley is beset by serious environmental problems. In the upper reaches, the removal of vegetation has led to soil erosion, mud flows and landslides, a deteriorating ecological situation, and the destabilization of agriculture.

Further downstream the situation is even worse. From the 1950s through the 1970s, large areas were enclosed and reclaimed for agriculture, thus causing many large and medium-size lakes to disappear, thereby aggravating flooding and making its control more difficult. Incomplete data suggest that even since the mid-1980s the area covered by water in the middle and lower reaches has diminished by some $12,000 \, km^2$, while the volume in the 2,240-km^2 Lake Taihu west of Shanghai has shrunk by 1,000 million m^3. Yet another problem still affecting Shanghai, despite strict limits on underground water extraction, is subsidence resulting from disturbances to the water-table.

Various schemes have been launched to try to rectify some of these environmental problems such as planting $28,600 \, km^2$ of forest in the upper and middle reaches of the river to halt soil erosion; building a dozen treatment plants to process water from cities in the Three Gorges reservoir area; closing some thirty small papermills polluting the upper reaches of the Changjiang River and replacing them with a couple of modern plants; and protecting flora and fauna (*Xinhua News Agency*, 26 June, 1 October 1996). Other notorious sources of pollution are also being curbed, an example being a loan of US$110 million from the World Bank to update technology in the iron and steel works at Chongqing (*Xinhua News Agency*, 29 June 1996).

Co-ordination of Development

Much has been said about the need to co-ordinate development along the Changjiang River. Some co-operation has occurred between neighbouring provinces, and wider organizations, like the

Changjiang Economic Joint Development Corporation, have been established (*Xinhua News Agency*, 2 June 1995). Economic links have also been developing, with the riverine provinces opening trade offices and enterprises in Pudong and Shanghai and promoting business by setting up industrial parks, as at Wanxian in Sichuan Province (*Zhongguo Xinwen She News Agency*, 22 February 1996). Other connections have emerged through the operation of stock, futures, and commodity markets in Shanghai.

The reality is that the competition between provinces for projects and investments has led to waste and duplication. While some discipline is imposed by the central government's control of national projects—the mainline railways, national highways, and trunk fibre-optic connections—each of the provinces has mapped out its own developmental blueprint. The Changjiang River will clearly remain the key artery, but the economic integration of the Valley as a whole can only be realized by putting in place a co-ordinated rail, road, waterway, and port transport system. Yet overland transport infrastructure is being laid out in a disconnected, piecemeal way, and ports, harbours, and anchorages are being built and operated without reference to any overall master plan. Compounding the problems are the poor administrative relationships among the central and local governments and overseas investors, and the lack of stable policy making (Chen, 1996b).

Some coherence may be introduced if a plan to establish shipping services linking China's inland areas with Japan via the Changjiang River—the subject of a feasibility study sponsored by the Japan–China Investment Promotion Organization—goes ahead. The proposal is for cargo to be shipped from Chongqing to Shanghai where it would be transferred to ocean-going vessels headed for Japan. In September 1996 Premier Li Peng had discussions with the Sino–Japanese Committee on Development and Cooperation in the Upper and Middle reaches of the Changjiang River (*Xinhua News Agency*, 23 September 1996).

What emerges from this chapter is that Shanghai is conscious of its past pre-eminence and is eager to regain it. Certainly it has come a very long way since opening its doors to foreign investment, but whether the momentum can be maintained and the goal reached of becoming an international city able to compete with those in other parts of Asia will depend on how much this Municipality can improve its quality and service (Bowring, 1996; *South China Morning Post*, 21 June 1996).

Legacies of the past also continue to hinder co-operation in the wider Changjiang region, an example being the division of responsibilities between the provinces and their local governments. The current arrangement of full local financial responsibility, management of credit and capital, and economic surveillance remain those of a managerial-type planned economy. With their eyes on immediate local benefits, the various administrations are making decisions aimed at aggrandizing and protecting themselves, thus leading to a scramble for resources, duplication of investments, lack of industrial diversification, higher costs, and lower profits.

6 The Bohai Sea Rim: Some Development Issues

LIU YI, ZHANG LEI, AND GODFREY LINGE

The Bohai Sea Rim (BSR) area is the leading political and cultural centre in China as well as the main economic focus of the northern part of the country. As defined for this chapter, it covers an area of 514,000 km^2 embracing Beijing and Tianjin Municipalities, and Hebei, Liaoning, and Shandong Provinces. About 64 million of its 214 million inhabitants (1995) live in urban areas, including Beijing (12.5 million), Tianjin (9.4), Shijiazhuang (8.4), Shenyang (6.7), and Jinan (5.4). The BSR—the main gateway to north-east, north, and east China—handles about 24 and 32 per cent, respectively, of the country's freight and passenger traffic.

The concept of these two Municipalities and three Provinces forming an economic region arose in 1984 as 'another manifestation of China's open policy' (Chang et al., 1992: 61). This northern proposal was rather different, however, from the Zhujiang (Pearl) River Delta and Shanghai economic regions proposed at about the same time because Guangzhou and Shanghai could be clearly identified as their core cities. Rather, the Bohai region was to be 'an aggregation of thirteen cities of different sizes', organized to promote mutual assistance 'as well as developing regional specialization and labor division in economic structure based on comparative advantages' in order to 'integrate economic activities of different cities and counties, to explore natural resources jointly with pooled technology and labor, and to share capital, urban and regional infrastructure, and harbor facilities for export-oriented industrial production' (Chang et al., 1992: 61).

Some of these considerations may have underlain the suggestion in the Ninth Five Year Plan that a Bohai Sphere Zone should be one of seven proposed economic regions to take shape gradually 'in accordance with the law of market economy, intrinsic economic association and special geographical and natural features', using the existing distribution of economic activities, central cities, and major traffic arteries as their foundation. The Plan statement emphasized that these regions were to be developed *irrespective of administrative boundaries* so, apart from the core components of Beijing and Tianjin Municipalities and Hebei Province only the Shandong and Liaodong Peninsulas—not the *whole* of Shandong and Liaoning Provinces—were included. The Plan document saw the strengths of the Bohai Sphere as being its well-developed communications, proximity to large and medium-size cities, concentration of qualified personnel, and rich coal, iron, and other resources. In practical political terms it is hard to see how such a regional concept could be operationalized other than at a very general level. It is inconceivable that Liaoning and Shandong Provinces would allow themselves to be bifurcated, even for planning purposes, with their most productive economic areas coming under the influence of some sort of regional planning authority.

Arguably, in any event, there are five reasons why the wider BSR definition is the more appropriate. First, much of it is within the Huabei Plain stretching south from the Taihang Mountains into Shandong Province, although Liaoning Province lies at the southern end of the Dongbei Plain (Figure 6.1). Second, it has seven of the country's sixteen principal seaports which, along with its well-developed road and rail system, link the northern part of China with the outside world. Third, its economy depends very much on its minerals (such as iron ore and coal) rather than on renewable resources (like grain and livestock products) which are a mainstay of Jiangsu Province further south. Fourth, because of this, the BSR is a leading exporter of mineral products, unlike the southern coastal areas which are mineral importers. Fifth, the relationships between the various parts of this region have historically been very close: between 1860 and 1910, for instance, large numbers of farmers migrated from Shandong Province to Liaoning Province so as to acquire enough agricultural land for survival. Prior to 1949, Beijing and Tianjin were part of Hebei Province, with Tianjin as its capital between 1958 and 1967. In addition, as a result of the Open Door policy, the economy of the BSR appears to be growing and maturing more quickly than those of the north-eastern and northern parts of the country.

As this chapter shows, the economies of the five main administrative areas both complement and compete with each other (Table 6.1). They also face many of the same problems. Yet the reality, discussed in Chapter 2, is that these political entities have long been in competition with each other, and it is only recently that they have

Figure 6.1: Main physical features of the Bohai Sea Rim.

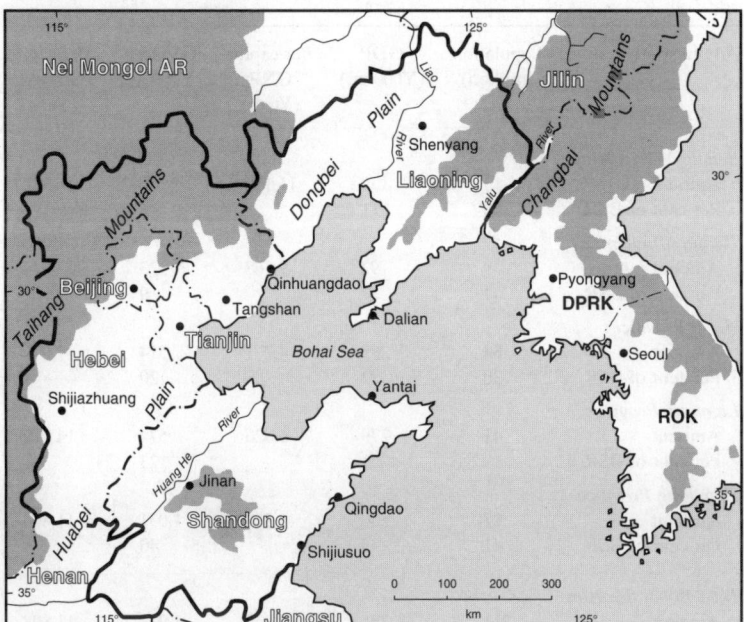

begun to recognize the need for greater co-operation. It is significant, then, that in August 1996 Beijing and Tianjin Municipalities
and Hebei Province announced that they had agreed on a fifteen-
year, US$125,000-million infrastructure investment programme
(*Xinhua News Agency*, 20 August 1996). Soon afterwards the two
Municipalities revealed that they had reached 'an understanding'
about the importance of co-operation, had 'pledged to push ahead
with economic integration', and were seeking favourable central
government policies 'conducive to bilateral economic integration'
(*China Business Weekly*, 13 October 1996).

There are several underlying reasons. Some concern has been
expressed about the widening development gap that seems to be
appearing between the north and the south of the country. Moreover, the BSR is no longer competing with just other parts of China
for investment funds and market outlets but also, as the national
economy becomes increasingly enmeshed into the outside world,
with a dozen or so cross-border zones that are emerging elsewhere

Table 6.1: Aspects of the Bohai Sea Rim economy by administrative area, 1995

Administrative area	Population (million)	GDP (Y000 m.)	Per capita GNP (Yuan)	GVOAI[a] (Y000 m.)	Per capita GVOAI[a] (Yuan)
Beijing Municipality					
Amount	13	139	11,150	207	16,572
Per cent of BSR	6	11		8	
Tianjin Municipality					
Amount	9	92	9,768	223	23,644
Per cent of BSR	4	7		9	
Hebei Province					
Amount	64	285	4,271	514	7,990
Per cent of BSR	30	22		20	
Liaoning Province					
Amount	41	279	6,826	574	14,019
Per cent of BSR	19	21		23	
Shandong Province					
Amount	87	500	6,214	1,031	11,848
Per cent of BSR	41	39		40	
Total Bohai Sea Rim					
Amount	214	1,295	6,049	1,934	11,898
Per cent of China	18	22	(4,811)[b]	23	(9,266)[b]

[a] Gross value of output of agriculture and industry.
[b] Average of China.
Source: State Statistical Bureau, 1996a.

in Asia. There is thus a growing imperative to rid the system of blockages and inefficiencies—whether these arise, for example, from shortages (as of water), lack of infrastructure (railways and ports) or the need to restructure state-owned enterprises (SOEs)—but the solutions often require the joint effort of neighbouring administrations. In addition, the policy of the central government for 'pillar industries' (like car manufacturing) to be reorganized into a few large enterprise groupings; the growing realization that, to become more competitive, manufacturers must aim for quality rather than quantity; and the recognition that high-technology processing may best be utilized in separate specialized establishments with different locational requirements are three among the many forces eroding the idea of spatial self-sufficiency being a virtue in itself.

Characteristics of the Bohai Sea Rim

The climate in most parts of the BSR is suitable for grain crops (wheat, rice, and corn), industrial crops (cotton), and specialized cash crops (peanuts and temperate fruits) and, as an added bonus, the slightly higher salinity of the waters along its 5,800-km coastline make them very suitable for aquaculture. The main agricultural areas along the Huabei and Dongbei Plains produce 20 to 45 per cent of the country's wheat, corn, cotton, seawater aquatic products, and peanuts, and 40 to 60 per cent of its orchard and viticultural output. However, agriculture is coming under pressure from increasing industrialization and spreading urbanization. In the early 1950s nearly 60 per cent of the BSR was farmland, with a further 38 per cent used for grazing and forestry. By 1990 this had shrunk to 42 per cent, while urban and industrial uses occupied 22 per cent, thus threatening the centuries-old intensive agricultural systems (Lu, 1995).

An example is Shandong Province, a major granary area, whose population jumped during these four decades from 45 million to 87 million, while the area under cultivation fell by a quarter to 6.7 million hectares, the minimum needed to guarantee each person 500 kg of grain annually (*Xinhua News Agency*, 27 April 1996). The Shandong authorities responded by promising to prevent further urban encroachment and implementing a programme to reclaim 130,000 hectares annually.

The BSR has long been one of China's major industrial areas with its rich array of minerals, including 40 per cent of the country's proven reserves of both iron ore and oil, leading to the emphasis on heavy industry that has dominated the BSR's economy since the late 1970s. Four of the country's eleven steelworks with annual capacities greater than 1 million tons are here—the Anshan Iron and Steel Company (7.7 million tons of steel in 1990) and the Benxi Iron and Steel Company (2.4) in Liaoning Province; the Shoudu Iron and Steel Company (4.4) in Beijing Municipality; and the Tangshan Iron and Steel Company (1.6) in Hebei Province—using local iron ore and coal railed 200 km from Shanxi Province (Figure 6.2).

The Shengli oilfield in north Shandong Province and the Liaohe oilfield lying between Shenyang and the Bohai Sea are the second and the third largest producers in the country with average annual outputs during the 1988–95 period of 30 million and 13.6 million

Figure 6.2: Main economic features of the Bohai Sea Rim.

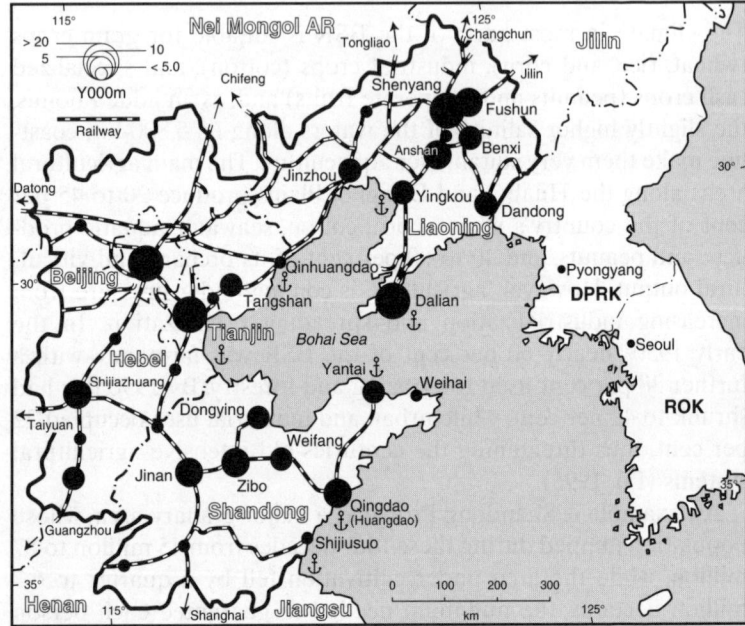

Sources: production data based on Li and Lu, 1995: 428, 455; railways based on Editorial Group, 1995: 104–9.

tons, respectively, and are expected to stabilize at 25.5 and 15.5 millions tons annually by 2000 (*Xinhua News Agency*, 24 April 1996). Shengli oil is refined at the Qilu Petrochemical complex at Zibo and also piped to Qingdao (formerly Huangdao) for shipment south, and to Nanjing for use along the Changjiang (Yangtze) Valley; Liaohe oil is mainly processed in refineries at Jinzhou. These and the other fields in the BSR produced 57 million tons of crude in 1995, nearly two-fifths of the national total. Coal output from the main fields in central Liaoning Province, south-east Hebei Province, and south-west Shandong Province totalled 235 million tons in 1995, 17 per cent of the national total.

Locally produced oil, natural gas, and sea salt are bases for a large-scale chemical industry, with Tianjin, Dalian, Beijing, Liaoyang, Zibo, and Jinzhou being nationally important centres for soda ash, caustic soda, plastics, sulphuric acid, ethylene, and chemical fibres. The producer and consumer goods made in the BSR

Table 6.2: Sectoral composition of GDP by administrative areas of the Bohai Sea Rim (per cent), 1984 to 1995

Administrative area	Primary[a]		Secondary[b]		Tertiary[c]	
	1984	1995	1984	1995	1984	1995
Beijing Municipality	14	7	72	46	14	47
Tianjin Municipality	14	6	67	56	19	38
Hebei Province	48	21	40	49	12	30
Liaoning Province	27	13	63	51	10	36
Shandong Province	51	20	40	49	9	31
Total Bohai Sea Rim	37	16	52	50	11	34

[a] Farming, forestry, animal husbandry, fishing.
[b] Mining, lumbering, processing, manufacturing, building and construction, electricity, water and gas production.
[c] Commerce, transport, and communication services.
Source: State Statistical Bureau, 1986, 1996a.

include heavy engineering equipment, electronic products, and textiles.

More recently there has been a significant rise in the tertiary sector's contribution to GDP: during the 1984–95 period the value of its output and the number of people employed increased annually by an average of 36 and 21 per cent, respectively (Table 6.2). The numerous universities, tertiary colleges, and state-owned research and development institutes located here give the region a width and depth of intellectual talent unsurpassed elsewhere in China. This may also help to explain why its per capita GNP is 26 per cent higher than that for China as a whole.

Main Industrial Areas

Most of the main cities and large and medium-size industrial enterprises are concentrated in three areas which contain about 40 per cent of the BSR's population and account for 62 per cent of its industrial output.

The Beijing–Tianjin–Tangshan triangle is the economic core, with about a quarter of its total industrial output. Both Beijing and Tianjin Municipalities have a relatively wide range of industrial activities, though with a particular emphasis on engineering, electronics, chemicals, metallurgy, textiles, and food processing. Beijing's particular strengths lie in metallurgy and petrochemicals, whereas Tianjin has better-developed textile and salt-based chemical industries. Since the mid-1980s, both municipalities have experienced a significant increase in tertiary sector activities—clearly shown in Table 6.2—especially business and personal services, real estate, and tourism in the case of Beijing, which anticipates that service sector activities will account for 50 per cent of its GDP by 2000 and 55 per cent by 2010 (*Xinhua News Agency*, 31 March 1996). Tianjin, China's second busiest container port after Shanghai, has well-developed transport and foreign trade-related services.

Central and south Liaoning Province, focusing on Shenyang, Anshan, Benxi, Fushun, and Liaoyang cities, is the second industrial area, and is dominated by iron and steelworks, petroleum refineries, and chemical and heavy engineering plants.

The Jinan–Qingdao railway belt, stretching some 380 km across central Shandong Province, has a balance of both heavy (oil refining and petrochemicals) and light (textiles and engineering) manufacturing activities. This area accounts for almost one-fifth of the region's industrial output.

Major port cities like Dalian, Qingdao, and Yantai have attracted the attention of foreign investors in recent years. Thus, at Dayao Bay New Port, 60 km north of Dalian near the Economic and Technological Development Zone (ETDZ) (Yeung and Hu, 1992), the Singapore Port Authority has a 51 : 49 joint venture with the Dalian port administration to construct the US$480 million Dayao Bay container terminal which by 1998 will be able to handle 1 million twenty-foot equivalent units (TEUs). At the end of 1996 it was already handling 110 vessels a month from twenty-one shipping lines even though only three of the berths were operating (Tan, 1996). This project is the second largest Singaporean investment in China (the other, Suzhou Industrial Park, is discussed in Chapter 5). When the whole Dayao Bay plan to build 70 to 80 berths for 10,000-ton vessels and others for larger ones (Lai et al., 1992: 31) is completed it will be one the Pacific Rim's leading ports. At Qingdao, too, Singaporean finance is behind a US$400-million, 3-km^2 industrial park being planned to accommodate some 450 advanced-technology factories within the existing Hi-Tech Zone by 2005 (Lu, 1996b; Teh Hooi Ling, 1996). Also in Shandong Province, Yantai Port secured a loan of US$63 million from the Asian Development Bank late in 1995 for the construction of additional conventional and container berths which will further boost the nearby ETDZ. Begun in 1985 and stretching 10 km along the coast, this had attracted over 130 foreign industrial ventures by mid-1996 making machinery, electronic goods, foodstuffs, and chemical fibres (*Xinhua News Agency*, 23 September 1996).

Industrial Structures Within the BSR

The provincial and municipal economies had mixed fortunes between 1952 and 1995, as indicated by the data for gross industrial output set out in Table 6.3. The shares of the national total produced in Beijing and Tianjin Municipalities increased until the mid to late-1970s and then began to decline; Hebei Province's share rose until the mid-1970s but its subsequent decline was arrested in the 1990s; the continuous fall in the output share of Liaoning Province is largely explained by the concentration there of

Table 6.3: Percentage of China's gross industrial output by Bohai Sea Rim administrative areas, 1952 to 1995[a]

Administrative area	1952	1957	1965	1974	1979	1984	1991	1995
Beijing Municipality	2.4	3.0	3.9	5.6	4.6	4.0	3.1	2.1
Tianjin Municipality	5.4	5.6	4.8	5.1	3.8	3.6	2.7	2.3
Hebei Province	3.9	3.6	4.7	6.6	4.4	4.1	4.7	4.3
Liaoning Province	13.3	14.4	13.4	11.9	9.1	8.2	6.6	5.4
Shandong Province	6.1	5.2	4.3	5.9	6.5	6.5	9.2	9.2
Total Bohai Sea Rim	31.1	31.8	31.1	34.9	28.4	26.4	26.3	23.3

[a] After 1984, village-run enterprises were transferred from agricultural to industrial output statistics.

Sources: Pannell, 1988: 22; State Statistical Bureau, 1992, 1996a.

loss-making state-owned heavy industrial enterprises (see Chapters 1 and 7); and Shandong Province has increased its share of the national total since the mid-1970s. These losses and gains—largely explained by changes in the relative importance of light and heavy industry—have tended to balance out across the BSR, so that it's relative position in China has remained much the same since the early 1980s.

Problems

Shortage of water has become a major concern. Although many rivers flow into the Bohai Sea, surface runoff is only 80 per cent of the national average, and the groundwater supply amounts to less than 7 per cent of the country's total. This problem has come about not only as a result of rapid industrialization and urbanization within the BSR but also because of the development of the areas beyond from which it draws supplies. Thus, the volume of river water reaching Hebei Province from Shanxi Province and Nei Mongol AR halved during the thirty-years to 1990. As a result, per capita water resources in the BSR now amount to only $510\,m^3$ (one-fifth the national average) as against about $800\,m^3$ thirty years ago.

At the same time, the demand for water has been rapidly increasing: per capita consumption in Beijing Municipality, for example, rose ten times during the four decades to 1990. Although its population only doubled, household use increased as running water and sanitation facilities were supplied to more dwellings. The low price charged for water gives little incentive to repair the wasteful reticulation system which is crumbling as a result of severe subsidence caused by excessive groundwater extraction. The main boost to demand, however, has come from industry whose value of output increased eighty-five times in real terms between 1952 and 1988 (Urban Social and Economic Survey Organization, 1990: 232). This same problem affects many other cities—particularly those along the coast like Tianjin, Dalian, Qinhuangdao, Huludao, Yantai, and Qingdao. The feasibility of diverting water here from the Changjiang River has been studied but such an undertaking would match the Three Gorges project in terms of the scale of investment, the lengthy construction time required, and its potential human and environmental impacts. It is also controversial because it raises conflicts of interest among the Coastal, Central, and Western Regions

(*Ping Kuo Jih Pao*, 8 March 1996: A12). Meanwhile, the shortage of water is becoming ever more serious (Lu, 1995).

Coal supply and related transport bottle-necks have jointly become obstacles to further development. As noted in Chapter 2, coal is the source of a very high proportion of the energy used in China for both industrial and other purposes, and the same is true in the BSR where 76 per cent of the 260 million tons of coal-equivalent consumed consists of coal itself. The growth of manufacturing, and especially of heavy industry, has further accentuated the regional imbalance between coal supply and demand. During the four decades to 1990, the BSR's coal self-supply ratio (coal production divided by coal consumption) fell from 1.2 to 0.6. Net coal imports in 1990 for local use amounted to 120 million tons, making the BSR the largest coal importing region in the country, while a further 70 million tons of coal passed through on its way from Shanxi Province to the southern coastal provinces. As a result, the BSR has become the busiest hub for the movement of coal, which takes up more than 85 per cent of the total available rail and coastal shipping capacity (Todd and Zhang, 1994).

Pressure on land is increasing: the population density in the BSR—about 412 per km^2 in 1994—is matched in only a few other areas, such as the Changjiang Delta (Shanghai Municipality and Jiangsu and Zhejiang Provinces) where it is about 470 per km^2. In built-up areas, of course, the pressure on space is much greater: the urban districts of Beijing and Shijiazhuang (capital of Hebei Province), had population densities in 1994 of, respectively, 2,405 and 4,590 per km^2, the latter being higher than any other major urban district in China. Indeed, the need to improve conditions, especially for people living in the older dwellings in inner city areas, is itself adding to the demand: as part of a national policy to upgrade urban housing, people are being relocated from these crowded districts to new suburban accommodation which provides about 10 m^2 per capita.

Environmental pollution is a greater problem here than in any other region in China. In 1995, waste gas emissions totalled 3,200,000 million m^3 (26 per cent of the national total); industrial waste water discharge amounted to 3,770 million tons (18 per cent), and industrial waste came to 192 million tons (30 per cent). In that year, the pollution densities (annual amount divided by total area) of air, water, and solid wastes in BSR were 20, 40, and 80 per cent higher, respectively, than along the east coast region as a whole, with densities in Beijing and Tianjin Municipalities and big industrial cities such as Shenyang, Anshan, and Benxi greater still. In Beijing coal still accounts for more than 75 per cent of the fuel burned compared to a mere 5 per cent for clean gas fuels (*Xinhua News Agency*, 29 May 1996). The growing number of vehicles on Beijing's streets (980,000 early in 1996 and 150,000 being added each year) is exacerbating traffic congestion so that restrictions have been imposed on their use by trucks and private cars (*Xinhua News Agency*, 6 February 1996).

Opportunities

The BSR was handed a major opportunity in 1984 when the leading seaport cities of Dalian, Qinhuangdao, Tianjin, Yantai, and Qingdao were declared open areas to encourage foreign investment. During the 1985–89 period, the BSR as a whole attracted US$5,750 million in foreign direct investment and loans (excluding 'Ministry' figures which are not disaggregated geographically), or about one-fifth of the national total.

During the following five years it received a further US$17,970 million (also about one-fifth of the national total), with most coming from Japan and the Republic of Korea (ROK), although there is now a growing interest by Singaporean business groups. Investors are recognizing that the BSR has the potential to become part of a wider regional co-operation zone that will benefit participating countries because of their geographical proximity, cultural and ethnic affinities, complementary and diversified economies, and large markets (Kong, 1993; Liang, 1995). Already, three-fifths of Tianjin's trade volume with the ROK consists of goods made up from materials supplied from there, with much of this work being done in over 600 ROK-funded factories (*Xinhua News Agency*, 3 May 1996). A more specific case is the proposal by the Daewoo Group to spend US$900 million on factories at Yantai, Qingdao, and Weihai to make car components for shipment to its ROK assembly plants (Cheung, 1996c).

The development of the BSR has also been assisted by its strategic location that gives it access to a hinterland consisting of much of the northern half of China and a market of 190 million people (about 16 per cent of the national total). The relationship is close. More than 80 per cent of the hinterland's domestic and international imports and exports are handled by the BSR's transport system. Some 40 per cent of the goods needed by the hinterland are manufactured in the BSR, while the hinterland supplies about 40 per cent of the raw materials and 30 per cent of the foodstuffs used in the BSR. The need 'to strengthen economic association and technological co-operation between the eastern coastal region and the central and western regions' was again stressed in the Ninth Five Year Plan, and the joint development of the inland's natural resources and the creation of employment opportunities for the abundant labour force there is helping to strengthen the bonds between the BSR and these hinterland regions. Some cross-border relationships have also developed. Mongolia, for instance, now ships all its exports through Tianjin to avoid the losses that occurred when sent out via Moscow or Nakhodka in Russia (*Tianjin Ribao*, 13 November 1995: 1).

The completion of several large-scale rail, road, and port projects is making the BSR even more accessible to the rest of China and to the outside world. Among others, the Beijing–Kowloon railway came into service as far as the Hong Kong border in September 1996; a 599-km railway, mainly for coal and due for completion in 2003, is under construction from Shenfu (Shaanxi Province) to a new port at Huanghua (Hebei Province); the 635-km coal line from Datong (Shanxi Province) to the country's leading coal port at Qinhuangdao (Hebei) has been upgraded to carry 100 million tons annually; an interprovincial highway system is being developed (see Chapter 3); and improvements are being made to several ports as has already been noted. A new deep-water port (Jintang) is being built to help develop the Tangshan Port Development Zone into 'a large international "shopping" town' (*Xinhua News Agency*, 17 July 1996); with a proposed handling capacity of 22 million tons by 2010, the export processing industries to be established there will have the advantage of being only 400 and 600 nautical miles, respectively, from the ROK and Japan (*Xinhua News Agency*, 22 April 1996).

Development Possibilities

The main goal of social and economic development in the BSR in the coming decade is to improve the economic structure and raise living standards without destroying the environment. This is no easy task. In Hebei Province, where 5.6 million mountain people (nearly 9 per cent of the population) do not have enough food or clothing, the Governor noted that only a robust economy could improve living standards and thus 'the province would encourage more foreign investment and develop infrastructure facilities' (Lai, 1995). The output of all parts of the primary sector—food and industrial crops, vegetable oils, and animal and aquatic products— will need to be steadily increased to meet the demands of the growing urban population and the developing international trade. Greater attention will have to be given to the development of water-saving dry-farming agricultural techniques and other inno- vations. To this end, a Sino-Canadian dryland agricultural research programme aimed at reducing water shortages in low-plain areas has been operating in Hebei Province since 1991 (*Xinhua News Agency*, 31 July 1995).

The restructuring of secondary industry will have to focus on intensive processing and the adoption of new technology that will make better use of raw materials, such as in the iron and steel, petrochemical, and chemical industries. The goals should be to upgrade the quality of products like rolled steel, chemical fibres, and fertilizers; to develop the ability to make large-scale equipment and electronic products for the mining, metallurgical, electric power, and other industries; and turn to the manufacture of mar- ketable kinds of micro-computers, kitchen appliances, and similar consumer items.

To improve the regional environment for international co- operation, special attention will need to be paid to the develop- ment of technology and education, as well as commerce, banking, insurance, real estate, tourism, and consultancy and other business services. The open cities, enjoying various forms of preferential treatment, will then be better able to deepen international and technological links through joint venture arrangements and inter- national tourism projects.

The regional division of labour and co-operation among provinces and municipalities in the BSR will have to take account of each area's advantages and help strengthen inter-regional co- operation. As an example of the scope for more co-operation by groups of enterprises, nearly 160 components for Tianjin's Charade car assembly plant are made in factories in Hebei Province (*Xinhua News Agency*, 6 July 1995).

Because of the diminishing amount of arable land, mounting traffic congestion, growing water shortage, and increasing environmental pollution, any new or relocated urban and industrial development should ideally take place near the coast. In such an arrangement, the key role will be played by port cities with their economic and technological development zones; multi-modal transport infrastructure; petrochemical, power, and export-orientated industries; and residential accommodation and facilities.

The Future for Major Industries

Energy industries. The BSR has to import energy in part because, as a result of its 63:37 heavy to light industry ratio, consumption per unit of output is higher than the national average (where the comparable ratio is 56:44). Even so, its manufacturing capacity is underutilized by about 15 per cent because, it is claimed, of energy shortages. The region's reliance on external supplies will continue to grow as local sources will only be able to provide 50 per cent of the 487 million tons of the raw coal and 70 per cent of the 405 GWh of electricity needed by 2000 (Rong, 1995).

Nearly 40 per cent of the country's oil comes from the Daqing oilfield in Heilongjiang Province, but this is now fully mature and production is maintained only by using expensive secondary oil recovery methods. As Daqing's output inevitably declines, the Shengli oilfield will take its place as the leading producer. This, together with the Liaohe, east Hebei, and the offshore Bohai Sea oilfields, will make the BSR the country's leading oil producer until the first decades of the next century when some of these fields, too, will start to run down.

Coal production will continue to be concentrated on the four main fields lying in south-west Shandong, around Handan and Kailuan in Hebei, and in central Liaoning: together these account for 70 per cent of the region's proven reserves and output. The decade to 2010 should see several new major mines come into production and these, along with proposed enlargements of existing ones, will increase annual output by perhaps 100 million tons, or roughly one-third more than current levels.

Power generating capacity will be increased by building a series of coal-fired power stations, some along the coast from Dandong in the north to Shijiusuo in the south (using seawater as the coolant) and others where there is adequate water or large quantities of low-quality coal. In addition, some medium-size thermoelectric plants will be located in urban areas where there is a heavy winter demand for residential, commercial, and industrial heating; they will not only be energy efficient but will help reduce the pollution from scores of small chimneys. In addition, 500 kV-transmission lines are planned from energy producing areas in Shanxi Province and Nei Mongol AR.

Basic materials industries. Iron and steel production will be increased by redeveloping plants and building new ones. The ore-mining, smelting, and cold rolling processes at the old plants at Anshan and Benxi in Liaoning are being upgraded so that by 2005 their combined capacity will reach 15 million tons. However, the expansion of the other old plants—such as the Capital, Tianjin, and Tangshan Iron and Steel Companies—should be severely restricted because there are already problems in relation to traffic, water supply, land use, and environmental pollution. The proposed locations for two new plants each has its own particular advantages: Wangtan in east Hebei is close to the local iron and fuel supplies, while Shijiusuo on the coast would have access to ore imported in bulk carriers.

Petrochemical industries are to be further expanded even though the 50 million tons of oil and 1.3 million tons of ethylene produced annually in the region represent 40 per cent and 50 per cent, respectively, of the national output. The large-scale petrochemical complexes at Yanshan (Beijing) and Zibo (Shandong), each with a capacity to make 300,000 tons of ethylene annually, need technical renovation and the addition of facilities to manufacture plastics, chemical fibres, and other downstream products. Medium-size complexes—as at Fushun, Liaoyang, and Dagang—could each expand ethylene production to 110,000 tons, while those at Tianjin, Dalian, and Qingdao should concentrate on fine petrochemical products. In terms of the overall development strategy, new large-scale ethylene plants would best be placed along the coast at Shijiusuo, Dagang, and Yingkou.

Salt-based chemical production is important, with two-thirds of the national production of soda ash, for example, being made here. The area under salt pans is extensive: those around Cangzhou in Hebei Province occupy 14,000 km^2 and produce 1.5 millions tons of raw salt annually. Many of the small, technologically backward plants will be made redundant by new 600,000-ton capacity soda ash plants under construction, whereas caustic soda producers will need to consider integrating further facilities with new large-scale petrochemical projects located at Dagang, Shijiusuo, and Dalian.

Transport Infrastructure

As China's most important transport hub, special attention is being paid to infrastructural improvements, particularly to the railway system. By 2000, some 200 million tons of coal alone will need to be brought in for local use, and perhaps half as much again will pass through the region on its way south. As noted in Chapter 3, several lines in a west–east 'coal corridor' are being upgraded or constructed, and north–south flows are improving as a result of work on the lines from Beijing to Hong Kong, Shanghai, and Guangzhou and from Qinhuangdao to Shenyang to enable passenger trains to double their speeds to 120 or even 140 km/hr. Development along the coastal zone will be greatly assisted when the proposed Dezhou–Longkou–Yantai and Qingdao–Shijiusuo–Lianyungang lines are completed early next century.

Examples have already been given of the improvements being made to most of the seaports so that they can cope with the growing volumes of domestic and international freight. Four expressways already completed or under construction— Shenyang–Changchun (290 km), Beijing–Shijiazhuang–Shenzhen (2,420 km), Shijiazhuang–Taiyuan (230 km), and Beijing–Tangshan–Qinhuangdao (284 km)—will form part of the inter-regional system shown in Figure 3.6. An important addition to the regional transport system would occur if the proposal, included in Shandong Province's Ninth Five Year Plan, to commence a train-ferry service across the neck of the Bohai Sea between Yantai and Dalian is approved and financially supported by the central government (Cheung, 1996c): these are only 90 nautical miles (165 km) apart by ferry but over 1,000 km by road.

Saving Water and Curbing Pollution

Use of seawater for industrial purposes is only 2 per cent in China as against 50 per cent, for example, in Japan. As the outlay involved in adapting plant adds no more than 3 per cent to establishment

Table 6.4: Urban population in administrative areas of the Bohai Sea Rim, actual 1990 and 1995, estimated 2000 and 2010 (millions)

Administrative area	1990		1995		2000		2010	
	Total population	Per cent urban	Total population	Per cent urban	Total population	Per cent urban	Total population	Per cent urban
Beijing Municipality	10.9	58.4	12.5	63.8	12.4	63.8	13.5	83.9
Tianjin Municipality	8.8	54.1	9.4	54.3	9.7	69.5	10.0	75.7
Hebei Province	60.3	13.3	64.4	17.1	70.6	24.4	77.5	30.1
Liaoning Province	40.0	41.5	40.9	44.0	44.1	63.5	47.4	74.1
Shandong Province	83.4	12.8	87.1	24.9	92.6	34.9	94.2	52.7
Bohai Sea Rim	203.4	22.8	214.3	29.7	229.4	40.9	242.6	52.3

Sources: State Statistical Bureau, 1991; Ye, 1995.

costs (Liu Wei-dong, 1995), seawater could be used by most industrial enterprises near the coast. Inland industrial enterprises might adopt new water-saving technologies and install water recycling systems, while farmers—especially market gardeners in the suburbs—could be taught dry-farming techniques. There are precedents for a longer-term, and more expensive, solution which is to relocate plants needing large quantities of water near the coast: in the late 1970s, for instance, a large power station and a large petrochemical complex were located at Dagang, a coastal district of Tianjin, which now has a population of about 100,000.

Urbanization and industrial emissions are the two major causes of environmental pollution in the BSR. As the estimates in Table 6.4 show, the urbanized parts are likely to contain 52 per cent of the region's population by 2010 as against the 23 per cent recorded there in 1990. Each year, therefore, they have to accommodate an average of 3.6 million new residents as well as upgrading the housing standards of many living there already. The first way of tackling the pollution problem is to disperse the population by speeding up the further development of county towns, including those in outer suburban areas and near the coast.

Then, second, an environmental management policy needs to be worked out, with each place and each enterprise being given discharge standards that would be monitored by each city's environmental agency. To help achieve these goals, expenditure on environmental programmes will have to amount to at least 1 per cent of the region's GNP, with much of it being used to build new sewage treatment plants so that the volume of domestic sewage treated can be raised from about 45 per cent in the mid-1990s to 65 per cent in 2001. The remaining funds could help finance the development of technology-intensive and energy-efficient industries. Loans have also been made by the World Bank and other bodies for environmental improvement projects such as the 17.5-km Shijingshan reticulation scheme on the western outskirts of Beijing which provides heat for 7 million m^2 of housing (*Xinhua News Agency*, 27 November 1995).

Potential and Constraints

The BSR has the potential to become one of the largest industrial centres along the western Pacific Rim and continue to project even stronger development impulses to the extensive inland areas throughout northern China. Such an optimistic outlook is mainly based on its favourable 'gateway' location and the way its regional economy has developed during the past four decades. No other part of the Coastal Region is so richly endowed with fossil fuels, ferrous minerals, and other raw material resources. These have formed the basis for the growth of a strong secondary sector dominated by heavy industry, and this is likely to remain the situation during much of the next two decades. The driving force, however, will be the economies of Beijing and Tianjin. This is because Liaoning Province is still weighed down by the old SOEs (see Chapter 7), and Hebei and Shandong Provinces—though rapidly growing— are still in the early stages of transition from agricultural to industrial bases and, according to the Governor of Shandong, have 'yet to develop "dragonhead" industries' (So, 1995).

Just as Hong Kong has powered the rise of south-east China and Shanghai is acting as the engine for development in the Changjiang Delta and Valley, so Beijing and Tianjin working together could become an even better catalyst for growth in the northern part of the country. Both have strong economies. However, some commentators (like Tang Xu in the *South China Morning Post*, 9 December 1995) have argued that, separately, these cities can achieve little, but by making joint use of their complementary resources, co-ordinating their development, and compensating for each other's weaknesses they can greatly build up their combined strength and influence. On the one side, Beijing has political, administrative, and scientific expertise and a good network of international contacts; on the other, Tianjin has commercial and trade know-how, strengthened by its port and industrial activities, as well as being historically a financial centre with many commercial banks still having their headquarters there.

Yet until recently Tianjin's performance has been sluggish because its SOEs have been slow to adjust to a market economy, and potential investors in service sector activities have perceived it to be a satellite of the national capital. It has also been short of money to modernize its ageing state-owned industrial facilities whereas Beijing has been relatively flush with funds brought in, for example, by the branches of southern companies being established there. A forceful argument for their working more closely together is that Beijing's scientific and financial institutions would find it profitable to invest in Tianjin and support its stated ambition to become the northern commercial and financial hub by the year 2010.

Yet, as this chapter has indicated, the BSR faces several serious problems which, if left unsolved, may thwart its development objectives. Water and energy shortages are affecting production; transport congestion and environmental pollution—particularly in urban areas—threaten the well-being of the population as a whole; and agricultural production has been stagnating since the mid-1980s due to the loss of arable land.

The BSR's industrial structure could be considerably enhanced if more emphasis were put on advanced forms of manufacturing—much of the technology for which would have to be imported—that would increase further the value added to raw materials. Access to both domestic and international markets could be improved if a multi-modal transport network were developed, along with the establishment of one, perhaps two, international trade centres. The goals of improving the regional environment and protecting the limited resources of arable land and fresh water, could be made more achievable by locating further productive activities along the coastal zone. The prosperity of the BSR will thus depend on how quickly it accepts the ideology of market reforms, and how well it makes the structural and spatial adjustments needed to make them effective.

7 The North-East: Searching for a Way Forward

CHEN CAI, YUAN SHU-REN, WANG LI, AND GODFREY LINGE

North-East China is a comparatively well-integrated if somewhat isolated region. Including Liaoning, Jilin, and Heilongjiang Provinces (totalling 790,000 km^2) as well as Hulun Buir Meng, Hinggan Meng, and Jirem Meng Counties and Chifeng City (456,000 km^2) in East Nei Mongol AR, it has a population of about 113 million. Although Liaoning Province has historically been considered part of the North-East, some—like the authors of Chapter 6—think it is more appropriately included in the Bohai Sea Rim. The Ninth Five Year Plan document suggests that the Liaodong Peninsula should be in the Bohai Sphere Zone but does not define what then should be embraced by its proposed North-Eastern Zone. In reality, it would be difficult (not to say impossible for political and administrative reasons) to divide Liaoning Province's spatial economy sensibly for such mega-region planning purposes as it has strong ties, and shares common problems, with both its northern and southern neighbours.

Three parallel north-east to south-west landforms—central plains flanked by mountains on the east and west—form a saddle-shaped natural base for economic activities (Figure 7.1). These mountainous areas, containing rich iron, coal, and other mineral deposits, also account for half China's forested area, while the central plains have over half the country's proved reserves of natural gas and oil. The considerable central tracts of fertile chernozem soil—about 4 per cent of China's total arable area—produce some 13 per cent of the nation's grain, while the wide steppes along the western fringe support animal husbandry. The continental temperate zone monsoonal climate and numerous rivers enhance the rich natural endowment and further reinforce the long-held view that this a favourable region for economic development.

Figure 7.1: Main physical features of the North-East.

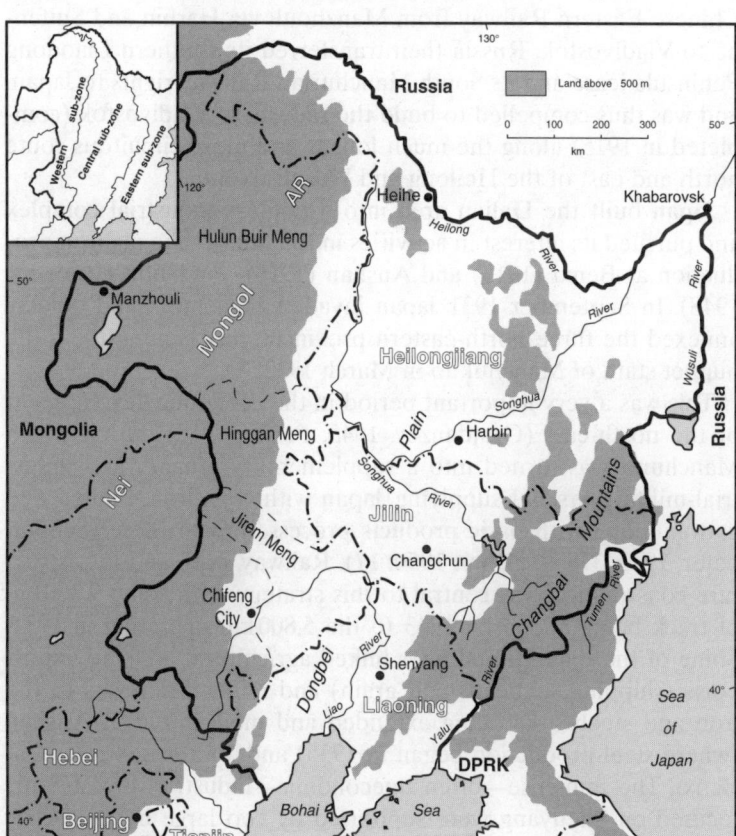

Regional Evolution

Many of the difficulties now facing the North-East are legacies of the territorial rivalries between China, Russia, and Japan, and a brief account of these is needed to understand some of the region's contemporary problems. Modern development accompanied railway construction, with the Shenyang–Beijing line, begun in 1880, being completed in 1907. Meanwhile, between 1896 and 1903, the Russians built the South Manchurian Railway from the southern tip of the Liaodong Peninsula—where they were developing the commercial (and ice-free) port of Dalian—to Harbin, and the Chinese Eastern Railway from Manzhouli via Harbin and Suifen-he to Vladivostok. Russia then transferred its southern Liaodong Peninsula lease and its South Manchurian Railway rights to Japan, and was thus compelled to build the railway to Vladivostok (completed in 1915) along the much longer and more circuitous route north and east of the Heilong and Wusuli rivers.

Japan built the Dalian area into a military-industrial complex and pursued its interest in activities in Liaoning—like pig iron production at Benxi (1915) and Anshan (1916)—and Jilin (Rodgers, 1948). In September 1931 Japan invaded Manchuria and quickly annexed the three north-eastern provinces, proclaiming them the puppet state of Manchukuo in March 1932.

This was a very important period in the economic development of the north-east (Grajdanzev, 1945; Peffer, 1958) during which Manchuria was turned into a supplementary granary and industrial-military arsenal supplying Japan with coal, iron, timber, and cotton, along with basic products processed from these (Schumpeter, 1940: 378–9; Fisher, 1950: 17). Railway, port, and infrastructure construction was central to this strategy, with some 9,300 km of track being added by 1943 to the 5,800 km operating in 1931. Some of these additional lines linked agricultural areas to export ports (shipping soybeans and grain) and mineral deposits to the iron and steelworks being extended and modernized at Anshan (where steel production began in 1935) and, to a lesser extent, at Benxi. The immense—often uneconomic—industrial investments focused on Shenyang were supported by two large hydroelectric stations built on the Songhua and Yalu rivers. In 1943, when the 'Ruhr of China' (as Manchuria had become known) was turning out 93 per cent of the country's steel, 66 per cent of its cement, and half its coal and electricity, the exigencies of war brought production to a standstill.

Then in 1945 the Japanese forces capitulated to invading Soviet troops. By the end of April 1946, the Soviet Union had withdrawn its forces from most of Manchuria—along with considerable quantities of plant stripped from the iron and steel and other industries—and the Chinese communist forces moved in, taking control of Changchun in May 1946, Shenyang in October 1948, and the whole area soon afterwards. Between 1949 and 1954 Manchuria was administered by the North-East People's Government based at Shenyang, and then its 790,000 km^2 and 63 million population (1964) came under the control of the provincial governments of Liaoning, Heilongjiang, and Jilin.

The Regional Economy after 1949

The spatial economy of the North-East can be divided into the central, eastern, and western sub-zones which accord with the natural landforms already described (Figure 7.2). The central zone, with the 945-km double-track railway—presently being electrified—from Dalian to Harbin as its backbone, is the most important economically as it contains many of the farming areas and the main iron and steel, machinery, oil, and chemical industries. The eastern zone, with only small to medium-size cities, is at a lower level of development with an economy largely based on supplying minerals and forestry products to the neighbouring central zone and other parts of China. The western zone, the least developed of the three, depends mainly on animal and forest products, but the discovery of three large coal deposits in Nei Mongol AR has boosted its potential. Although the outer fringes lag behind the central zone, they have been receiving more attention since the late 1980s as' trade has developed across the border with Russia and, to a lesser extent, with the Democratic People's Republic of Korea (DPRK). As indicated later, steps are also being taken to link Hunchun with deep-water ports in Russia and the DPRK which would greatly increase the North-East's accessibility to world markets.

Thus, the evolution of the North-East has had four characteristics. First, its economic development has always been linked with the outside world. Second, the basic structure of the transport network formed during the Russian and Japanese occupations left good connections with neighbouring countries. Third, the relations between China and its neighbours have been, and remain, important influences on its development and spatial organization. Finally, the location and natural endowments of the area have stamped their mark on its economy. While its rich resources, geographical location, and political relationships have been the principal influences on its spatial economy in the past, it is the latter two that will remain the key to its future.

Figure 7.2: Main economic features of the North-East.

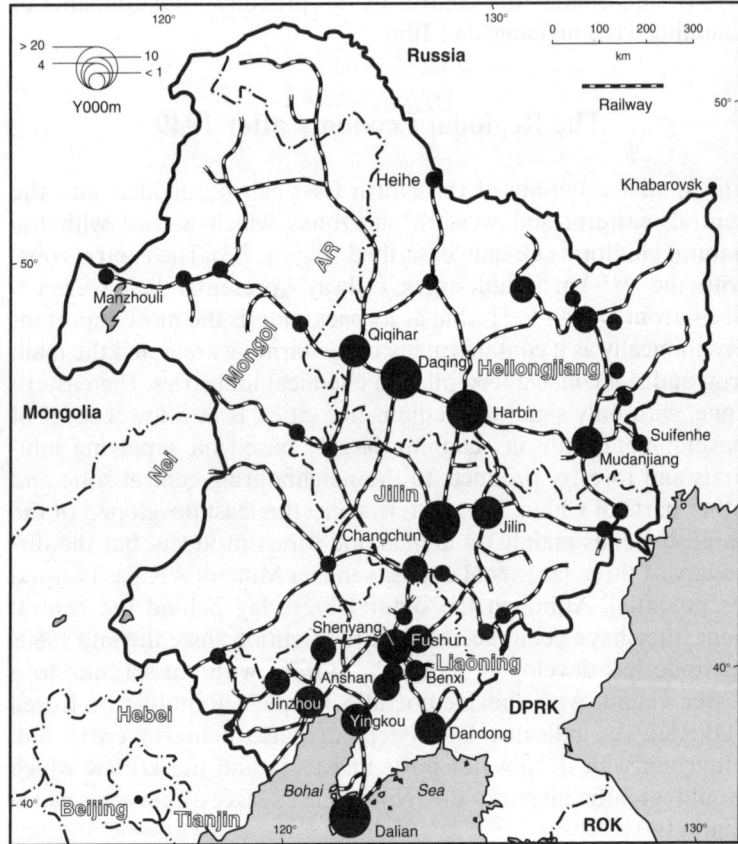

Sources: production data based on Li and Lu, 1995: 455; railways based on Editorial Group, 1995: 104–9.

Problems Hindering Development

For the first couple of decades after the establishment of the People's Republic of China in 1949, the North-East regained its role as one of the country's leading industrial areas. During the First Five Year Plan (1953–57), the fifty-six large industrial businesses built there—mostly with Soviet support—absorbed one-third of all state investment outlays, with stress being laid on heavy industries like iron and steel (Anshan, Benxi), coal (Fushun,

Table 7.1: Percentage of China's gross industrial output by North-East administrative areas, 1952 to 1995[a]

Administrative area	1952	1957	1965	1974	1979	1984	1991	1995
Liaoning Province	13.3	14.4	13.4	11.9	9.1	8.2	6.6	5.4
Jilin Province	3.2	3.1	3.6	2.7	2.7	2.9	2.1	1.6
Heilongjiang Province	5.6	5.2	5.6	4.6	4.7	4.5	3.5	2.4
North-East[b]	22.1	22.7	22.6	19.2	16.5	15.6	12.2	9.4

[a] After 1984, village-run enterprises were transferred from agricultural to industrial output statistics.
[b] Excluding the part in Nei Mongol AR for which data are unavailable.
Sources: Pannell, 1988: 22; State Statistical Bureau, 1992, 1996a.

Hegang), heavy equipment (Shenyang, Qiqihar), transport equipment (Changchun, Dalian), power generators (Harbin, Shenyang), and chemicals (Jilin City). The country's first locally developed oil-field came into production at Daqing in the early 1960s and then other north-eastern fields were developed at Liaohe and Jilin; oil refineries followed at Daqing (the first to be locally designed and built and using advanced technology), Panjin, Jinzhou, and Jilin City. By the late 1970s the North-East was producing 54 per cent of China's petroleum, 32 per cent of its motor vehicles, 25 per cent of its pig iron, and 22 per cent of its steel. Agricultural and forestry activities were also flourishing.

For some years prior to this, however, the area's share of China's gross industrial output value had been declining (Table 7.1). Heavy industry, formerly its strength, was becoming a liability as the post-1979 reforms exposed the gross inefficiencies of many of the large and medium-size state-owned enterprises (SOEs). More especially the shift to a socialist market system continued to be frustrated by inflexibilities which inhibited economic and industrial growth and widened income disparities between the North-East and other parts of the country. These problems—widely known in China as 'the phenomenon of the North-East'—have five principal causes.

First, the substantial cut-backs in central government investment since the mid-1980s have left most of the disproportionately large number of inefficient SOEs here shackled in triangular debt chains (estimated in 1994 to be as much as US$4,000 million in Jilin Province and US$5,000 million in Heilongjiang Province), thus tying-up funds needed to modernize equipment and meet taxes. In Heilongjiang Province alone, SOEs lost US$61 million in 1993 and US$132 million in 1994 (Yue, 1994); in 1995 35 per cent of them were making losses and 68 per cent of their assets were in debt. As a particular example, a state-owned heavy machinery plant at Qiqihar, with 30,000 employees and assets of US$225 million, produced goods in 1993 worth only US$88 million and a profit (even after using only a 4 per cent depreciation rate) of US$25,000. Despite efforts to privatize, amalgamate, or close SOEs their numbers continue to grow: Jilin Province, for example, had 2,170 in 1985 but 2,730 a decade later (*Jilin Ribao*, 30 July 1996: 2). Reform efforts by provincial governments are fettered because many large enterprises in key or sensitive industries are directly controlled by central ministries, and their in-house health, education, and other worker-support facilities reduce the burden on local government expenditures. A further constraint is the lack of a fully fledged social security system to look after laid-off and retired workers, although all the provinces are developing unemployment insurance and retraining schemes. None the less, a vice-chairman of the National People's Congress noted in September 1996 that a quarter of the enterprises in Jilin Province were losing money, but argued that they should not lay off the more than 800,000 redundant workers unless they have worked out settlements with them (Kwan, 1996b).

Second, the over-exploitation of energy, minerals, and other resources during the 1950s and 1960s has sharply reduced economically exploitable reserves so the industrial activities based on them have been declining. Thus, Daqing City, which relies on crude oil and petrochemicals for 90 per cent of its GDP, is trying to diversify its economic base to cope with the expected decline in oil output (despite the use of costly secondary oil recovery technology) from 56 million tons in 1996 to 50 million tons by 2010.

Third, the entrenched and prominent role played by large SOEs and other heavy plants continues to create an inflexible local economy that cannot easily adjust to the changing market demands occasioned by economic reform. In 1995, 67 per cent of industrial output in Heilongjiang came from SOEs (as against 76 per cent in 1993 and 80 per cent in 1986); in Jilin the proportion in 1995 was 62 per cent (68 and 75 per cent); and in Liaoning it was 42 per cent (52 and 65 per cent). In order 'to speed up the transformation of this old industrial base and display its abilities', Vice-Premier Wu Bangguo said in June 1995, 'we must emancipate our minds, change our traditional ideas, improve our train of thought and the reforms' (*Xinhua News Agency*, 12 June 1995). Illustrating what this means in practice are the changes made at three plants in Qiqihar, said to be 'the large key enterprises of the ordnance industry in China', which incurred deficits after 1989 when the demand for military hardware diminished. They could not even pay wages. Since 1993 they have introduced foreign investment and technology, and 'adjusted the product mix in line with market demand' (*Hei-longjiang Ribao*, 24 November 1996: 1). By the end of 1996 one-fifth of the output of their 33,000 employees consisted of civilian goods (such as sanitary ware made under licence from a Swiss firm) but, in addition, they had also transferred 7,000 of their previous workforce to newly established farms, retail stores, health clinics, and other service activities. An even more striking example is the Anshan Iron and Steel Company, a sprawling conglomerate that embodies 103 plants and mines, 11 research institutes, 10 colleges, and 16 hospitals, which has redeployed no fewer than 300,000 people on its payroll (including retirees on company pensions and 170,000 children) by setting up 17 non-steel subsidiaries, including hotels, restaurants, shops, and other businesses, in Anshan City; 24,000 more will lose their jobs by 2000, leaving 50,000 workers to make 8 million tons of steel annually (*Reuter Australasian Briefing*, 24 April and 20 September 1996).

Fourth, the comparatively weak infrastructure and undeveloped tertiary sector impedes the circulation of goods, people, capital, and information, slows the development of village and township enter-prises, and saps the vitality of the regional economy. A related problem is that many of the cities in the North-East have grown up, in some cases since the 1930s, as 'enterprise towns' whose for-tunes are closely linked to a few large state undertakings. Report-edly, the 'unitary structure and product mix' of the city itself has been changed as a result of the new directions adopted by the defence plants in Qiqihar (*Heilongjiang Ribao*, 24 November 1996: 1). The same is true of many other urban areas: in Liaoning

Province alone, 200,000 people were forced to change jobs in 1996 because more than 100 SOEs had gone bankrupt (*Xinhua News Agency*, 6 December 1996).

Fifth, the need to send about three-quarters of the region's exports through the overloaded ports in Liaoning Province adds to costs and delays, reduces the market value of products like grain, and has made it more difficult for enterprises to establish close and convenient linkages with foreign investors—the main stimulus for development elsewhere in China.

The three underlying causes of this 'phenomenon'—the changing resource base, the influence of economic reform, and international circumstances—deserve closer examination.

Changes to the Resource Base

Although the North-East has long been regarded as richly endowed with natural resources, the current reality and future outlook are very different. Jilin Province, for example, plans to tap 1,700 million m³ of natural gas by 2000 but, as this will not meet the expected demand, contracts have already been signed to import the 900 million m³ shortfall from overseas (*China Daily*, 5 August 1996). Over-exploitation has run down—even exhausted—mineral, forest, and other resources. Coal-mines, like those near Fushun, are closing as seams are worked out. Until about 1980 substantial quantities of coal were exported, but now some 30 million tons a year have to be brought into Liaoning Province alone, mainly from Shanxi Province. Or again, although the Anshan and Benxi steelworks are still using ore mined nearby, increasing quantities are being imported from overseas. In some areas tree felling has exceeded planting since the 1930s so that the proportion of mature forest has declined and ecosystems have been adversely affected, although Liaoning Province has used World Bank funds to restore its forest coverage to 42 per cent, while at the same developing a lucrative high-density charcoal product for export to Japan.

Many cities and industrial enterprises face water shortages. The amount available per person in Liaoning Province is only one-third of the national average, and in places like Dalian and Huludao (formerly Jinxi) supplies to industry have to be restricted. There are numerous examples of air and water pollution: sulphur dioxide from the local smelter pollutes the air in Shenyang; untreated toxins from coke ovens at Benxi flow into the Taizi River; untreated waste water pollutes the Shenfu Irrigation Canal in Fushun; and until late in 1996 untreated waste water from the Jilin Chemical Industry Corporation's plants at Jilin City flowed into the Songhua River.

These resource and environmental concerns have not, however, been fully appreciated by government officials and other decision makers who have continued to formulate their development planning on the old idea that the North-East can support heavy metallurgical and chemical industries using local resources. This attitude simply aggravates the problem.

Impact of Economic Reform

The economic reform programme has impacted on the North-East in three main ways. First, the central government changed its emphasis from supporting the old industrial bases to promoting and aiding coastal areas in eastern and southern China that were better able to generate revenue and develop international markets and business linkages. Second, for many years under the centrally planned system the North-East supplied raw materials and agricultural and industrial products to other parts of China at very low fixed prices. This drained the region financially and curtailed the funds available for updating industrial plants and upgrading infrastructure. Finally, the growing obsolescence of the old-established resource and energy-consuming enterprises makes it difficult for them to adapt and, hence, compete with newer factories elsewhere.

These problems have been exacerbated in some instances by central government decisions. Steel makers now have to pay cost price for their coal and yet see their markets being undercut by cheap bartered steel imported without tariffs from Russia. The short-lived experiment with car loans is another example. In June 1996, the China Construction Bank reached agreement with the First Automotive Works (FAW)-Volkswagen of Changchun to offer US$98 million in consumer loans to boost sales of Jetta cars—the first consumer financing scheme of its kind in China. Without warning, on 13 October after just 800 vehicles had been sold, the central government ordered banks to stop processing loans under this scheme even though the car industry throughout China—and one of two main pillar industries in Jilin Province—had rapidly growing stocks of unsold vehicles.

Many managers, workers, and officials are unfamiliar with the way a market economy system operates and thus continue to look to government for support and guidance. This ignorance about how to adapt to changing circumstances and adopt market-driven performance and quality criteria greatly hinders attempts to upgrade regional economic conditions. Late in 1994 the Secretary of the Heilongjiang Provincial CCP Committee drew attention to the ideological legacies when he called for people to

break with the rigid idea of being absolutely obedient to books and higher levels; eliminate such traditional concepts as pursuing 'iron rice bowl', being reluctant to give up the 'big common pot', being accustomed to 'taking from those who have too much and giving it to those who have too little'; eliminate the habitual thinking trend of strengthening 'leadership' over everything, having the government run and manage everything, and having the state own and operate everything; change the development idea of depending solely on state investment and on the expansion of scale . . . (Yue, 1994).

International Influences

The North-East has been particularly influenced by changes in China's international relationships because it shares lengthy borders with Mongolia (789 km), Russia (4,288 km), and the DPRK (1,416 km). The 1990s have seen warmer relations evolving with Russia—symbolized for the North-East by the mid-1995 agreement to construct a bridge linking the frontier towns of Heihe and Blagoveshchensk across the Heilong River and due for completion in 1998. In contrast, a more ambivalent attitude developed towards the DPRK, though some signs of a *rapprochement* appeared late in 1996. This included an agreement to allow North Korean settlers to farm the fertile 145,000-km^2 Sanjiang Plain in the far north-east of Heilongjiang Province (*Hangyore Sinmun*, 16 December 1996: 3), and another to establish a 1.6-km free trade zone on Sindo Island at the mouth of the Yalu River near Donggou (*Korea Economic Weekly*, 31 October 1996).

Despite these uncertainties, the possibility of increased trade with Russia and the DPRK, and the growing hope of a cross-border development zone taking shape in the Tumen River area (see later) has stimulated activity at border settlements like Suifenhe, Heihe, Manzhouli, and Hunchun. Arguably, however, the attention paid to these places has diverted the attention of regional leaders, policy makers, and potential foreign investors from the pressing need to upgrade technology in the older enterprises in the central area.

Reorganizing the Spatial Economy

Three strategies—strengthening the central economic belt, developing the border areas, and realizing the Tumen River Economic Development Area (TEDA) project—are being considered to try to overcome some of these short-term obstacles and put longer-term solutions in place.

Strategy 1: Strengthening the Central Economic Belt

The backbone of the central sub-zone, as indicated already, is the trunk railway and expressway linking Harbin and Dalian, the oil pipeline from Daqing to Dalian, and the industrial cities along it like Anshan, Liaoyang, Shenyang, Siping, and Changchun. In recent years, the modernization of industry and agriculture in land-locked Jilin and Heilongjiang Provinces has been retarded by the chronic congestion on the railways and in the southern ports of Dalian and Yingkou. At peak periods Liaoning can handle only one-tenth of the demand for rail freight (*Reuter Australasian Briefing*, 19 September 1994). This has now been recognized with an announcement in June 1995 of a long-range transport blueprint for Liaoning Province involving a complex network of water, land, and air transport links (*Reuter Australasian Briefing*, 20 June 1995), including the upgrading of port facilities at Dalian, Yingkou, and Dandong; an 800-km canal linking the Songhua and Liao rivers; and the construction of highways between Shenyang and Shanhaiguan (near Qinhuangdao) and from Changchun to Harbin. Much also needs to be done to improve the efficiency of the transport system at a more local level: as a case in point, the 128-km railway between Changchun and Jilin can handle only a third of the demand, as the track needs rehabilitating completely with diesel power replacing steam.

Other infrastructural deficiencies are also being repaired, often with outside assistance. The World Bank has provided a loan of

US$110 million to finance waste treatment and air pollution ameli-
oration projects; the Canadian government has lent money to cut
sulphur dioxide emissions at Shenyang City; the Asian Development Bank is partly funding a new bypass road to the port at
Dalian; and the Republic of Korea (ROK) is assisting construction
work at Yanji airport. A fifteen-year US$2,000-million low-interest
loan from Russia was to have helped pay for two 1,000 MW nuclear
power plants Wafangdian (80 km north of Dalian), but towards
the end of 1996 the site was changed to Lianyungang (Jiangsu
Province), ostensibly because the need for power was greater there
(*Reuter Australasian Briefing*, 4 November 1996).

Several examples have already been given of the ways in which
SOEs are being reformed. Some have been bankrupted or reorganized. Others have been given a new vitality by an infusion of foreign
capital, in so-called 'marry and connect' deals, such as FAW at
Changchun in which Volkswagen AG now has a 41 per cent
holding, and the Dalian Rubber Company in which the US tyre
maker Goodyear has a financial interest. Others have concentrated on higher-quality products or linked up with major conglomer-
ates operating in other parts of China.

Each of the provinces has announced plans to form groups of
so-called 'pillar' industries. Among those listed by Liaoning, for
example, are automobiles, aircraft, video cameras, computer mon-
itors, and digitally controlled machine tools (*Xinhua News Agency*,
8 January 1995). In Heilongjiang the task is to develop petrochemical projects in the west, non-coal substitute industries in the
east, wood product industries in the forested areas, and intensive
processing of farm products. In Jilin the list is headed by the motor
vehicle and associated industries at Changchun (see later), which
provide about one-fifth of the provincial government's revenue.
Next in importance is the state-owned Jilin Chemical Industry Corporation with 135,000 employees working in more than 300 owned
and part-owned production units on its 40-hectare complex at Jilin
City, the largest chemical production centre in the country. A new
phase of chemical manufacturing began early in 1997 with the
completion of a US$1,800-million, 300,000-ton per year ethylene
cracker plant, which obtains its feedstock from a new 600,000-ton
per year hydrocracker and is linked to a polyethylene plant rated
at 100,000 tons and an ethylene glycol unit (*Chemical Marketing
Reporter*, 23 September 1996: 26). These developments will raise

the Corporation's annual revenue to US$2,000 million (*EIU Electronic Publishing*, 13 September 1996).

Already most of the North-Eastern cities have started to overcome their infrastructural deficiencies by building modern hotels, improving water supplies, and reducing traffic congestion. In October 1992, Dalian (population 2.4 million) announced a twenty-year development plan to make it the 'Hong Kong of the North': to this end it is using a US$160 million loan from the Asian Development Bank to upgrade its water supply and reticulation system, installing high-tech urban traffic control systems, and seeking funds to build a 14-km subway. Or again, at Changchun, a Malaysian property developer has contracted to build 80,000 medium-cost residential and commercial units by 2005. Taken together, these kinds of changes will help to make conditions more attractive to investors from other parts of China and from abroad.

Economic development zones of various kinds are multiplying throughout the North-East—by the end of 1996 Jilin Province alone had four state and twelve provincial-level zones. Changchun has both an Economic and Technological Development Zone (ETDZ) (which by the end of 1995 had 172 foreign-funded enterprises, including 10 multinationals) and a High-Tech Development Zone (with 194 foreign-funded enterprises in place, including GE Motors, Ford Motor Co., C. Itoh, and Siemens) (*Zhongguo Xinwen She News Agency*, 18 October 1996). Many of these are associated with the US$1,200-million FAW-Volkswagen joint venture which was completed in July 1996 with a capacity to build 150,000 Jetta and 30,000 Audi-200 cars per annum.

In Liaoning Province, Dalian set up a 24-km^2 ETDZ (30 km from the city centre) in 1984, which by mid-1995 had become a comprehensive commercial, industrial, and residential area with a permanent population already of 100,000 out of a planned total of 700,000 by 2010. The main source of investment initially was Japan, with companies like Toshiba Corp., Sanyo Industries Ltd, and Canon Inc. being attracted principally by the low labour costs. Thus, Mabuchi Motor Co. Ltd employs 7,500 making micro-motors for products as diverse as cars and cameras, and claims to save 20 per cent on its wages bill compared with its operations in Japan.

The inauguration of direct flights with Seoul early in 1995 spurred interest among firms in the ROK which then became the leading source of investment. Firms like Lucky-Goldstar

International Corp., Pohang Iron and Steel Corp., and Hyundai were also attracted by the low cost of labour as this makes up less than 5 per cent of total production outlays here as against 20 per cent back home. At the provincial capital, Shenyang, the Nanhu Science and Technology Development Zone has more than 200 joint ventures making computer peripherals, biotechnology apparatus, numerically controlled machine tools, and telecommunications equipment.

Two spatial consequences are flowing from these developments. First, the economies of the cities in the central area are being enlarged and diversified. Second, the upgrading of the transport facilities in the central corridor has helped to strengthen the region's external connections. For example, in 1990 the Dalian–Harbin railway was extended 567 km to the border city of Heihe. If in due course a railway track were added to the 3-km road bridge currently being built across the Heilong River to connect Heihe with the Russian city of Blagoveshchensk opposite, a link could be created with the Trans-Siberian Railway 109 km away at Belogorsk (although this—like all such cross-border links—has to have bogie exchange or cargo transfer facilities because of the difference in the Russian broad gauge and Chinese standard gauge systems). Yet another proposal is for a rail link from Hunchun to connect with the Trans-Siberian Railway at Borzya (see later).

Strategy 2: Developing the Border Economic Belt

As tensions eased along the sensitive militarized border with the Soviet Union in the north-east, informal trading began in about 1987 with fruit from China, for example, being exchanged for Russian fertilizer. By 1993 the *total* recorded value of Sino-Russian trade had reached US$7,700 million (with a surplus in Russia's favour of US$2,100 million), largely consisting of foodstuffs, clothing, and consumer goods from China and steel, trucks, and machinery from Russia. Most of the border trade, accounting for about US$2,500 million, passed through the twenty or so crossing places in Heilongjiang, some of which (like Heihe and Suifenhe, that became designated border open cities in March 1992, are on the border itself) and others (like Harbin) are ports on the Songhua River which feeds into the Amur River. Nei Mongol AR reported a US$770 million cross-border trade in 1993 through its eighteen posts, but mainly through Manzhouli (US$611 million) opposite the Russian town of Zabaykalsk which is connected to the Trans-Siberian Railway at Chita. After being declared a border open city in March 1992, Manzhouli (population 130,000) started to construct a 12-km^2 free trade zone which came into operation late in 1996.

Thus, in the early 1990s the prospects of trade stimulating development north and south of the border looked very positive. After 1993, however, *total* Sino-Russian trade fell to only US$5,100 million in 1994, US$5,500 million in 1995, and about US$6,900 million in 1996 (*Xinhua News Agency*, 21 April 1997). Among the explanations were the depressed state of the Russian economy; the austerity measures in China which for a time reduced the demand for construction materials; changes in tariffs; the shoddy quality of merchandise; and a fall in the value of the yuan against the Swiss franc—the currency of choice among those border traders not involved in barter arrangements.

Trade across the border with the DPRK also began to develop but on a smaller scale. Much of it was in the hands of Chinese merchants and pedlars who were allowed to operate, albeit unofficially, in such Korean cities as Sinuiju, Hoeryong, Chongjin, and Najin. By early 1995 the Yanbian Korean Autonomous Prefecture had eight border gates through which China exported mainly grain and soybeans in exchange for fish and lumber. This 'official' trade through Yanbian was worth US$310 million in 1993 but then slumped as a result of the collapse of the DPRK's economy and amounted to a mere US$55 million in 1995 (Dickie, 1996a). Late in 1996, China banned border trade with the DPRK unless payments were made in advance until traders in that country settle debts of US$100 million that have been outstanding since the end of 1995 (*Chungang Ilbo*, 17 December 1996: 2).

The initial rapid growth of the border trade encouraged local communities and provincial leaders to see this as a new development opportunity. Yet the reality is that the total external trade of Heilongjiang and Jilin Provinces together totalled only US$6,350 million in 1995, about 40 per cent of this being border trade—roughly two-fifths in the form of barter deals. The extent to which border trade will invigorate economic activity around the margins of the North-East is unclear, although a few communities are benefiting. Trade through Suifenhe (population 40,000), for example, reached US$150 million in 1995 and US$253 million in the first eight months of 1996.

Although border cities like Heihe, Suifenhe, and Manzhouli have been authorized by the central or provincial governments to apply special policies to encourage foreign investment, much of the effort has gone into developing tertiary activities like tourism rather than upgrading industry. Long-running discussions about joint free trade zones led in September 1996 to an agreement between Heihe and Blagoveshchensk to build a visa-free 10-hectare Sino-Russian Economic and Trade Town on an island in the middle of the river (*BBC Monitoring Service*, 4 September 1996).

Strategy 3: The Tumen River Project

For most of its length, the Tumen River, which rises in the Changbai Mountains and flows 516 km to the Sea of Japan, forms the border between China and the DPRK, but for the final 15 km it marks the boundary between the Russian Republic and the DPRK (Figure 7.3). In 1938 China's centuries-old access to the Sea of Japan via the Tumen River was cut off and trade through its river port at Hunchun ceased. This whole border area then became an inaccessible militarized zone, and Hunchun remained closed to foreigners until 1991. In that year Russia agreed to restore navigation rights to China but, in the absence of a similar gesture by the DPRK, by early 1997 no Chinese vessel had ventured down this final stretch of the Tumen River (Linge, forthcoming).

By the late 1980s each of the three riparian countries was independently investigating the idea of establishing separate special economic zones (SEZs) near the coast. Some years previously, however, geographers at the Northeast Normal University in Changchun had quietly floated the concept of the three countries jointly establishing an economic zone in the Tumen area, possibly with financial support from Japan and the ROK. This idea had much in its favour: the manpower, mineral, and forestry resources in the three riparian regions could be better exploited; northeastern China and Mongolia would get more-direct access to the open sea and hence to international markets; and the feasibility of a rail 'bridge' linking Asia with Western Europe (which might be of particular interest to Japan) could be enhanced. The protagonists were further encouraged by accounts of the 'growth triangle' being promoted by Singapore, Johor (Malaysia), and Riau (Indonesia), although none of the potential Tumen participants stood out as being an economically advanced and financially well-

Figure 7.3: The Tumen River project.

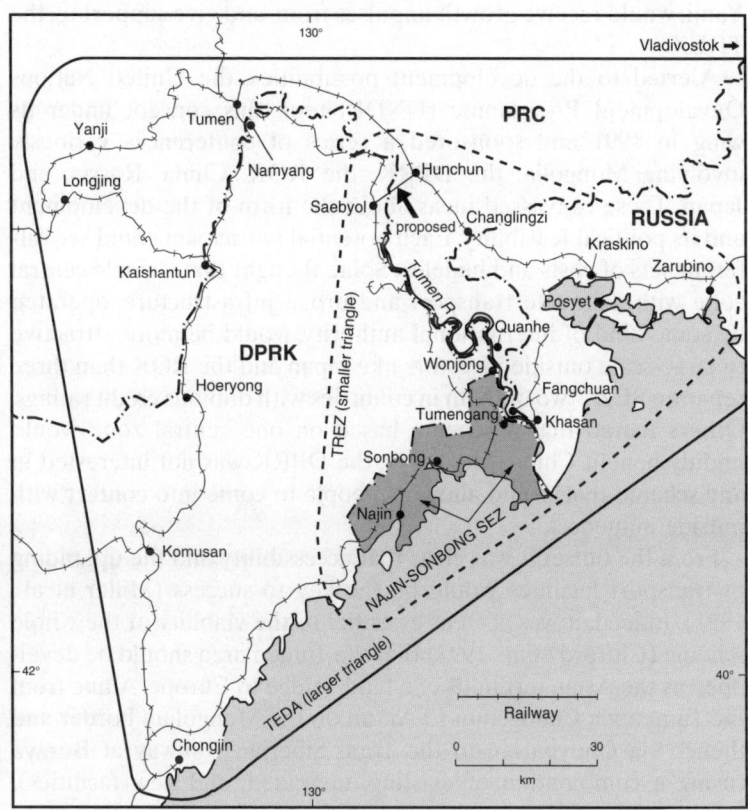

Sources: authors' fieldwork and unpublished reports.

connected 'dynamo' able to drive the whole project. However, the three key cities—Vladivostok (Russia), Chongjin (DPRK), and Yanji (China)—in what some saw as the potential scope of the Tumen region all had status as provincial or prefectural capitals, a political reality that could not be ignored.

By July 1990 the project had become conceptualized in the form of two triangles (Figure 7.3). The smaller one of about 1,000 km^2— labelled the Tumen River Economic Zone (TREZ) with apexes at Hunchun, Sonbong (or Najin) in the DPRK, and Posyet in Russia— would be a transport, warehousing, and industrial hub. The larger triangle, the Tumen River Economic Development Area (TEDA) covering 10,000 km^2 with apexes at Chongjin, Vladivostok, and Yanji, would receive growth impulses from, and give support to, the TREZ.

Alerted to the development possibilities, the United Nations Development Programme (UNDP) took this concept under its wing in 1991 and sponsored a series of conferences variously involving Mongolia, the DPRK, the ROK, China, Russia, and Japan. These canvassed ideas about the form of the development and its political feasibility. Each potential participant could see different sets of costs and benefits. Some thought that a single central zone with adequate transport and urban infrastructure, operated by some kind of international authority, would be more attractive to large-scale outside investors like Japan and the ROK than three separate SEZs, two of them in countries with dubious credit ratings. Others feared that a scheme based on one central zone would unduly benefit China. Moreover, the DPRK was not interested in any scheme that would allow its people to come into contact with outside influences.

From the outset it was clear that accessibility and the upgrading of transport facilities would be the key to success (Miller et al., 1991). Indeed, it was seen as essential to the viability of the whole scheme (Clifford et al., 1992) that the Tumen area should be developed as the Asian terminus of a land-bridge to Europe. A line from the Tumen via Changchun to Arxan on the Mongolian border and thence via Choybalsan to the Trans-Siberian Railway at Borzya (using a combination of existing, upgraded, and new facilities), would save 1,750 km compared with the existing all-Russian route from Nakhodka, Vostochnyy, and Vladivostok via Ussurijsk and Khabarovsk. It would also provide Mongolia with more-direct access to the Sea of Japan and stimulate the development of its resource-rich eastern region.

It became apparent that the initial idea of dredging or canalizing the Tumen River itself would be expensive and of limited utility during winter. The more practical and politically acceptable alternative that had emerged by mid-1992 was a major inland freight-handling facility at Hunchun linked by new or upgraded railways and roads to existing deep-water ports of Zarubino in Russia and Najin in the DPRK, both of which needed enlarging and modernizing. These discussions continued during 1993 and 1994 but against a background of rising international tensions about the nuclear intentions of the DPRK and a flurry of diplomatic stand-offs that this and other issues were generating in the region. Lack of progress led the UNDP to downgrade its involvement in the project at the end of October 1994.

No sooner had it done so than a series of unrelated events removed some of the political obstacles, so that by May 1995 China, the DPRK, the ROK, Russia, and Mongolia had all revived their willingness in principle to co-operate in a Tumen scheme. On 6 December 1995 these countries signed agreements to (i) establish a ministerial-level co-ordinating committee (with the three riparian countries as members); (ii) form a consultative committee to manage the development plan and to take account of issues involving nearby areas of North-East Asia; and (iii) consider environmental conservation matters in the region.

These agreements marked the beginning of a second phase in the Tumen River project, which has become part and parcel of the macro-level geopolitical manœuvring which is taking place throughout North-East Asia as countries test new-found strengths and weaknesses. In addition, China, the DPRK, and Russia are each trying to come to terms with the collapse of the socialist market economy and the consequences of opening up, widely or more narrowly, to the outside world. This is requiring fundamental changes to financial, legal, and administrative rules and procedures as well as the development of mechanisms that can enable privately owned joint ventures to interact with monolithic SOEs. For each country, too, the Tumen project is raising a mix of unprecedented issues, including the respective roles and responsibilities of the political core and the distant periphery; the management of contradictions arising from domestic and foreign policies; the sovereignty of territory; the inviolability of borders; and the codification of three different sets of rules and procedures in such a way that trade and commerce can operate in a cross-border zone without bureaucratic inefficiency.

Given all these circumstances, the many local legacies of long-standing territorial disputes, and the intra-regional jealousies and conflicting political ambitions, it seems unrealistic to imagine that an international transport and industrial zone straddling the borders of the three riparian countries and administered by some tripartite or international authority will be up and running much before 2010 at the earliest. Rather, the signs are that the three countries will promote their own SEZs within the larger triangle and operate them in separate and competitive ways. Even this will require considerable co-operation on a series of practical matters, including the construction and upgrading of railways, roads, bridges, border crossing points, and telecommunications facilities, to say nothing of the procedures relating to visas, customs, currency, and banking, as well as laws regarding taxation, repatriation of profits, and intellectual property rights.

While much of the detail has yet to be worked out, places like Hunchun, Tumen, and Yanji are already benefiting from the improved access to Najin and Zarubino ports, which are both being upgraded. Hunchun (population 300,000), with the status of a 'border open city' since March 1992, has a strategic position: in the south-east it has a 233-km common border with Russia, and for 139 km in the south-west faces the DPRK across the Tumen River. By the end of 1996, its economic development zone had signed contracts for twenty-nine projects with an investment value of US$140 million (*Zhongguo Xinwen She News Agency*, 18 October 1996).

Prospects

When in July 1996 the Provincial Party Secretary noted that 'Heilongjiang has a deep tradition of central planning and has been slow adopting economic reforms' (Kattoulas, 1996), he was in effect articulating the main problem facing the whole of the North-East. It is illustrated by Honghe north-east of Harbin, a collective of 104 individual farms supporting 1.6 million people (and one of the largest state-run farms in China), which only began introducing mechanized methods—commonplace by the early 1980s in the Changjiang Delta—to help in the 1995 harvest of 5 million tons of grain and soybeans.

All three provinces and Nei Mongol AR have programmes aimed at upgrading agricultural and industrial efficiency and technology, but their leaders also admit that it will take time to 'rip off the fetters of central planning' and build 'red-blooded market economies'. The Governor of Jilin Province, in a report on progress during the first nine months of 1996, wanted his administration to 'squarely face the problems', most notably the downturn in industrial economic returns: 'losses increased, and some SOEs had increasing difficulties with production and management ... some departments failed to adapt themselves to the market' (*Jilin Ribao*, 16 October: 1, 8).

New approaches are needed to make the industrial structure of the North-East less dependent on state-owned heavy industry and central government finance. One possibility is to give further encouragement to township and village enterprises which, in Jiangsu and Zhejiang Provinces, have shown themselves adept at merging and acquiring small and medium-size state businesses. Indeed, the Governor of Liaoning Province has said that township enterprises 'have become the driving force of the provincial economy' as they accounted for two-fifths of its output (*Xinhua News Agency*, 6 June 1996). During the five years to the end of 1996 this province had given approval for about 2,200 foreign-funded township enterprises and had plans to attract another 1,000 similar export-orientated ventures by the end of the decade.

Less emphasis has to be placed on resource development and more on making better use of existing assets, such as raising crop yields. As part of its campaign to foster the non-state sector, Helongjiang Province is encouraging small entrepreneurs to develop the 'five deserts' (wasteland, barren hills, deserted beaches, ditches, and water surfaces) that occupy 47,000 km^2 still 'sunk in slumber'. Opportunities exist for processing local products into higher-value exportable goods (such as grain into starch and animal feed), and for strategies aimed at replacing imports: for example, China imported 10 million tons of rolled steel in 1996 to make up a shortfall in good quality domestic supplies (*Financial Times*, 3 January 1997: 4).

Though considerable efforts have been made to improve railway, road, communications, and information networks, a range of tertiary services—banking, commerce, hotels, and real estate—still needs to be widened and deepened to attract overseas investors, especially to places in the north with inhospitable climates. Multinational companies—like Gillette Razor and Tampax (Shenyang), Slumberland (Harbin), and Ericsson (Dalian)—have found the local market for consumer and household goods to be undeveloped, product distribution difficult, and some services (like advertising agencies) non-existent.

Much weight has been placed by regional leaders on developing foreign trade, especially with countries in North-East Asia, as a significant engine for growth. While there are signs of a revival in the border trade with Russia it seems unrealistic, given the economic problems facing the Russian Far East, to imagine that this will significantly boost the North-East's economy. The total value of Liaoning Province's exports to Russia in 1995 was a mere US$130 million (*Xinhua News Agency*, 14 June 1996). Suggestions that Sino-Russian trade may be boosted to US$20,000 million by 2000 may not assist the local area because it involves mainly the supply by Russia of big-ticket items like equipment for the Three Gorges project and nuclear power plants.

Considerable hope, too, has been pinned on the stimulus that could flow from the Tumen River cross-border zone but, as already made clear, it will probably be at least 2010 before this comes to fruition, and even then much depends on very large slices of investment capital being made available to a region that continues to be surrounded by political uncertainties and power plays. A key part of this scheme is the proposal to build, at an estimated cost of US$1,000 million, a rail link from Hunchun to connect with the Trans-Siberian Railway at Borzya which, if it were to proceed in competition with other 'land-bridges' being built or considered, would generate a certain amount of construction and maintenance activity along its route. Revived from time to time are several other major schemes that would also change the North-East's relationships with the outside world. Among them is a proposal for an undersea tunnel linking Shimonoseki in Japan to Pusan in the ROK, thence a road to Dandong in Liaoning Province and a further road from Dandong to Beijing. Were this to eventuate (and the cost has been estimated at US$20,000 million), Liaoning Province would find itself becoming the centre of the 'North-East Asian Economic Circle' (*Reuter Australasian Briefing*, 14 December 1994). Proposals are revived from time to time for a series of bridges and tunnels to link Dalian with Yantai in Shandong Province which would bring this North-East area physically and symbolically closer to the more prosperous part of the eastern seaboard. These schemes might seem fanciful but illustrate the kind of imaginative thinking—like Dalian's ambition to become the 'Hong Kong of the North' by 2010—that seems necessary to lift this region out of the doldrums.

8 Regional Disparities in Rural Development

ANDREW WATSON, HARRY X. WU,
AND CHRISTOPHER FINDLAY

In a large country with a diversity of local endowments, regional disparities in the course of rural growth and development are inevitable. Before 1978, the regional pattern of rural development in China was largely determined by the direction of central planning and was subject to national priorities. The policy of self-reliance and the emphasis on the production of basic agricultural commodities for local consumption prevented regional specialization on the basis of comparative advantage. The structure of commune organization restricted mobility, and the diversion of labour and other resources to non-agricultural activities was constrained by the requirements of agricultural planning and the lack of access to markets for inputs and for products. Regional disparities were thus largely the result of local resource endowments and of the ability of local cadres to balance the interests of the administrative hierarchy and the needs of their village.

Economic decentralization after 1978 transformed this situation. As part of the process of transition to a market economy, local governments and rural producers both gained greater autonomy in resource allocation, investment, production, and trade enabling them to base their economic activities more directly on their own resource endowment and comparative advantage. The decentralization that has occurred, however, has involved two quite different forms of change. One is decentralization within the established administrative system, which does not change the nature of the economy but serves to highlight local economic interests. The fiscal contracting discussed later is the key example of this process. The second type involves granting autonomy to independent economic agents who are then free to relate to each other through the market. This change was embodied in the rural reforms of late 1978 and their subsequent evolution, and implies a basic shift in the nature of economic operation. These two types of decentralization have been the source of most of the key developments in the rural economy over the last two decades. The diversification of rural output, the growth of regional specialization and inter-regional trade, and the emergence of the rural enterprise sector have combined to generate a new dynamism.

As a result of this process, the forces influencing regional disparities and inequalities in rural China have passed through a number of phases, a process that has been well reviewed by Rozelle (1996). The initial surge of growth in the rural economy was associated with the liberalization of farm management, the rise in agricultural prices, and the introduction of free markets. It not only led to a rise in rural incomes but also appeared to offer the hope of reducing both urban–rural and inter-regional inequalities. After the mid-1980s, however, the rise in real incomes in the countryside slowed and some areas of China even experienced stagnation or decline. At the same time, the rapid growth of the rural enterprise sector became the main source of both increases in rural incomes and in regional disparities. Those areas which were able to develop large rural enterprise sectors not only avoided the worst effects of the rural slowdown but even managed to pull away from the others. The coastal development strategy also further intensified the locational, infrastructural, and market advantages enjoyed by the countryside along the coast. By the early 1990s, therefore, it was becoming clear that the goal of 'let some get rich first' was succeeding, but the hope that this would 'trickle down' to the less prosperous areas in central and western China began to seem more remote. Income disparities began to widen.

In response to this situation, the central authorities devoted more attention to the problems of regional poverty, inequality, and disparities, so in 1991 the thrust of central policy began to shift the emphasis from a regional to a sectoral bias, though the momentum for coastal development remained strong as indicated in the 'Outline of the 10-year program and the Eighth Five Year Plan' (*People's Daily*, 16 April 1991). Rozelle (1996: 64) also notes that between September 1993 and October 1994, four national workshops were convened to address rural problems. Eventually, the State Council's 'Outline for State Industrial Policy in the 1990s' of March 1994 confirmed the sectoral focus (*BBC, Summary of World Broadcasts*, 28 June 1994). By 1996, the regional variations had become the source of economic, social, and political tensions, with the result that regional development and efforts to balance the relationship between rich and poor areas became a major theme of the Ninth Five Year Plan adopted by the National People's Congress in March (*Xinhua News Agency*, 18 March 1996).

This chapter examines the implications of economic decentralization in China for rural economic development and regional disparities. It provides an analytical discussion of how rural producers are reacting to the new economic environment. It also assesses the implications of regional differentiation for the rural economy and for some of the key concerns of the central government, especially in terms of improving agricultural output and efficiency. Based on this analysis, it sheds light on the policy implications for China's future rural economic growth.

It first briefly reviews how the rural reforms contributed to development and the transformation of the rural economy, then explores the formation of local interests due to fiscal decentralization and the debate over the effects of the emergence of those interests. The impact of economic decentralization on the growth of rural enterprises and the consequences for regional disparities are then assessed. This focus is followed by a discussion of the role of 'marketization' and its potential to encourage further specialization in ways which will lead to greater efficiency in the rural sector and to changing relationships between regions. Finally, some of the implications of these trends for future rural economic growth and regional disparities are considered.

The Sources of Rural Development in the Reform Period

China's economic transition started with a series of reforms in the rural economy in the late 1970s, which began in the farm sector and were carried over into the rural non-farm sector (reviewed in Findlay et al., 1993). The subsequent evolution of change in the two sectors then played a central role in the process of rural development, regional differentiation, and overall economic decentralization. Three key initiatives were introduced: the reintroduction of household farming, the increase in prices for the agricultural products procured by the state, and the liberalization of markets for after-quota agricultural products. All these reforms were interrelated, and each served to reinforce the impact of the others. Together they had a strong decentralizing effect on the economy.

The reintroduction of household farming was a process which

went through several stages over the 1978–83 period (Watson, 1983) but, in essence, it liberalized planning controls over the use of land and labour. Households rapidly became conscious of the opportunity costs of different activities, and the effect was to pre- cipitate the surplus labour which had previously been hidden within the commune system, releasing it for other employment. At the same time, households became freer to plan production accord- ing to their resources, skills, and relative returns. The price in- creases for agricultural products purchased by the government from the countryside represented a large injection of funds into the rural economy, thus stimulating a strong production response, which further increased the flow of funds. It also meant that more capital, in the hands of both collectives and households, became available for reinvestment in the local economy. The liberalization of the market system then became the catalyst which brought the surplus labour and new sources of capital together. After fulfilling their sales quotas farmers were free to use their labour and funds to specialize in production for the market and to develop activities which were subject to local resource endowment and could maxi- mize their returns.

As a result of these developments, there was a sharp rise in rural incomes, which was associated with a decline in urban–rural inequalities while regional disparities seemed to remain stable. Some observers began to argue that the regional inequalities may even have declined (Selden, 1988). Following on from the changes in the farm sector, however, in March 1984 the Central Committee and the State Council approved the 'Report on Creating a New Situation in Commune and Brigade-Run Enterprises' which sig- nalled a new phase of development for rural enterprises (*Zhong- guo Nongye Nianjian* Editorial Group, 1986). This Report envisaged that the former collective enterprises, now run by town- ships and villages, together with the co-operative and private undertakings that had grown up since 1978, would become the focus of a new phase of integrated rural development, providing inputs for agriculture, absorbing rural labour, helping to raise rural incomes, and producing for the market. It stressed that the rural enterprises were responsible for their own profits and losses but that their development should be supported and encouraged by government at all levels. In effect, this was an acceptance that rural development could not be based primarily on the growth of agri- cultural production as under the old Maoist approach. Instead, the diversification of production, the shift of labour to non-agricultural activities, greater mobility for the rural population, and the relative decline of agriculture in the rural economy became the hallmarks of the new strategy. By 1984, therefore, the key changes which generated the momentum for the following profound transformation of the rural economy were in place. This strategic change also meant that regional disparities would become increasingly related to the potential for different areas to diversify their rural economy.

Fiscal Decentralization

Alongside these basic changes affecting the supply of labour and capital, changes in administrative systems, in particular the introduction of fiscal contracting (*caizheng baogan*), created a strong sense of local economic identity (Findlay et al., 1991; Oksenberg and Tong, 1991; Wong, 1992). This crystallization of local economic interests made the development of local and rural enterprises a priority for all levels of government. Although the new fiscal arrangements were similar to experiments in the pre-reform period (Deng et al., 1990), they gave local governments much greater levels of autonomy. More importantly, they were implemented in an institutional environment in which planning was being replaced by markets.

The new arrangements determined the financial relationship between different levels of government. Experiments began at the provincial level in 1977, at the county level in 1980, and during the early 1980s spread to all provinces and counties. Under this system, each level of government made an agreement with the next level up to meet certain income and expenditure targets. Any additional revenue was to be shared with its next superior level according to an agreed ratio set out in the contract, although in some cases all such income might be fully retained at the local level. Local governments were then free to use this revenue for their own purposes.

The major aim of the change was to provide the incentives to increase revenue and to improve financial efficiency. The crucial difference with the pre-reform situation was that local governments now found themselves in a much freer environment, with the ability to develop local enterprises—their own or those owned by the rural community—as a source of revenue and local employment. This flexibility promoted the decentralization of the economy as a whole and created the conditions for China to 'grow out of the plan'. Indeed, Naughton (1995) argues that the rapid growth of the non-plan sector has been a major factor in transforming the Chinese economy.

County-level government is part of the overall budget system. It is also the owner of local industrial enterprises. In many ways, its industrial network is like a miniature state system, therefore to some extent its industries can be expected to share some of the inefficiencies and problems of state-run enterprises, being subject to administrative control and lacking the integrity and financial discipline of independent economic agents. Nevertheless, since they are locally owned and cannot rely on funds from upper levels, they are under strong pressures to improve efficiency and to generate profits for local government. In effect, they face relatively hard budget constraints. At the same time, they provide a focus of economic activity which can, through subcontracting and the economies of agglomeration, stimulate enterprises run at lower levels by rural communities. Encouraging the growth of rural enterprises provides county-level governments with the opportunity to exploit vertical and horizontal linkages, to promote local comparative advantage, and to increase revenue in the form of taxes and other levies. This complex set of relationships was observed in a survey of Ling County in Shandong Province carried out in 1987 and 1988, in which close linkages between county, township, and village authorities were found in the development of cotton production and processing, fruit and vegetable marketing, and the development of animal husbandry and dairy production.

Unlike counties, township and village governments have no established budgets. They obtain funds from county government for some of their activities, but they are primarily dependent on the income they receive from the local community. As a result, they have a primary interest in developing and protecting their collective and private rural enterprises, both of which are a source of revenue. Furthermore, the distinction between collective and private sectors is often difficult to make (Young and Yang, 1994): both have a close relationship with township and village officials and both are subject to market forces.

In sum, fiscal decentralization has had major implications for government behaviour at county level and below. It has meant that local economic interests have become very clearly defined and that local governments have the independence to achieve their economic goals. There is thus a strong incentive to promote local enterprise development as the major source of income for governments at the basic level. These factors have formed the basis for the explosive growth of the non-farm sector across the Chinese countryside. They also led to the promotion of regional specialization and to the patterns of regional variation in both farm and non-farm activities that have emerged.

Economic Decentralization and Regional Disparities

In a partially reformed economy in which local authorities still have the powers to intervene in economic activity, however, these developments have had mixed effects. Some aspects of the local economy tend to reflect the operation of market forces, while others reflect the interests of the local authorities. The result is intervention in market operations and economic decisions to protect local interests. This not only tends to create local inefficiencies and distortions but also affects regional differentiation. Driven by these pressures, therefore, fast growing local economies have been characterized by competition and conflicts and by local protectionism in ways that were never seen under the central planning system. The strongest expression of this conflict was found in the various 'commodity wars' of the late 1980s. In an effort to promote local development, regional governments stepped into the markets to control the flow of raw materials and products across administrative boundaries. The aim was to ensure local market supplies and stability and to protect local enterprise growth, a case in point being the 'wool war' described by Watson et al. (1989). While by the mid-1990s the more extreme aspects of this behaviour had been curbed by both central government action and the intensification of market interaction, regional intervention remains common. In 1995, for example, reacting to national decisions to stop maize exports and to increase the transfer of maize from north-east China to the rest of the country, authorities in Shanxi Province sealed off the local maize markets and stopped it flowing out of the province. The decision backfired since local supply exceeded demand and prices tended to drop (Anon., 1996b: 1).

In the face of this competitive regionalism, Chinese observers have basically adopted two different perspectives. One view argues that regionalism has strong negative effects which distort growth and inhibit macro-economic control; the other sees regionalism as a mechanism which promotes reform. Among those who are concerned with the negative effects of independent local interests on national economic development, regionalism is described as 'economic warlordism' (*zhu hou jingji*)—a view held, for example, by Shen and Dai (1990). They have three main criticisms of regionalism.

First, decentralization tends to enhance 'investment hunger' and contributes to overheating: to increase their revenue, local governments pursue a fast rate of growth, which requires increasing investment in profitable manufacturing activities. As a result, these grow faster than raw material industries, agriculture, and infrastructure. Shortage of raw materials and the investment induced in the bottle-neck sectors tend to push inflation further upwards. Furthermore, when the central government attempts to cool the economy, local governments always try to weaken the central austerity programme and to protect their area from its effects.

Second, decentralization tends to lead to structural similarity and market segmentation across regions, which increase the costs of development. To expand and protect local revenue sources, each region develops those industries that are profitable in the current market, leading to duplication. Each region also tries to make its own industrial structure as complete as possible in order to reduce the degree of reliance on outside regions. Administrative measures may be used to create barriers to inter-regional trade by stopping the outflow of local resources and the inflow of products from outside.

Third, decentralization also tends to reinforce the relationships between the different levels of government and economic enterprises, which therefore runs counter to the underlying reform goal of the separation of administrative and economic powers. Local governments intervene in enterprise development to protect their revenue base, while enterprises are encouraged to rely on local government support.

In contrast to this position, the opposing view affirms the positive effects of economic decentralization (Wu, 1990), claiming that decentralization has promoted the reform of the old planning system and encouraged the economic transition towards a market system.

First, it argues that economic decentralization has lowered the costs of decision making. Given China's size and the great differences across regions, centralized decision making was bound to have a high cost. On the one hand the higher authorities were remote from the locality and lacked knowledge of local conditions for economic development, so that they could not make sensible and timely decisions. On the other, since local governments played no role in the decision-making process, they had less incentive to implement central decisions. Decentralization to the local government or to the enterprises themselves removes this source of inefficiency.

Second, economic decentralization has encouraged competition between regions and hence has contributed to marketization and the opening up of the economy. This position contradicts the view that decentralization has largely created market segmentation. Although local governments have dual standards, both protecting local markets and competing for outside markets, the nature of the decentralization will ultimately favour the latter outcome. Local markets cannot be completely closed off, and differences in regional resource endowment and existing industrial structures mean that local development cannot be successfully achieved in the absence of trade with other markets, both domestically and internationally.

Third, while regionalism has caused some problems, such as short-sighted local investment and local resistance to macro-economic control, these have arisen largely because the market system was far from perfect and the new fiscal arrangements were poorly designed. The distorted price structure, with low raw material prices, was also partly responsible for the chaotic 'wars' for raw materials. As market structures improve, these problems can be expected to decline gradually.

Both sides in the debate have, to some extent, exaggerated their arguments. 'Regionalism' is the rational outcome of a form of economic decentralization that creates clearly defined, independent local government interests. It becomes 'warlordism' when development of a legal system to control the behaviour of local authorities is lacking and there are no effective instruments for macro-economic control. China's experience since the mid-1980s illustrates many of the negative effects of this form of regionalism, but in many ways these problems can be seen as part of the price it has to pay for its gradual approach to economic reform, while avoiding the dislocation that can be created by the 'big bang'. It is also reasonable to argue that, as market structures improve and their legal and technical environment is strengthened, the gains from regional specialization and market interdependence will tend to offset local protectionism.

The following two sections illustrate these themes and their implications for regional variations in rural development by examining first the role of rural enterprise growth and, second, the potential for integrated agricultural product markets.

Township and Village Enterprises and Regional Differentiation

As indicated already, the emergence of the township and village enterprises (TVEs) has been one of the key features of the change in China's rural development strategy since 1978, and such enterprises have promoted the structural changes occurring in the rural economy (Findlay et al., 1994). The growth of TVEs during the 1990s has been particularly rapid. Between 1990 and 1994, they increased their contribution to total national output value from just over 25 per cent to 30 per cent, and to total rural output value from 58 per cent to around 70 per cent, while the value of their export deliveries in 1994 was over 30 per cent of all of China's exports. Over the same period, their industrial output value rose from 30 per cent of the national total to some 42 per cent. What is more, over 49 per cent of the growth in peasant net income came from the TVEs. Such dramatic increases have not, however, taken place evenly in all provinces. Variations in TVE growth have thus been a major component of regional disparities in rural development during the reform period.

Given their nature as enterprises owned and operated by local communities, a priori it can be expected that there will be major differences between regions in the growth, characteristics, and structure of TVEs, depending on local endowments and existing levels of development. In the more advanced areas, with better infrastructure, more capital, better educational systems, and proximity to major cities and foreign trade, the growth of rural enterprises is likely to be strong and rapid. By contrast, less developed areas with poor infrastructure, marginal agriculture and hence less capital, and more distant from markets and foreign trade are likely to grow much more slowly. The speed and extent of structural change in the local economy are thus likely to vary widely.

This expectation is borne out when comparisons are made of the regional differences in rural enterprise growth (as in Watson and Wu, 1994) using the Coastal, Central, and Western Regions (defined in Figure 1.1) commonly used by Chinese planners and social scientists. In 1989, for example, the distribution of total rural enterprise output value was: Coastal Region 66 per cent, Central Region 25 per cent, and Western Region 9 per cent (Wang, 1991); by 1994, these proportions had changed to 69.4, 23.1, and 7.5, respectively, indicating an even greater concentration in the Coastal Region (Ministry of Agriculture, 1995: 436). In 1994, the latter accounted for 91.3 per cent of the gross value of production of TVE exports, the Central for 6.7 per cent, and the Western for only 1.6 per cent (Ministry of Agriculture, 1995: 507). When compared with the 1988 figures of 83, 15, and 2 per cent, respectively (Ke, 1990), this also indicated a further concentration in the Coastal Region. Such distributions illustrate considerable imbalance in development, with rural enterprises increasing in concentration and significance as one moves eastwards across the country. As a result, TVEs in the Coastal group of provinces generally have well above the national average shares of industrial enterprises, employment, output value, capitalization, fixed assets, and output per enterprise. They also have higher levels of productivity.

Nevertheless, it is important to underline that the broad regional aggregates disguise internal inconsistencies: the profile of Guangxi Zhuang AR, for example, is much closer to that of the Central Region provinces than those of the Coastal Region. Furthermore, there are also marked variations within provinces. TVEs in southern Jiangsu Province are much more highly developed than those in the north.

Analysis of the variations in the attributes of TVEs in different regions indicates that three issues are important: sectoral structure, ownership type, and enterprise behaviour. Sectoral structure refers to the regional variations in the types of activities undertaken by rural enterprises: less developed areas have poorer infrastructure, are capital and skill short, and are also more distant from major markets. They will therefore tend to have less-mechanized industrial enterprises. In contrast, the more developed regions, with a firmer overall economic foundation, have better industrial and service sectors. Ownership type refers to differences in the levels of community (township and village) and private (individual or co-operative) ownership. Given its potential impact on levels of capitalization, differences of ownership will be reflected in the scale of operation and technical levels. Finally, enterprise behaviour will be influenced by the relationship between local government and enterprise managers, especially in respect of such attributes as the distribution of profits, levels of reinvestment and employment, and plans for development.

In terms of sectoral structure, industry is much more dominant in the Coastal group. In 1988 the level of TVE industrial output value as a percentage of the national total in the Coastal, Central, and Western Regions was 74.1, 18.9, and 7.0 respectively (Watson and Wu, 1994: 82); these remained relatively unchanged in 1994, at 74.8, 19.1, and 6.2 (Ministry of Agriculture, 1995: 438). This dominance of the Coastal Region in industrial output was also reflected in each Region's ratio of TVE industrial output value to total TVE output value. This was 81.8 per cent in the Coastal Region (up from 77.3 in 1988), 62.7 in the Central (55.4), and 62.3 in the Western (52.3). The proportion of industrial output value thus clearly plays a key role in regional disparities. Nevertheless, the figures indicate that TVEs as a whole are becoming more concentrated in industry and that the rate of change in the Central and Western Regions is accelerating.

The data in Table 8.1 for ownership of TVEs in 1988 and 1994 also indicate that changes are occurring among the Regions. In the Coastal Region, the proportion of TVEs (collective or local government-owned) remained higher than the national average but declined slightly. Meanwhile the private and co-operative sectors were smaller than the national average, but the private sector was growing. In the Central Region, the private sector was the largest of all and the township and village sectors remained fairly stable. In the Western Region, however, the township sector had grown remarkably to become the largest and well above the national average, while the private sector share had declined sharply to be below it.

The initially high level of collective enterprises in the Coastal Region reflects the higher level of development achieved there under the commune system, which was the inevitable result of their locational advantages in an era when local self-sufficiency was stressed. More collective capital was thus available for rural enterprise development. The difference also underlines that in many more-developed areas collective organizations have retained greater strength, as is indicated by some of the development

Table 8.1: Ownership structure of Township and Village Enterprises, 1988 and 1994 (percentage of gross output value)

	National	Coastal	Central	Western
Townships				
1988	37.5	41.4	27.9	34.7
1994	35.3	37.0	27.6	43.3
Villages				
1988	29.6	33.7	22.9	17.7
1994	32.5	35.0	26.2	13.5
Co-operative				
1988	8.8	7.9	11.2	8.9
1994	5.7	5.1	8.1	3.9
Private				
1988	24.2	17.0	38.7	38.7
1994	26.5	22.9	38.2	24.0

Source: State Statistical Bureau, 1989, 1995a.

models discussed below. Despite this initial emphasis on the collective sector, however, the rapid growth of the coastal economy has meant that more wealth has accumulated in the hands of individuals and this may explain the later increase in the size of the private sector.

In the Central Region, the township and village sectors have remained below the national average, again reflecting the legacy of the commune period. Since the collectives were less developed in this zone, the accumulated capital available for TVE growth was less. At the same time, the general levels of infrastructure and economic development were also less conducive to rapid development, with a higher proportion of TVE development dependent on private individuals, also implying that their level of capitalization and scale would be smaller. As a result, their growth lagged behind the Coastal Region.

The Western Region has the smallest and least developed TVE sector. The problems of lack of capital, poor infrastructure, and distance from markets have been major constraints. Nevertheless, it is interesting to note the marked increase in the importance of the collective sector over this period. In part this underlines the low levels of capital available to individuals to develop private enterprises. It also reflects the fact that official policy to promote growth in poor areas tends to channel funds through the administrative system into development initiatives by townships and villages.

Overall, therefore, the relative proportions of enterprises under different types of ownership are indicative of the constraints facing development in the different regions. The sources of these regional differences in TVE development can be found in several key factors: the level of development of local infrastructure, capital availability, the level of labour skills, access to cities and urban industry, as well as access to foreign trade and domestic markets. (A regression analysis of these issues is available in Watson and Wu, 1994.)

As may be expected, differences in enterprise ownership structure also affect enterprise behaviour and the relationship between TVEs and the local government. Jiang (1992) argues that several factors influence enterprise behaviour in poor areas. Their economic environment is, by definition, more unsettled and risky: poor natural conditions; lower levels of commercialization; fluctuating local government behaviour; and less economic security all act as constraints. Enterprises in these less developed areas are thus less able to compete with either state enterprises or rural enterprises elsewhere.

A second issue is the subordinate relationship all TVEs have to their local governments. On the one hand, this may provide protection and support; on the other, it also means that they are subject to pressures to meet local government goals, which may not be purely economic. These pressures can be expected to be more intense in poor areas than in rich ones, where local government has a greater range of sources of income. Issues of this kind thus raise questions about the trade-off between enterprises solely meeting economic efficiency criteria and enterprises filling other social functions, including employment provision, local revenue creation, and welfare support. These sorts of pressures may also lead to local officials using their powers to protect local enterprises from outside competition and to duplication of investment as each local community tries to develop a full range of activities.

The differential growth of rural enterprises has had a number of consequences for inter-regional relationships. One outcome is the transfer of labour from the poorer western areas to the east where rapid development has placed pressures on labour supply for both agriculture and rural enterprises. A second outcome is that the less developed Western and Central Regions are now in a position to compete on price and labour costs with the developed Coastal Region, much in the way that China's labour-intensive industries compete with industries in outside countries. Nevertheless, the lack of efficient capital markets, the poor infrastructure, and the absence of effective market institutions still present many difficulties for the more backward areas

A further important outcome of the variations in regional enterprise growth has been that they are an important source of the disparities in rural output and income. Rozelle's (1996) work has shown convincingly that it is the growth of TVEs which has been the major contributor to rural inequality among China's provinces over the years 1983 to 1992, and their impact has tended to cause it to rise over time. These findings underline their significance for the disparities in the general processes of rural economic growth across China. Ultimately, this situation emphasizes the need for more integrated labour, raw material, and product and capital markets which can help balance the relationship between the different regions and enable them to compete on a more equal basis. Some of the models for local development that have been derived from the growth of TVEs during the 1980s can now be briefly summarized.

Models of Local Development

The emergence of the rural enterprise sector generated considerable speculation within China over the nature of the development processes involved. By the late 1980s a large number of 'models' reflecting differences in the pattern of rural growth in various areas had been identified. During 1986 and 1987 many articles appeared in China's newspapers and journals describing the nature and merits of various models (Yang et al., 1986; Anon., 1986; Feng, 1987; Lin, 1987), and useful discussions of the key examples and their characteristics can be found in Rural Development Research Institute (1987) and Chen (1988). These models were defined with reference to several key characteristics: (i) the dominant forms of enterprise ownership; (ii) the role of local government; (iii) the sectoral distribution of rural enterprises; (iv) the relationship between rural enterprises, the local agricultural economy and the local state-owned economy; (v) the extent of foreign involvement; and (vi) the level of export orientation. The differences in the achievements of these various models led to consideration of their relative merits and of the implications for China of greater regional diversity in economic structure and operation. The long-established custom of using models as mechanisms for promoting policy initiatives also meant that this discussion could be seen as reflecting a competition to form the basis for national policy decisions. Some of the most significant examples are briefly described.

The Wenzhou model (southern Zhejiang Province). This was based on a flourishing private economy operating through free markets. It was seen to reflect the spontaneous operation of market forces and the system of private ownership. Capital accumulated in the hands of individuals or groups of families, who invested in TVEs and employed workers as needed. Free markets for inputs and outputs enabled exchange to take place across administrative boundaries. The main focus was consumer goods and services, often produced by small-scale operations.

The Sunan model (southern Jiangsu Province). This approach relied on development by villages and townships in an area with highly developed agriculture. Because of its relatively successful development before the reforms, the collectives in this area had the resources to invest in and develop large new rural enterprises. There was a strong focus on industrial manufacturing and the processing of agricultural products, and close links with urban industry were fostered. Income distribution was managed through the collective using the new incentive schemes encouraged by the reforms. In addition, some of the wealth generated by the TVEs was diverted to investment in agriculture and support for farming families. Although mainly under collective ownership, the TVEs still operated in a free-market environment.

The Daqiuzhuang model (Tianjin Muncipality). This was characterized by a strong collective economy in a suburban setting, with cross-subsidies to agriculture and links to urban state industry. Enjoying the advantages of close proximity to a large urban market and industrial infrastructure, this model involved a rejection of the individual private economy and focused on collective operation of non-agricultural activities. Agriculture rapidly ceased to be a significant source of community income, and most labour was redirected to industrial activity. Daqiuzhuang therefore reflected the complete transformation of the local economic structure under collective management.

The Gengche model (northern Jiangsu Province). This combined both private and collective ownership in an area with a poor agricultural foundation. The link between collective and private activity was seen as a mechanism for encouraging growth in difficult circumstances. Investment focused on labour-intensive processing of raw materials. At the same time, labour was able to flow freely between industry and agriculture according to the season. In general, however, the local economy remained quite distinct and separate from urban industry.

The Pingding model (central Shanxi Province). This was based on exploitation of local raw materials through collective action. Located in an area with good coal and mineral resources and convenient transport routes, extraction and processing industries developed rapidly, with agriculture quickly becoming a minor activity. Although private household enterprises also developed, the collective TVEs remained dominant since the industries involved the exploitation of collectively owned local resources.

The Jinjiang model (Fujian Province). This involved a large volume of foreign investment coming from Overseas Chinese who had originated in this area, a point emphasized in Chapter 4. Given the foreign involvement, enterprises in the Jinjiang area were mainly established as shareholding operations, enabling joint investment by foreign and domestic capital and the introduction of foreign technology. It also meant that products were sold to both the domestic and international market. In addition, there was a pattern of specialization and contracting between enterprises.

The Zhujiang Delta model (Guangdong Province). This was also based on extensive involvement in foreign trade and foreign investment. With a good location and access to the Hong Kong market and capital, this area rapidly became one of the key growth centres of the reforms. Its development focused entirely on export-orientated manufacturing and the various support services required, importing foreign technology aimed at improving the quality of output to become internationally competitive. It involved a major role for collective management and investment at township and village level, but it also encouraged all forms of ownership and operation.

In general, the definition of each tended to reflect its specific development, as much as any fundamental principles which could be generalized. Nevertheless, the clarification of the various developmental patterns also served to underline how the decentralization generated by the reforms had enabled regional growth to follow different paths. It also reflected the underlying political debate over the economic impact of different forms of ownership— the private-ownership Wenzhou model could be seen as competing with the collective-ownership Sunan model. It was also argued that the regional variations in development should not be taken to represent competing models, but that they merely reflected the pre-reform patterns of development and the variations in local endowments (Lin, 1987: 61). Ultimately, therefore, this discussion of models did not lead to any attempt to impose unifying policies across regions, but it did provide considerable insights into the growing diversity in the patterns of regional development in various parts of China.

Marketization and Regional Development

Theory predicts that regional specialization will lead to greater efficiencies as comparative advantage is exploited. Given the increasing diversity of regional production structures, levels of development, and organizational models described above, the potential exists for market competition to encourage more efficient development in the various regions, even though regional disparities could remain large. (The preceding discussion was based on the three broad planning zones used in China and shown in Figure 1.1: an analysis at provincial level would reveal even greater diversity.) It is likely that the differences in endowments, in existing levels of development and infrastructure, and in the impact of previous regional biases in economic policies will mean that government action and transfers through the fiscal system will be needed to help overcome regional disadvantages. Nevertheless, increasing commercialization of the rural economy, more competition, and the removal of economic barriers between regions through the development of integrated capital, labour, and commodity markets also offer a path to greater local efficiencies. Analysis of grain markets, still largely subject to government intervention, and of fruit and vegetable markets, broadly liberalized since 1984, suggests that such an outcome can be expected.

Grain market reform, as Watson and Findlay (1995) have elaborated elsewhere, has been among the slowest of the market reforms in the Chinese countryside. Given the central government's long-standing concern with grain self-sufficiency and a stable supply of food for urban areas at low prices, it has been reluctant to liberalize grain markets at a time when the returns to agriculture are low and the shift of rural resources to non-agricultural activities has been substantial. The initial attempt at market reform in 1985, with the abandonment of the unified purchase and sales system, was followed by a drop in grain production and by a relative stagnation in output, a situation detailed by Oi (1986) and Sicular (1988). The government responded by making the new contractual system more coercive and by increasing the flow of subsidies to producers through the provision of cheap inputs and other incentives. When these subsidies were added to those to consumers, caused by the difference between the purchase and handling costs of state grain and the low selling price, the pressures on government budgets became substantial. Though grain output recovered during the 1990s, the fiscal pressures on the government for further market reform were strong.

The second major phase of grain market reform came between 1991 and 1993. Consumer prices were increased and the markets were deregulated in most parts of the country (Watson and Findlay, 1995). Once again, however, the government faced difficulties. A decline in rice output and the absence of a well-structured free marketing system led to rapid price rises and a market panic. Fears were expressed that grain production could fall, and the government once more intervened to subsidize producers and to enforce production levels through a 'governor responsibility system', whereby provincial governors agreed to maintain their sown acreage in order to minimize reliance on interprovincial transfers. Then, in turn, they began to exert administrative pressures on local governments to sustain grain output. While it was not a complete return to the previous system, these policies represented a retreat from the hopes of full marketization raised during the 1991 to 1993 reforms.

Hidden within this reform process is a significant issue of economic transfers among different groups and different regions. Farmers were made to produce a low-value crop for sale at low state prices using resources which might have been better employed in other activities, with consumers enjoying cheap food subsidized by the state. Meanwhile, depending on the size of state purchases for each province or county, the volume of grain transferred in or out, and the extent to which an area was in surplus or deficit, there were differences in the subsidies to be provided from central and local budgets (Chu, 1989: 1; Lardy, 1990). Surplus regions supplying grain to other areas at base prices were forgoing profits that might be made by selling the grain at higher free market prices. In contrast, deficit regions were subsidized through transfers at base prices and were anxious to minimize additional purchases at higher prices, since the extra costs had to be met from the local budget without central government support. Ironically, therefore, the relatively poorer areas specializing in agricultural production found themselves disadvantaged compared to the richer areas with higher levels of manufacturing but low levels of grain production.

In such a situation, the development of a more efficient free market system, whilst it could lead to higher consumer prices, should generate a more equal level of exchange between regions in ways which provide higher returns to grain-producing areas and might stimulate a positive producer response.

In contrast to the situation in grain production, an analysis of the reform of vegetable marketing in China demonstrates that regional interdependence through markets can bring gains to all sides, even if it involves complex issues of political economy (Watson, 1992, 1996). The expansion of free markets in many agricultural commodities began as soon as the rural reforms were initiated in late 1978 (Watson, 1988). Peasants shifted surplus output of state-controlled goods and other household products to the free markets which rapidly spread across the countryside and into the cities. Initially formed as traditional fairs where producers sold their own products, economies of scale and the requirements of aggregation and disaggregation soon led to the emergence of intermediate traders and independent retailers. During the 1980s this process accelerated and, after liberalization of state controls over the marketing of such items as meat, fruits, vegetables, and aquatic products in 1984, the range and volume of goods traded through free markets steadily increased. Between 1978 and 1995, the number of free markets grew from 33,302 to 82,892 and the trans-action value rose from Y12,590 million to Y1,159,000 million in current year prices, at growth rates well above both the rate of economic growth and the rate of inflation (State Statistical Bureau, 1996b: 104).

While this growth in free market trade was taking place, structural changes were also occurring in the nature of food consumption, especially in urban areas. Consumers were shifting away from direct consumption of grains and bulk vegetables towards better quality foods and greater variety—a change prompted by the steady rise in incomes. As a result, urban residents were no longer satisfied with a supply of local staple fruits and vegetables but wanted finer vegetables and out-of-season products. This shift in demand began to conflict with the planned system's emphasis on local self-sufficiency, especially in the northern cities. Beijing residents were no longer willing, for example, to spend the winter primarily consuming large amounts of cabbage produced through subsidies. At the same time the expansion of economic opportunities for suburban peasants and the rise in the value of their land as cities expanded meant that it became uneconomic for them to specialize in vegetables for urban consumption.

By the late 1980s these trends were stimulating the emergence of a more national network of fruit and vegetable marketing. Large cities tended to become less self-reliant, and the free markets became more complex as a nationally integrated network of fruit and vegetable marketing developed (Watson, 1992, 1996). The benefits of this process to both producers and consumers soon became apparent. Urban residents found they could choose from an expanding range of better quality foods; suburban producers moved towards alternative forms of production with higher returns; and more-distant producers were able to shift from lower value crops to higher value products for the urban market. This change was also assisted by the development of more sophisticated marketing systems so that, for example, banana traders in Beijing maintained links with producers in southern China and were able to regulate the flow of supplies into the market to match demand.

This case study provides a textbook example of the way in which markets can evolve to promote regional specialization along the lines of comparative advantage, with benefits for consumers, local producers, and more-distant regions. Developments of this kind not only stimulate growth but also create forms of regional interdependence which act to overcome the economic localism that the pressures within a partially reformed economy have generated. Further market reforms in capital, labour, and commodity markets can potentially also deliver similar benefits for inter-regional relationships. The real problem, however, is the costs of the transition as prices and production structures between regions are adjusted, and it is here that government action will be important to ameliorate inter-regional tensions and disparities.

The Future for Rural Economic Growth

Economic decentralization has been both a source of dynamic growth in China's rural economy and a source of increasing regional disparities. One of the important signs of the changes taking place has been in the growth of the non-state sector and in the regional variations in ownership structure. In addition the extent of openness to trade has also played an important role in increasing the differentiation between the regions, especially between the coast and the other areas.

Generally, coastal provinces lack natural resources, not only because of low natural endowment but also because of a high population to resource ratio. However, they do enjoy some topographical advantages. Their coastal location allows easier access to foreign trade and the relatively flat terrain allows development of transport infrastructure at low cost. By contrast, the western provinces have, on the one hand, the nation's richest natural resource endowment and the least population and, on the other, the most unfavourable location and the most difficult topography. The central provinces, having fewer topographical advantages than the Coastal Region but sharing some of the resource advantages of the Western, represent a transitional level of development compared to the other two. Furthermore, earlier development in the Central and Western Region provinces tended to rely heavily on large-scale state industry established with capital transfers from other areas.

A shift towards market regulation thus represented a major challenge to the interior economies as a whole. These features have determined that, compared with provinces in other regions, the rural economy in the coastal provinces developed earlier during the reforms and was orientated towards diversification of output, light-manufacturing, and exports. The inland provinces have lower levels of development, a weaker infrastructure and a large state-owned sector which has experienced relative decline. As a result, their rural economies have also faced greater difficulties. In this situation, it can be expected that each individual region's development pattern will depend more on local resource endowment and hence on local comparative advantage.

The impact of this regional development on the national rural economy has also been significant. Growth in the Coastal Region has been the largest contributor to total rural growth, and its contribution has been increasing. The development of large TVE sectors, with labour-intensive manufacturing industries and exports, have magnified the variations in regional growth patterns and the disparities in regional development. As a result the coastal provinces are the ones that have benefited most from China's economic decentralization.

Decentralization in China can be seen in terms of two inter-related processes. One is a process of fiscal decentralization within the established administrative system. While this has had very important implications for the functioning of the economy, it does not, of itself, imply a complete transformation of the economic system. Its main impact has been to clarify and highlight the identity of economic interests at the local level. The gains in economic efficiency from this change should not be ignored. Nevertheless, because such decentralization maintains the role of local administrators in economic decision making, it also maintains distortions and inefficiencies associated with the centrally planned system at the local level. The second is one of decentralization of decision-making power to independent economic agents and enterprises, and is characterized by a shift away from planning towards market-based resource allocation. This second form of decentralization is, inevitably, more profound in its implications for the functioning of the economy. This analysis has shown that both dimensions of change have been at work in China since 1978. They have in many ways reinforced each other and promoted both economic growth and economic restructuring in the rural economy. At the same time they have also generated conflicts between pressures for local protectionism and pressures for greater inter-regional interaction.

Overall, therefore, decentralization has had both positive and negative effects on the rural economy. It has encouraged diversification and specialization along the lines of comparative advantage.

It has also encouraged interdependence between regions through market relationships in ways which benefit both sides. At the same time it has led local governments to protect their local economy and to build barriers to the inter-regional flow of resources and commodities. In addition, the coastal bias of government policy and the nature of regional variations in the levels of pre-reform rural development have tended to reinforce the disparities in rates of development and income levels that the emergence of the TVE sector has generated.

To some extent, the current patterns of rural development suggest that overcoming these disparities will be difficult. The different models of regional development listed above underline that the basic parameters of local economies vary widely, as do the institutional structures. The models are not easily transferable, and they reflect local endowments and accumulated advantages. What is more, once the development process accelerates, economies of agglomeration tend to reinforce the importance of the capital accumulated in the more developed localities. The absence of an integrated capital market also tends to prevent capital flowing to less developed areas.

Given the pragmatic and gradual nature of the reforms to date, a process of compromise and incremental change can be expected to continue. Against a background of further market reforms in commodity and factor distribution, further changes to the state enterprise system, and continued strong growth in rural enterprises and the non-state sector, maintaining the decentralization of economic authority to individual economic agents remains the likely long-term outcome. In that situation, regional development will increasingly have to depend on regional comparative advantage, rather than on the ability of local levels of government to protect local interests. While improvements in market institutions should enable regions to compete more efficiently, however, the experience of growing regional disparities in the rural economies over the period since the mid-1980s suggests that government interventions through fiscal transfers and investment in infrastructure, welfare, and human capital will be important if the interior provinces are not to be disadvantaged.

9 Towards 2020: Crossing the River by Feeling the Stones

GODFREY LINGE

There are as many views about the possible future course of China's development as there are commentators on it: the one thing they have in common is uncertainty, in part brought about by the political manœuvring still taking place in the region after the demise of the Soviet Union, the stand-off between China and Taiwan, and the several territorial disputes over islands around its coastline. The assumption made for present purposes, however, is that the external environment will remain relatively harmonious, and that the mood prevailing in the mid-1990s of cautiously encouraging and welcoming China's further opening to the outside will continue.

Importantly, but seldom recognized in all the discussion, this country's renewed contact with the world coincided almost precisely with the development and rapid diffusion of new microelectronics-based computer and communications technologies that were rapidly reshaping the global organization of finance, of production, of competition, of supply, and of demand. It is difficult to quantify the quickening pace of change in any sensible way other than to note that after industrial take-off in 1780 it took Britain fifty-eight years to double its real income per head; after 1839 it took the United States forty-seven years; after 1885 it took Japan thirty-four years; after 1966 it took the Republic of Korea eleven years; and after 1985 it has taken China barely ten years. In other words, not only did China 'telescope' this initial stage of its progress from a mainly agrarian society to a more industrialized-urbanized one, but it did so at a time when all countries were trying to find appropriate responses to an uncertain, fast-changing, and pervasive environment. In effect, it was jumping on a bus already accelerating to a rather uncertain destination.

What happens to its external trade relationships will be crucial, of course, to its ability to manage the dossier of domestic problems that are mounting in complexity. If China's rate of GNP growth were to continue for the next decade or so at around 8 or 9 per cent—the rate the government is anticipating and, if most things go right, the majority of analysts are accepting—exports could grow to US$350,000 million by 2005 and US$840,000 million by 2015 (Perkins, 1996: 22). Were this to eventuate, and inflows of foreign direct investment and loans maintained, the significance of two major potential constraints would be eroded because China would be well able to import increasing amounts of crude oil, and also grain if the strategies in hand to boost food production only partially succeed. The questions which arise, of course, are whether the world economy will continue to grow strongly enough, and the trading system remain open enough, to absorb exports of this magnitude. These in turn depends on the composition and comparative advantage of the products on offer and whether trade surpluses build up if imports do not rise at the same rate, in the event, for example, that the import replacement strategies—advocated by some provinces to help absorb labour—are carried through.

The chapters in this book have demonstrated the breadth and depth of the challenges facing this country. Among them are the inadequacies of the transport system; the shortages of electricity and water; and a series of environmental problems. All sectors of the economy will have to get used to continuous restructuring in place of the periodic upheavals that have characterized the past half century. Agriculture, for instance, will be hard-pressed to meet not only the continuing growth in demand but also to keep abreast of changing consumption patterns as an increasingly urbanized population continues to shift its preference from rice and cereals to fish and meat (the ramifications of which become apparent when it is realized that one kilogram of beef requires seven kilograms of feed grain). Manufacturing has to keep its sights on moving up the industrial ladder and shifting its focus away from exporting labour-intensive goods, like basic textiles, clothing, and footwear, towards more sophisticated products, which in turn require access to technology and the honing of shopfloor skills and management prowess. Many parts of the tertiary sector are relatively undeveloped, none more so than banking, financial services, and information technology which will underpin the restructuring and modernization of the entire system. Overarching all these issues is the drag caused by the moribund state-owned enterprises (SOEs) and the associated problems of job creation and the provision of welfare nets.

Arguably, only a strong central government will be able to steer through all these problems in ways that maintain growth without overheating the economy; reduce the burden of the SOEs without exacerbating social tensions; and curb environmentally harmful practices without adding to unemployment. It is most unlikely in any event that the political structures at the centre will allow power to slip away, but many would agree that, if economic progress is to be maintained, the archaic political and bureaucratic arrangements will need to go through the same sort of modernization and efficiency tests being demanded of others. In particular, remnant legacies of the Soviet-style central planning arrangements are ill-adapted to the needs of a rapidly expanding, increasingly market-orientated and internationalizing economy. To paraphrase a comment made in Chapter 3, the danger is that central ministries will continue to make decisions about issues from their own sepa-rate perspectives and without considering the likely impacts, indi-vidually and collectively, on the structure and operation of the various modes of transport. The same can be said about the deci-sion-making process in other areas of the economy. Underlying some of these problems is the inadequacy and inconsistency of the legal system, the uncertainty as to who has the authority to make decisions, and the bureaucracy and formalism that characterize some organs of government.

Yet another balance to be worked out is that between the centre and the provinces and between these and the local governments within their jurisdiction. Here it is salutary to remember that 'local' in China usually means administrative entities that are consider-ably larger in area and population than many nation states: thus the inland city of Chongqing, enlarged and redesignated as a municipality (a status similar to that of a province) early in 1997, has twice as many people as Scandinavia. One theme taken up in Chapter 2 is the way the decentralization of fiscal power, intro-duced after 1979, reduced the central government's share of revenue thus greatly weakening its capacity to guide social and economic development, while at the same time accentuating the problem of 'dual subordination', where the responsibility of orga-nizational units was both to their line ministry superiors and also to the same level of the local government. In addition, the variety of non-unified preferential arrangements and the power of local governments to alter them have enabled provinces to determine their own economic strategies and policies, ignore the views of the centre, and 'make a detour when the red light is on'.

The relationship between the central administration and other levels of government has been vigorously debated since the 1970s and even before that. The issues have been well summarized by Ma Hongbo (1994):

On the one hand, we must continue to arouse the enthusiasm of localities for economic development and must maintain their economic vigour. On the other hand, while further transforming enterprise operational mechanisms and cultivating the market system in order to strengthen local economic capabilities, the central administration will increase the weight of macroeconomic regulation and control, with emphasis on finance, tax, monetary matters, investments, the planning system and so on, so as to prevent anarchy in economic operations, or an economy of feudal princes.

The problem is to reach agreement on their respective responsibilities and powers, but this seems to be yet another river that has to be crossed by feeling the stones. Some scholars both in and outside China see the end result being some form of federal system, perhaps made up of constitutional hybrids unfamiliar to Western political scientists.

Spatial Implications

The way that these issues are resolved will have a direct bearing on how the spatial economy of China is configured during the next two or three decades. The geographical dimension presents governments with two difficulties. First, it forces greater precision into what may previously have been stated as generalities, and reveals policy goals that seem achievable at the national level to be unrealistic when applied to particular areas. Second, the urban, transport, and other infrastructure already in place, and which can feasibly be augmented given the availability of time and money, acts as a 'shock absorber' modifying some of the extreme oscillations in policy (Linge and Forbes, 1990a: vii) while at the same time constraining flexibilities that might otherwise have been desirable.

Discussions about China's space economy seldom recognize that much of what is happening has parallels elsewhere in the world, even though the scale of the events and the political circumstances in which they are taking place are rather different. It is not drawing too long a bow to suggest that the problems of the North-East mirror those of other decaying smokestack regions, like the north-east of England; that the decline and revival of Shanghai has features in common with events in Birmingham, UK; and that the overnight rise of the South-East is not dissimilar to the way that export-orientated platforms have appeared on more or less 'green-field' sites elsewhere in South-East and East Asia. Or, again, it would not be hard to incorporate discussion of the prospering Coastal Region and the struggling Central and Western Regions into the huge 'core–periphery' literature (summarized, for instance, in Linge, 1988). Bodies of literature of this kind are, if anything, becoming more relevant. The few (mostly unpublished) studies of Western firms' behaviour in China suggest that they have tried to use much the same location selection criteria as in other parts of the world. Moreover, as growing numbers of indigenous enterprises are to be left to fend for themselves without subsidies, and are no longer shielded from the real costs of freight, energy, and other inputs, they, too, will be paying more attention to the friction of distance and other locational considerations in order to remain competitive. Their response will be lagged, not just because of geographical inertia, but because locational choice is not something with which they have had much familiarity.

Copy-cat Industrial Structure

The unreal world of subsidies and managed pricing, along with the stress laid on quantity rather than quality or utility, has resulted in an enormously wasteful industrial structure. Early in 1995 the Governor of Zhejiang Province noted that, during the sixteen years since reform began in 1979,

the province's economy has been characterized by a copy-cat industrial structure, low levels of technology and poor efficiency. All in all, these have been key factors hindering a sustained, rapid and healthy development of the province's economy. We shouldn't feel so great about ourselves. On the contrary, we should feel a strong sense of urgency . . . the province will make output value a less important economic indicator and put economic efficiency and quality at the top of its list of factors in judging a region's economic development (*Xinhua News Agency*, 17 January 1995).

This diagnosis was, and remains, equally true of the other provinces and autonomous regions.

The extent of this copy-cat phenomenon emerges clearly from the 1995 production data which record that television receivers were made in twenty-nine provinces, and refrigerators and washing machines were both built in twenty-three. Of the eighteen provinces hosting a total of 122 car-manufacturing enterprises, only nine recorded annual outputs of more than 5,000 vehicles; just sixteen of the twenty-nine provinces sharing 1,700 iron and steel enterprises claimed a steel output for the year of more than 2 million tons (*Zhongguo Xinwen She News Agency*, 6 August 1996). Such examples can easily be multiplied. Only 15 of the 200 motorcycle makers in China are equipped to make more than 100,000 units a year, and only 80 of the 700 breweries can produce more than 10 million gallons of beer annually (Korski, 1997). What emerges, then, is that there is a vast array of small, inefficient, locally owned firms that have been kept going by subsidies, preferential purchasing by local government, and by various forms of protectionism, including border taxes, 'quality' and 'environmental' inspections, and the banning of competing products from neighbouring regions.

As a result, the industrial structures across the provinces in each of the three major Regions are remarkably similar, a matter of concern to the State Planning Commission, which in August 1996, appealed to all local and provincial governments to avoid the development of similar industries. Yet, ironically, the emphasis now being laid on the need to promote 'backbone', or 'pillar', industries may exacerbate this problem because several of the provinces have listed much the same handful of pillars in their Five Year Plans to 2000, and in their longer-term plans to 2010. Twenty-four have nominated electronics (embracing telecommunications equipment, computers, and audio-visual products); twenty-two have included car manufacturing; and sixteen have said they would give priority to machinery and chemical industries. Moreover, the bidding continues for investment, especially from overseas, seemingly of any kind: Chongqing, for instance, implemented tax breaks early in 1997 exempting foreign-funded firms from paying any income tax for six years after becoming profitable, and at reduced rates thereafter.

The Coast Versus the Inland

The most enduring issue relating to the spatial organization of China has been the relative development of the areas along the eastern seaboard as against the rest of the country. This was the main theme running through Chapter 2, where it was noted that a small army of researchers had ploughed through the statistics endeavouring to ascertain whether the Central and Western Regions (shown in Figure 1.1) were making progress or falling behind the Coastal Region. There are all manner of statistical and conceptual problems involved in measuring 'progress', and some of the more sophisticated analytical techniques (such as the Human Development Index constructed by the United Nations Development Programme) cannot be used in this instance because the data are lacking.

Table 9.1 sets out information about the shares of gross industrial output (a crude measure, but one of the few for which a reasonably consistent time series can be compiled) in each of the regions used in this book (Figure 1.2). This suggests that, taken as a whole, the Central and Western Regions have maintained a fairly constant share of around one-fifth of the country's industrial production during the last three decades, a remarkable result in the light of the emphasis given to coastal development since 1979. However, the downturn shown for 1995 gives the hint that the balance is now swinging in favour of the Coastal Region, where the average annual increase in GNP was 16 per cent during the 1991–95 period compared to 9 per cent in the remainder of the country. In any event these production statistics give only part of the story because it is clear from per capita income, wealth, and other unpublished (and confidential) measures of 'well-being' that the standard of living of a substantial proportion of the inland population, though improving, still lags behind that of a substantial proportion of that living along the coast.

Such discrepancies have long been a bone of contention. At the Fourth Plenary Session of the Fourteenth CCP Central Committee in September 1994, voting on the proposal for Wu Bangguo and Jiang Chunyun to be admitted to the Central Committee

Table 9.1: Percentage of China's gross industrial output by region, 1952 to 1995[a]

Region	1952	1957	1965	1974	1979	1984	1991	1995
North-East[b]	22.1	22.7	22.6	19.2	16.5	15.6	12.2	9.4
Bohai Sea Rim[c]	17.8	17.4	17.7	23.0	19.3	18.2	19.7	17.9
Changjiang[d]	38.4	34.6	33.0	32.9	36.3	37.7	35.9	39.3
South-East[e]	6.3	6.7	6.8	6.3	6.1	6.8	11.5	13.6
Rest of China	15.4	18.6	19.9	18.6	21.8	21.7	20.7	19.8
Total China	100.0	100.0	100.0	100.0	100.0	100.0	100.0	100.0

[a] After 1984, village-run enterprises were transferred from agricultural to industrial output statistics.
[b] Liaoning, Jilin, and Heilongjiang Provinces.
[c] Beijing and Tianjin Municipalities; Hebei and Shandong Provinces.
[d] Shanghai Municipality; Jiangsu, Zhejiang, Anhui, Hubei, Hunan, and Jiangxi Provinces.
[e] Guangdong, Fujian, and Hainan Provinces.
Sources: Pannell, 1988: 22; State Statistical Bureau, 1992, 1996a.

Secretariat and for Huang Ju to be promoted to the Central Political Bureau was delayed by an argument that this would give even greater representation to the Coastal Region (and especially Shanghai) and thus further bias development away from the north-west, north-east, and south-west. Concern about the possibility of its undermining social stability is implicit in the priority given in the Ninth Five Year Plan to inland development, and the constant refrain by top-ranking leaders about the 'strategic importance' of rectifying this imbalance.

Within a few months of the Ninth Five Year Plan being approved in March 1996, some of the inland provinces began protesting that, despite all the talk, there had been little action to formulate a long-term development plan, something which they had been promised for several years and, more specifically at the Fifth Plenary Session of the CCP Central Committee in September 1995. It was said then that plans were being made for 'coordinated regional development in the next five to fifteen years'. These were to include five new major policy measures: the stepping up of resources development and infrastructure projects; guiding the transfer of resource-processing and labour-intensive industries to the central and western parts of the country; rationalizing the prices of resource products so as to enhance self-development; improving the invest-ment environment and directing more foreign funds there; and strengthening economic association and co-operation and encour-aging the eastern areas to invest more in inland projects.

Instead of the promised plan, senior officials continued to make soothing noises about what the government had in mind to assist these regions (Kwan, 1996a; *Zhongguo Xinwen She News Agency*, 17 July 1996). In June 1996 it was announced that most of the soft loans received by China from international financial agencies, and two-thirds of the State Development Bank loans, would be used there, and that earnings from minerals could be used to pay off some of the inland provinces' foreign debts. The State Council's agreement soon afterwards to enlarge Chongqing City (now, with 30 million inhabitants, the largest in China) and upgrade it to municipality status was viewed by some as a sop to deflect such criticism. For their part, the authorities saw it as a way of stabiliz-ing and developing this part of Sichuan Province—which is being greatly affected by the Three Gorges project (see Chapter 5)—as well as a much wider area including Qinghai and Gansu Provinces. In further moves, the State Council also permitted authorities in the Central and Western Regions to give approval for foreign-funded investments of up to US$30 million (triple the previous limit), and overseas investors in these Regions were given permis-sion to sell all their output in China instead of having to export part of it.

A report prepared by the State Planning Commission, entitled 'Focus of China's future economic development and the opening up of the central and western part', was released in October 1996 but added little depth to what had already been stated in the Ninth Five Year Plan (*Zhongguo Xinwen She News Agency*, 25 October 1996). In reality, the goal of accelerating development across large parts of the inland, which covers about 86 per cent of the national land area and accommodates about 59 per cent of the population, seems overly ambitious, at least in the short to medium-term. It will take time and considerable funds to upgrade the poor transport and communications facilities; to modernize the industrial enter-prises (about three-quarters of which are state owned); and to raise living standards and thus enlarge the consumer market and make it more sophisticated. Claims that there are abundant natural resources, a relatively unexploited domestic market, land and raw materials, and less intense competition are generalizations that have to be treated with caution because the physical and social conditions vary widely. Half the Western Region, for example, is sparsely settled desert, mountain, or plateau. The story is not entirely gloomy. In some places significant developments are in hand, like the very large petrochemical complex being built in conjunction with the 140,000-ton ethylene plant at Sushanzi, 270 km west of Ürümqi in Xinjiang Uygur AR, while the opening of the 943-km Jining–Tongliao railway in 1995 has made it possible to link the economies of the eastern and western parts of Nei Mongol AR. In the south-west, Yunnan Province—one of the poorest in China—sees the scheme to create the Greater Mekong Sub-region (a grand vision of a network of road, rail, river, and air links powered through an electricity grid) as the fast lane to help it, Myanmar, Cambodia, Laos, and Vietnam achieve the level of development reached by the sixth participant, Thailand. Yet this, like so many of the other proposals to develop the inland areas will mainly hinge on the availability of funds. The central government has a declining share of tax revenue at its disposal. The State Development Bank has limited lending capacity and the value of its loans to inland areas have remained much the same at US$6,450 million in 1994, US$7,000 million in 1995, and about US$6,600 in 1996, most of it in the form of seed money to start industries, launch infrastructural projects, and improve farming (*Xinhua News Agency*, 14 May, 4 October 1996). The loan programmes of the World Bank, the Asian Development Bank, and the Japanese government are all giving priority to inland projects, but these are not without problems. As the State Planning Commission has explained, although the government's aim is to direct at least 70 per cent of the low-interest loans to projects in these regions, 'their economic foundations are usually very weak, and inadequate supporting funds, low repayment capability and poor management of the loans have made it difficult for many foreign-funded projects to become operational' (*Zhongguo Xinwen She News Agency*, 7 January 1997).

Foreign investors are given optimistic pictures about the opportunities available in power, transport, and telecommunications projects; in energy and key manufacturing sectors such as raw materials, agriculture, electronics, chemicals, vehicles, and construction industries; in joint ventures with military enterprises; and in projects using advanced technology to improve product quality, save energy and materials, improve enterprise efficiency, or to produce new equipment and materials to meet market demand (Wang, 1996). Many foreign firms are already involved in joint ventures in some parts of the inland, especially in cities along the Changjiang (Yangtze) Valley and in industrial centres even further away from the coast like Chongqing, which by the end of 1996 had attracted nearly 250 foreign-funded enterprises involving a total investment of US$910 million, to its Economic and Technological Development Zone (*Xinhua News Agency*, 29 January 1997). The main attraction for both local and overseas investors in the Western Region remains the availability of cheap labour, especially as wages and other labour-related costs in some parts of the coastal zone doubled during the 1993–95 period. Some potential overseas investors who have done the arithmetic say, however, that any savings on labour inputs are negated by increased freight costs.

The central government has already ruled out the possibility of Special Economic Zones (SEZs) being established in inland areas (*China Daily*, 20 July 1995), but it is unclear what, if any, other kinds of incentives may be offered to promote investment and how these will be incorporated into the revised policy directions that emerged during 1995 and 1996, when the emphasis turned from geographically specific incentives towards support for newly prioritized sectors, like agriculture and housing. The question arises, for example, as to whether more cities will be granted 'open' status as only 40 of the 359 open to foreign investment at the end of 1996 are in the eighteen inland provinces and autonomous regions. The significance to investors of the tax and other preferential measures is illustrated by the choice of the open city of Wuhan by Chevron for its plant rather than Shiyan (also in Hubei Province) which is the headquarters of its partner, the Dongfeng Automobile Company, but is not an open city (*China Business Weekly*, 15 October 1995). The proposed gradual opening up to foreign investors of such sectors as banking, insurance, and retail chains may in time provide the kinds of services at inland locations that would make them more attractive to investors in other fields.

Apart from a few large infrastructural and mineral-based projects, much of the investment is likely to be on a small scale, thus continuing the pattern of the last few years when the amount invested per project in the hinterland was about half that of the Coastal Region. In part, this will be an outcome of the restructuring programme being undertaken by coastal cities like Shanghai and Tianjin, which involves the relocation of their labour and resource-intensive SOEs to places where wages are lower and the raw materials are close at hand. In the eyes of the central government, this is the perfect example of east–west co-operation, since it frees up inner city land in places like Shanghai which can be better used for professional and high-tech service activities, while providing employment opportunities and markets for wool, cotton, and leather in, for instance, Xinjiang Uygur AR. It also fits well with the increased emphasis being placed on activities associated with agricultural development following 'Project Grain Self-Sufficiency' introduced throughout China in 1996, but with the inland areas being more heavily subsidized by the central government. The Hong Kong Trade Development Council, for example, is advising people to consider investing in pesticides, fertilizers, agricultural machinery, food processing, packaging, and similar activities (Cheung, 1996a). It is perhaps no coincidence that this advice comes at a time when smaller investors—especially the Overseas Chinese in Hong Kong, Singapore, and Taiwan—have been told that they will not be included in the central government's plans to open up some service sector activities to handpicked foreign companies (Lu, 1996a).

What is striking about all this is the seemingly random nature of the various proposals and the lack of any underlying comprehensive plan that incorporates places with various kinds of development potential into a phased plan for action. Reportedly, ideas of this kind have already been floated (*China Business Weekly*, 16 July 1995). One identified five types of inland area that might be opened up and given their own specific goals. The first group would include the capitals and main regional centres in each of the provinces and autonomous regions, and the second would consist of areas already known to be rich in mineral resources (such as Panzhihua–Xichang in southern Sichuan Province). A third group would be the places where defence-related enterprises were set up during the 1966–75 period in the Third-Line region (Figure 2.2) which the People's Liberation Army has been struggling to convert to civilian use. In a fourth category could be the thirteen border cities (some of them also railway crossing places as shown in Figure 3.1) that were officially opened to foreign investment in 1992 and given further tax privileges in April 1996. However, the total value of trade recorded through all these places in 1995 came to only US$1,300 million (down from a high of US$1,700 million in 1993), and their selective tax privileges may become an issue when China is admitted to the World Trade Organization (*Reuter Australasian Briefing*, 16 June 1996). A fifth group might consist of centres like Mudanjiang and Jiamusi in Heilongjiang Province and Yanji in Jilin Province that are serving as gateways between provincial capitals and border cities.

The Coastal Region

The other major spatial conundrum is the future role of the four main regions lying along the eastern seaboard. Each has been discussed in detail in earlier chapters and little need be added here. All have problems in common, ranging from the burden of the SOEs through to water shortages and environmental pollution. Each has its own set of strengths and weaknesses and all are facing, or are already undertaking, massive programmes of structural adjustment.

North-East. Nowhere is this more so than the North-East which, as Table 9.1 indicates, has been in a state of decline, in terms of its share of China's gross industrial output, for more than three decades. It is, not to mince words, the rust belt of China suffering all the agonies of declining employment opportunities. Not everything of course is bad. The chemical complex at Jilin is already very significant and has ambitious plans for expansion, and Dalian seems to have a fair chance of becoming one of the leading freight handling and container transhipment ports in the Asia–Pacific region. Other possibilities appear to have become less certain. Changchun's hopes of becoming an even more important vehicle manufacturing centre may have been dented now that the idea of a 'People's Car' has been side-tracked for, it seems, the foreseeable future. The Tumen River cross-border development scheme (Figure 7.3) has so far failed to live up to the over-optimistic expectations of some of its original protagonists and is unlikely to produce a significant development thrust until the early years of the twenty-first century; even this will depend on whether Japanese business interests are prepared to make a very expensive and long-term commitment to the proposed high-speed rail link from Hunchun across China, Mongolia, and Russia to the Netherlands. Similarly, the notion of a roaring border trade developing with Russia, much less the Democratic People's Republic of Korea, remains at best a possibility for the future, although the gradual appearance of bridges and trade zones will at least keep the idea alive.

Bohai Sea Rim. This region seems to have suffered from its lack of cohesiveness. It is probably fair to say that, despite lip service being paid from time to time to the need for co-operation, no 'grand plan' has emerged for the region as a whole. The annual reports and planning 'visions' of these municipalities and provinces are couched almost entirely in terms of their own achievements and ambitions, with scarcely a reference to any wider co-operative issues. During 1996 each published economic planning goals for the Ninth Five Year Plan period emphasizing their own sets of priorities; all want to attract more investment, especially from outside China. Yet, as Chapter 6 has indicated, this region would be in a much stronger position if differences were set aside and strengths were pooled. As one planner said during a personal interview in 1995: 'the central government should bang our heads together'.

South-East. The restructuring faced by the South-East is of a different kind, and largely stems from the fact that since the early 1980s it has been attracting two kinds of foreign-invested enterprises—those wanting to establish themselves for the long haul, and those more internationally footloose activities that were searching for low costs and quick profits. For this latter group the cheap labour and land and the array of concessions offered by Guangdong and Fujian Provinces, and more particularly by the Zhuhai, Shenzhen, Shantou, and Xiamen SEZs, were a bonanza for turning imported materials and components into watches, television sets, and clothing for world markets. For the central government, the export income generated, now about 40 per cent of the national total, was a bonus. Yet it was a situation that could not last. By 1994 land and labour prices had risen (and the footloose industries were starting to move to cheaper sites inland or abroad), and hardliners and jealous provinces were fuelling a debate about whether the SEZs had outlived their usefulness. Although the central government made clear late in 1995 that it wanted the SEZs to continue for the foreseeable future, it had in fact already started to whittle away their special status by phasing out some of the legal and policy advantages, or granting them to other places. By the end

of 1996, in fact, only two of the privileged policies remained: the
low (15 per cent) income tax rates for foreign investment projects,
and the tax-free entry (due to be phased out by 2000) of capital
goods imported to build the zones' infrastructure. This is not to
suggest that the South-East is in decline but rather that there are
signs, like falling levels of contracted investment, that its growth
may be levelling off, with the SEZs (in the official language) entering 'a period of conventional and balanced growth'.

By late 1994, in fact, the provincial and SEZ authorities had seen
the writing on the wall and recognized that their comparative
advantage was being eroded. They also understood the weaknesses in their industrial structures and of the human and physical
environments that had developed around them. Unfortunately, too,
they were stuck with loss-making infrastructural and other projects
built hastily during the real estate boom of the early 1990s, and
these still continue to tie up funds now badly needed to pursue their
restructuring goals, including the very serious levels of air and
water pollution. The SEZs, in particular, have shifted their investment focus away from labour-intensive activities towards
high-technology ones, while the provinces are encouraging the
formation of large enterprise groups in the hope that these will lead
to greater efficiency, economies of scale, and flows of new investment. This process is being slowed, however, by the low educational
standard of its workforce which is largely made up of peasants
originally recruited from rural areas more for their nimble fingers
than their knowledge. Gone are the days when Guangdong and
Fujian could make up this deficiency by recruiting 20,000 graduates
a year from other places as these are now paying more competitive salaries.

All this is taking place in an atmosphere of uncertainty stemming
from the absorption of Hong Kong into China on 1 July 1997 and
the constantly churning relationship between Taiwan and the mainland. Some observers, like Tracy in Chapter 4, take the optimistic
view that the conjunction of a restructured and modernized industrial system in Guangdong and Fujian Provinces and the sophisticated commercial and financial system in Hong Kong will continue
to make South-East China a force to be reckoned with. At the end
of the day, much will turn on the perceptions, experiences, and attitude of the Overseas Chinese business community, and whether the
kinship ties with the people of southern China are as deep and
durable as sometimes supposed. In any event, the flamboyance that

has characterized this region will disappear not just because of the more sober assessment of the times ahead, but also because there are powerful figures in the central government who want the South-East brought back into line.

Shanghai and the Changjiang dragon. One need look no further than Shanghai and its environs to see the importance of political influence on the reoganization of space in China. The account given in Chapter 5 of the demise of Shanghai after 1949 and its resurrection during the 1990s indicates how a few people in positions of power can crush or create regional growth. There seems no doubt, for instance, that the development of Pudong was given immense moral and financial support in order to create a counterweight to the South-East, which was perceived to be getting dangerously big for its boots. It may have been a happy coincidence that President Jiang Zemin was a former mayor of Shanghai, and that when Zhu Rongji (now the economic tsar) held that same office in the late 1980s he was 'very active both in and out of China to push the reform and takeoff of Shanghai's economy' (Wang Chi, 1992: 39). Qiao Shi, President of the National People's Congress, toured Shanghai in January 1997 and reportedly opined that it 'would certainly rise above other Chinese cities'. Too much, of course, can be made of the supposed existence of a 'Shanghai faction' or of individual remarks, but the evidence is quite plain that, individually and collectively, the central leadership has a great stake in ensuring the success of Shanghai–Pudong at the head of the dragon and the Three Gorges Scheme at the end of the tail. Whether or not Shanghai will regain its 1930s place as a first rank international financial and commercial centre only time can tell, but it cannot escape notice that every reform in the financial system is being tried out first in Shanghai and, more specifically, in the newly established Lujiazui Financial District in Pudong. China is large enough already to sustain two financial centres: in the short-run Hong Kong may retain its pre-eminent role but in the longer-run the cards may become stacked in Shanghai's favour.

The Evolving System

The important message of this book is that China is not a single space but rather a series of regions which in terms of transport and

communications are being linked more closely whilst in other ways
they are growing apart. Although they share many of the same
problems, they have different characters: the ageing North-East,
the sedate Bohai Sea Rim, the thrusting Shanghai, the adolescent
South-East, and the inchoate inland. All are evolving in the face
of different historical and contemporary pressures. The shape of
China in 2020 will owe much to the way the central government
uses the powerful tools at its disposal to favour some parts of the
country as against others. Yet the more market orientated that
China becomes, the more difficult it will be for any government, no
matter how powerful, to push against spatial trends dictated by the
very motives of efficiency—in effect profitability—that it is trying
to engender in the economy as a whole. Part of the problem of
the SOEs—the single most important and most intractable issue
thwarting reform—stems from a failure to acknowledge that
several of the key plants were located irrationally in the first place,
and that some of the funds being used to resuscitate them would
be better spent on new plants elsewhere. Perhaps this is what Deng
Xiaoping meant when he said 'we must not act like women with
bound feet'?

References

Anon. (1986), '*Guanyu "Wenzhou moshi" de taolun* [Discussion of the "Wenzhou Model"]', *Jingji Yanjiu* [*Journal of Economic Research*], No. 8, 58–67.

Anon. (1995), 'City must come to terms with its mighty neighbour', *South China Morning Post Weekly*, 13 July.

Anon. (1996a), 'No truck with trains: China's joint ventures take to the highway', *Far Eastern Economic Review*, 18 January, 46.

Anon. (1996b), '*Shanxi "yumi zhanlüe" yu "mai liang nan" chansheng maodun* [Shanxi's "maize strategy" creates contradictions with the "lack of a market"]', *Jingji Cankao Bao* [*Economic Reference News*], 3 May, 1.

Baldinger, P. (1992), 'The birth of Greater China', *The China Business Review*, May–June, 13–17.

Barret, C. (1994), 'Provincial disparities in requirements and resources short-circuit planners', *South China Morning Post Weekly*, 2 November.

Baum, J. (1994), 'Taiwanese takeover', *Far Eastern Economic Review*, 22 September, 77–80.

Becker, J. (1995), 'Across China by white elephant', *South China Morning Post Weekly*, 7 October, 11.

Becker, J. (1996), 'Chongqing becomes new self-administration zone in wake of dam project', *South China Morning Post*, 30 August.

Bo Yibo (1991), *A Retrospect of Some Important Policy Decisions and Events*, Chinese Communist Party University Publisher: Beijing.

Bowring, P. (1996), 'Hong Kong's star role may be shanghaied', *Australian Financial Review*, 23 September, 26.

Bradbury, N. (1996), 'Guangdong stands out in kaleidoscope of markets', *South China Morning Post Weekly*, 8 February.

Cao Yong (1995), '3 multinationals lead the way', *Shanghai Star*, 21 April.

Chan, E. (1996), 'Retailer boosts land value', *South China Morning Post*, 30 October.

Chan, T. (1985), 'Financing Shenzhen's economic development', *Asian Journal of Public Administration*, 7(2), 170–97.

Chan, T. (1993), *Foreign Direct Investment in China and its Relationship with Overseas Chinese Capital from Hong Kong, Taiwan and the ASEAN Countries*, China Business Centre: Hong Kong.

Chan, V. P-K. (1996a), 'Beijing facing financial ruin, says researcher', *South China Morning Post*, 13 June.

Chan, V. P-K. (1996b), 'Alarm at misuse of development capital in overlapping projects', *South China Morning Post*, 21 November.

Chang, S-D., Hu, X-W. and Sun, J-J. (1992), 'Tianjin: north China's reviving metropolis', in Y-M. Yeung and X-W. Hu (eds), *China's Coastal Cities: Catalysts for Modernization*, University of Hawaii Press: Honolulu, 41–68.

Chen Hang and Zhu Jinchu (1995), 'Industrial development and distribution before 1949', in Li Wen-yan and Lu Da-dao (eds), *Industrial Geography of China*, Science Press: Beijing, 30–45.

Chen Hang, Zhang Wenchang, Jin Fengjun, Rong Chao-he et al. (1993), *Transport Geography of China*, China Social Sciences Publishing House: Beijing.

Chen Jiyuan (ed.) (1988), *Xiangzhen Qiye Moshi Yanjiu* [*Research on the Models for Township Enterprise Development*], Zhongguo Shehui Kexue Chubanshe: Beijing.

Chen Qide (1995a), 'Lack of public facilities block use of new housing', *Shanghai Star*, 23 May.

Chen Qide (1995b), '2-step strategy envisions finance, trade hub by 2010', *Shanghai Star*, 15 December.

Chen Qide (1996a), 'Urban plan maps city's future form', *Shanghai Star*, 21 May.

Chen Qide (1996b), 'Yangtse projects seek funds', *Shanghai Star*, 24 May.

Chen Yao (1994), *Regional Development Policy in China*, School of Development Studies, University of East Anglia: Norwich.

Cheung Lai-kuen (1996a), 'Foreign investors heed call from China's impoverished hinterland', *South China Morning Business Post*, 23 November, 8.

Cheung Lai-kuen (1996b), 'China's poorer regions need extra resources to catch up with richer coastal areas', *South China Morning Post Weekly*, 8 February.

Cheung Lai-kuen (1996c), 'Yantai open to foreign cash on highway project', *South China Morning Post*, 2 April.

Cheung Tai Ming (1990a), 'Clogged arteries: Shanghai's revival hinges on better transport', *Far Eastern Economic Review*, 4 October, 68–9.

Cheung Tai Ming (1990b), 'Pudong investment lures', *Far Eastern Economic Review*, 4 October, 68–9.

Cheung Tai Ming (1993), 'Life is a beach? China's Hainan aspires to become an island paradise', *Far Eastern Economic Review*, 5 August, 60–2.

China's Customs Statistics (various years), China Statistical Publishing House: Beijing.

Chu Yijie (1989), '*Liangshi diaochushi de ku zhong* [The difficulties of grain transfers are heavy]', *Jingji Cankao* [*Economic Information*], 8 June, 1.

Clayton, D. and Foo Choy Peng (1996), 'Power mega-giant stalled by resistance: regional and Beijing opposition delays plans for national energy company', *South China Morning Business Post*, 15 June, 3.

Clifford, M., do Rosario, L. and Kaye, L. (1992), 'Trade and trade-offs:

potential partners weigh benefits of cooperation', *Far Eastern Economic Review*, 16 January, 18–19.

Corporate International (1994), *Corporate International's Company Handbook*, Hong Kong.

Crothall, G. (1996), 'Long haul ahead for extensive road network', *South China Morning Weekly Business Post*, 27 January, 1.

Dai Gang and Li Jishen (1992), 'New financing for Shanghai markets', *Beijing Review*, April, 20–26, 29–32.

Dalton, G. (1995), 'Tolls hold "key to revival"', *South China Morning Weekly Business Post*, 4 November, 5.

Darwent, D. F. (1969), 'Growth poles and growth centers in regional planning—a review', *Environment and Planning*, 1, 5–31.

Deng Nan (1995), 'China agenda for the 21st century—sustainable development strategy', *Proceedings of the XVIII Pacific Science Congress, Population, Resources and Environment: Prospects and Initiatives*, Beijing, 30–6.

Deng Yingtao, Yao Gang, Xu Xiaobo and Xie Yuwei (1990), *Zhongguo Yusuanwai Zijin Fenxi [An Analysis of Extra-budgetary Funds in China]*, Zhongguo Renmin Daxue Chubanshe: Beijing.

Denny, D. L. (1992), 'Provincial economic differences diminished in the decade of reform', in Joint Economic Committee (ed.), *China's Economic Dilemmas in the 1990s: The Problems of Reforms, Modernization and Interdependence*, M.E. Sharpe: Armonk (Conn.), 186–208.

Department of Resources Conservation & Comprehensive Utilization (1994), *China Energy Annual Review 1994*, State Economic and Trade Commission: Beijing.

Development Research Centre (1994), *China's Regional Development Strategy and Policy* (ADB TA Project 1696-PRC), DRC: Beijing.

Dickie, M. (1996a), 'China border trade highlights N. Korea ills', *Reuter Australasian Briefing*, 2 July.

Dickie, M. (1996b), 'China says 7–8 percent of urban workers lack jobs', *Reuter Australasian Briefing*, 15 July.

Earnshaw, G. (1996), 'Dirty Shanghai gets high marks for trying', *Reuter Australasian Briefing*, 2 August.

Economist Intelligence Unit (1995), 'Investment development trends', *Business China*, in *Reuter Australasian Briefing*, 26 April.

Economist Intelligence Unit (1996), 'Obstacles hinder conversion of defence sector', *EIU Country View*, in *Reuter Australasian Briefing*, 11 July.

Editorial Group (1995), *Zhongguo Jiaotong Dituji [Atlas of China's Transport]*, Zhongguo Shehui Chubanshe: Beijing.

Feng Lanrui (1987), '*Daqiuzhuang moshi de sikao ji qi bijiao* [Thoughts on the Daqiuzhuang model and some comparisons]', *Zhongguo Nongcun Jingji [China's Rural Economy]*, No. 1, 46–51.

Fincher, J. (1990), 'Rural bias and the renaissance of coastal China', in G. J. R. Linge and D. K. Forbes (eds), *China's Spatial Economy: Recent*

Developments and Reforms, Oxford University Press: Hong Kong, 35–58.

Findlay, C., Martin, W. and Watson, A. (1993), *Policy Reform, Economic Growth and China's Agriculture*, Organisation for Economic Co-operation and Development: Paris.

Findlay, C., Watson, A. and Chen, C. L. (1991), 'The growth of rural enterprises in China: the impact of fiscal contracting', unpublished paper presented to the conference on 'China's Growth and Economic Reforms', The Australian National University, Canberra, November.

Findlay, C., Watson, A. and Wu, H. X. (eds) (1994), *Rural Enterprises in China*, Macmillan: London.

Fisher, C. A. (1950), 'The expansion of Japan: a study in oriental geopolitics', *Geographical Journal*, 115, 1–19.

Foo Choy Peng (1996), 'State-sector jobs to go', *South China Morning Post*, 10 October.

Fossey, J. (1996), 'Inland—Wuhan woes', *Containerisation International*, September, 75.

Fujian's Statistical Yearbook (various years) [in Chinese], China Statistical Publishing House: Beijing.

Fung, K-I., Yan, Z-M. and Ning, Y-M. (1992), 'Shanghai: China's world city', in Y-M. Yeung and X-U. Hu (eds), *China's Coastal Cities: Catalysts for Modernization*, University of Hawaii Press: Honolulu, 124–52.

Gao Shangquan (1984), 'Reform of China's economic system', in Xue Muqiao (ed.), *Almanac of China's Economy 1983*, Modern Cultural Company: Hong Kong, 243–8.

Goldstein, C. (1993), 'Resisting the centre', *Far Eastern Economic Review*, 2 September, 42–3.

Goodman, D. and Feng Chongyi (1993), *Guangdong: Greater Hong Kong and the New Regionalist Future*, Asia Research Centre, Murdoch University: Perth.

Grajdanzev, A. J. (1945), 'Manchuria: an industrial survey', *Pacific Affairs*, 18, 321–39.

Higgins, A. (1996), 'Ambitious Shanghai reaches for sky', *The Guardian Weekly*, 1 June, 13.

Ho, L. S. (1993), 'Central-provincial fiscal relations', in J. C. Yu-shek and M. Brosseau (eds), *China Review 1993*, Chinese University Press: Hong Kong, 12.1–23.

Hull, T. H. (1990), 'Spatial aspects of the natural increase of China's population', in G. J. R. Linge and D. K. Forbes (eds), *China's Spatial Economy: Recent Developments and Reforms*, Oxford University Press: Hong Kong, 109–28.

Huus, K. (1994a), 'One province, no system', *Far Eastern Economic Review*, 2 June, 46–8.

Huus, K. (1994b), 'Come as you are', *Far Eastern Economic Review*, 2 June, 50–2.

Huus, K. (1994c), 'Heartbreak hotel', *Far Eastern Economic Review*, 2 June, 52.

Hyslop, J. S. (1990), 'The spatial structure of Shanghai City Proper', in G. J. R. Linge and D. K. Forbes (eds), *China's Spatial Economy: Recent Developments and Reforms*, Oxford University Press: Hong Kong, 144–59.

International Monetary Fund (various years), *Direction of Trade Statistics Yearbook*, IMF: Washington DC.

Jiang Changyun (1992), '*Pinkun diqu xiangcun qiye de jingji xingwei fenxi* [An analysis of the behaviour of rural enterprises in poor areas]', *Zhongguo Nongcun Jingji* [*China's Rural Economy*], No. 1, 39–43.

Jiang Jian (1994), 'Improved services', *Shanghai Star*, 25 January.

Kattoulas, V. (1996), 'China fights to smash legacy of central planning', *Reuter Australasian Briefing*, 4 July.

Ke Bingsheng (1990), '*Wo guo xiangzhen qiye fazhan shuiping de quyue chayi ji qi qishi* [Regional differences in the level of rural enterprise development and their lessons]', *Nongye Jingji Wenti* [*Issues in Agricultural Economics*], No. 10, 33–6.

Kohut, J. (1993), 'Shanghai to be the pioneer of reforms', *South China Morning Post*, 11 December.

Kong De-yong (1993), *Studies of Regional Economic Development in Huanghai and Bohai Rim* [in Chinese], Chinese Technology and Sciences Press: Beijing.

Korski, T. (1996), 'Huge write-offs for banks', *South China Morning Post*, 4 November.

Korski, T. (1997), 'Top economist sees billions lost by duplication and rivalries between enterprises', *South China Morning Post*, 28 January.

Kueh, J. J. (1989), 'The Maoist legacy and China's new industrialization strategy', *China Quarterly*, No. 119, 420–47.

Kueh, Y. Y. (1987), 'Economic decentralization and foreign trade expansion in China', in J. C. H. Chai and C-K. Leung (eds), *China's Economic Reforms*, Centre of Asian Studies, University of Hong Kong: Hong Kong, 444–81.

Kwan, D. (1996a), 'Ambitious scheme unveiled to help poor provinces bridge financial divide', *South China Morning Post*, 18 June.

Kwan, D. (1996b), 'Streamlining and delays blamed for downturn', *South China Morning Post*, 9 September.

Kwang, M. (1996), 'Don't blame ailing state firms blindly, Zhu tells critics', *Straits Times*, 5 December.

Lai, D. C-Y., Zhao, X-Y. and Liang, X-X. (1992), 'Dalian: industrial development and urban growth', in Y-M. Yeung and X-W. Hu (eds), *China's Coastal Cities: Catalysts for Modernization*, University of Hawaii Press: Honolulu, 25–41.

Lai, R. (1995), 'Peasants target of Hebei growth', *South China Morning Post*, 20 June.

Lai, R. (1996), 'Railways behind times on investment', *South China Morning Weekly Business Post*, 20 April, 8.

Lam, W-L. (1997), 'Propagandists spin on tales of rural hardship', *South China Morning Post Weekly*, 1 February, 7.

Lam, W. W. (1995), 'Jiang boost for Shanghai', *South China Morning Post*, 22 May, 6.

Land, T. (1995), 'World Bank boosts revitalisation of China's inland waterways', *Lloyd's List*, 10 July.

Lardy, N. R. (1980), 'Regional growth and income distribution in China', in R. F. Dernberger (ed.), *China's Development Experience in Comparative Perspective*, Harvard University Press: Cambridge (Mass.), 153–90.

Lardy, N. R. (1990), *China's Interprovincial Grain Marketing and Import Demand*, United States Department of Agriculture, Economic Research Service, Agriculture and Trade Analysis Division: Washington DC, September.

Lardy, N. R. (1992), *China in the World Economy*, Institute for International Economics: Washington DC.

Li Wen-yan (1988), 'Industrialisation in peripheral China with special reference to the Greater Northwest', in G. J. R. Linge (ed.), *Peripheralisation and Industrial Change: Impacts on Nations, Regions, Firms and People*, Croom Helm: London, 94–112.

Li Wen-yan (1995a), 'The changes and basic experiences of industrial allocation in China since 1949', in Li Wen-yan and Lu Da-dao (eds), *Industrial Geography of China*, Science Press: Beijing, 46–77.

Li Wen-yan (1995b), 'Appendix: current industrial change and spatial-industrial structure in China', in Li Wen-yan and Lu Da-dao (eds), *Industrial Geography of China*, Science Press: Beijing, 603–15.

Li Wen-yan and Fan Jie (1993), 'An analysis on the relationship between the hierarchy of economic regions and energy strategy in China', in She Zulin (ed.), *Proceedings of UNESCO Round Table on Strategic Energy Issues in China*, Atomic Energy Press: Beijing, 69–84.

Li Wen-yan and Lu Da-dao (eds) (1995), *Industrial Geography of China*, Science Press: Beijing.

Liang Yun-bin (1995), 'International environment and foreign economic development of Bohai Rim' [in Chinese], in Lu Da-dao (ed.), *Studies of Sustainable Development of China's Bohai Rim*, Science Press: Beijing, 208–19.

Lin Jian (1987), '*Shilun Zhongguo nongcun jingji fazhan moshi de yanjiu* [A discussion of research on models of rural development in China]', *Jingji Yanjiu* [*Journal of Economic Research*], No. 8, 59–62.

Linge, G. J. R. (1988), 'Peripheralisation and industrial change', in G. J. R. Linge (ed.), *Peripheralisation and Industrial Change: Impacts on Nations, Regions, Firms and People*, Croom Helm: London, 1–21.

Linge, G. J. R. (forthcoming), 'The Tumen River cross-border economic development area', in G. Wijeyewardene (ed.), *Southeast Asian Borders in Regional Context*, Institute of Southeast Asian Studies: Singapore.

Linge, G. J. R. and Forbes, D. K. (eds) (1990a), *China's Spatial Economy: Recent Developments and Reforms*, Oxford University Press: Hong Kong.

Linge, G. J. R. and Forbes, D. K. (1990b), 'The space economy of China', in G. J. R. Linge and D. K. Forbes (eds), *China's Spatial Economy: Recent Developments and Reforms*, Oxford University Press: Hong Kong, 10–34.

Linge, G. J. R., Karaska, G. J. and Hamilton, F. E. I. (1978), 'An appraisal of the Soviet concept of the territorial production complex', *Soviet Geography: Review and Translation*, 19, 681–97.

Liu Hong (1996), 'City adds industries: Shanghai targets biomedicine, high-tech materials', *China Business Weekly*, 11 August, 5.

Liu Wei-dong (1995), 'Industrial development and water resources exploitation' [in Chinese], in Lu Da-dao (ed.), *Studies of Sustainable Development of China's Bohai Rim*, Science Press: Beijing, 224–8.

Liu Weiling (1995), 'Commercial banks gain strength', *China Business Weekly*, 22 January.

Lu Da-dao (ed.) (1995), *Studies of Sustainable Development of China's Bohai Rim* [in Chinese], Science Press: Beijing.

Lu Ning (1996a), 'When big is beautiful', *Business Times*, 21 November.

Lu Ning (1996b), 'Singapore manufacturers group to build Qingdao industrial park', *Business Times*, 2 October.

Lu Ning (1996c), 'China redirecting FDI', *Business Times*, 30 October.

Lyons, T. P. (1987), 'Spatial aspects of development in China: the motor vehicle industry, 1956–1985', *International Regional Science Review*, 11(1), 75–96.

Ma Hongbo (1994), 'Handle well relations between central administration and localities in economic development [in Chinese]', *Qinghai Ribao*, 12 January, 3.

Michalski, M., Miller, R. and Stevens, B. (1996), 'China in the twenty-first century: an overview of the long-term issues', in OECD, *China in the 21st Century: Long-term Global Implications*, OECD: Paris, 7–19.

Miller, M., Holm, A. and Kelleher, T. (1991), 'Mission report on Tumen River area development', paper presented at Pyongyang Conference, 16–18 October.

Ministry of Agriculture (1995), *Xiang-zhen Qiye Caiwu Tongji Huizong Ziliao 1994 [Collected Financial Statistical Materials on Rural Enterprises 1994]*, Beijing.

Mu Ren (1996), 'Go bankrupt or dodge creditors?—expounding on the issue of enterprise bankruptcy', *Renmin Ribao*, 9 December.

Murata, F. (1996), 'Old communist foes turn allies in business: railways seen as locomotive of flourishing Sino-Vietnamese trade', *Nikkei Weekly*, 8 April, 22.

Naughton, B. (1988), 'The Third Front: defence industrialization in the Chinese interior', *China Quarterly*, No. 115, 351–86.

Naughton, B. (1995), *Growing out of the Plan: Chinese Economic Reform 1978–1993*, Cambridge University Press: Cambridge.

Ngai, A. (1995), 'Massive test to put infrastructure back on track', *South China Morning Post Weekly*, 11 February, 5.

Nyaw Mee-kau (1993), 'Direct foreign investment in China: trends, performance, policies and prospects', in J. C. Yu-shek and M. Brosseau (eds), *China Review 1993*, Chinese University Press: Hong Kong, 16.1–38.

O'Neill, M. (1996a), 'China's military makes clothes, shoes, machinery', *Reuter Australasian Briefing*, 16 April.

O'Neill, M. (1996b), 'Pudong stops land sales for commercial development', *Reuter Australasian Briefing*, 3 June.

Oi, J. C. (1986), 'Peasant grain marketing and state procurement: China's grain contracting system', *The China Quarterly*, No. 106, June, 272–90.

Oksenberg, M. and Tong, J. (1991), 'The evolution of central-provincial fiscal relations in China, 1971–1984: the formal system', *The China Quarterly*, No. 125, March, 1–32.

Overholt, W. H. (1993), *The Rise of China: How Economic reform is Creating a New Superpower*, Norton: New York.

Paine, S. (1981), 'Spatial aspects of Chinese development: issues, outcomes and policies 1949–79', *Journal of Development Studies*, 17, 132–95.

Pannell, C. W. (1988), 'Regional shifts in China's industrial output', *Professional Geographer*, 40(1), 19–32.

Peffer, N. (1958), *The Far East: A Modern History*, University of Michigan Press: Ann Arbor.

Perkins, D. H. (1996), 'China's future: economic and social development scenarios for the twenty-first century', in OECD, *China in the 21st Century: Long-term Global Implications*, OECD: Paris, 21–35.

Press House (1996), *Yearbook of China's Transport* [in Chinese], Press House for Yearbook of China's Transport: Beijing.

Quinn, A. (1992), 'Dreams clash with reality in Shanghai', *Reuter Australasian Briefing*, 26 March.

Rodgers, A. (1948), 'The Manchurian iron and steel industry and its resource base', *Geographical Review*, 38, 41–54.

Roell, S. (1996), 'Urban Chinese growing poorer—slowdown has implications for multinationals', *Financial Times*, 24 October, 6.

Roll, C. R. and Yeh, K. C. (1975), 'Balance in coastal and inland development', in Joint Economic Committee, *China: A Reassessment of the Economy*, Government Printing Office: Washington DC, 81–93.

Rong Chao-he (1993a), *On Transportation* [in Chinese], China Social Sciences Publishing House: Beijing.

Rong Chao-he (1993b), 'Transport's impact on regional development', *First Collection of China's Post-doctoral Academic Articles*, 1, 1088–94.

Rong Chao-he (1995), 'Prediction of energy consumption and supply' [in Chinese], in Lu Da-dao (ed.), *Studies of Sustainable Development of China's Bohai Rim*, Science Press: Beijing, 125–43.

Rozelle, S. (1996), 'Stagnation without equity: patterns of growth and inequality in China's rural economy', *The China Journal*, No. 35, January, 63–92.

Rural Development Research Institute (1987), *Xiangzhen Qiye Moshi Yanjiu* [*Research on the Models for Township Enterprise Development*], Zhongguo Shehui Kexue Chubanshe: Beijing.

Ryuji Sato (1995), 'Foreigners find business in Shanghai no picnic', *Nikkei Weekly*, 22 May.

Schumpeter, E. B. (1940), 'Japan, Korea and Manchukuo, 1936–1940', in E. B. Schumpeter (ed.), *The Industrialization of Japan and Manchukuo 1930–1940*, Macmillan: New York, 271–450.

Seidlitz, P. and Murphy, D. (1996), 'Beijing may have raised stakes too high for investors', *South China Morning Post*, 22 September.

Selden, M. (1988), 'Income inequality and the state in rural China', *The Political Economy of Chinese Socialism*, M.E. Sharpe: Armonk (Conn.), 129–52.

Sender, H. (1997), 'Wrong number', *Far Eastern Economic Review*, 9 January, 74–6.

Shanghai Pudong New Area Administration (1993), *Shanghai Pudong New Area Handbook*, Shanghai Far East Publishers: Shanghai.

She Qijiong and Yu Renlin (1993), 'Telecommunication services in China', *IEEE Communications Magazine*, 31, 30–3.

Shen Liren and Dai Yuanchen (1990), '*Woguo "zhuhou jingji" de xingcheng ji qi biduan he genyuan* [The formation of the "warlord economy" in China: defects and origin]', *Jingji Yanjiu* [*Journal of Economic Research*], No. 3, 12–19.

Shen Wei-cheng (1990), 'Development and problems of China's seaports', in G. J. R. Linge and D. K. Forbes (eds), *China's Spatial Economy: Recent Developments and Reforms*, Oxford University Press: Hong Kong, 96–108.

Sicular, T. (1988), 'Agricultural planning and pricing in the post-Mao period', *The China Quarterly*, No. 116, 671–705.

So, I. (1995), 'Shandong aims for the top', *South China Morning Post*, 4 December.

So, I. (1996), 'Billions needed to save environment', *South China Morning Post*, 18 June.

State Statistical Bureau (1986–1996a), *China Statistical Yearbook*, China Statistical Publishing House: Beijing.

State Statistical Bureau (1995b), *Urban Statistical Yearbook 1995*, China Statistical Publishing House: Beijing.

State Statistical Bureau (1996b), *Zhongguo Tongji Zhaiyao, 1996 [China Statistical Abstracts, 1996]*, Zhongguo Tongji Chubanshe: Beijing.

Statistical Survey of China (1994, 1995), China Statistical Publishing House: Beijing.

Statistical Yearbook of Guangdong (various years) [in Chinese], China Statistical Publishing House: Beijing.

Stevens, H. (1994), 'On the fast track to success: Wu close to reaching goal', *South China Morning Post Weekly*, 22 July, 2.

Summers, L. H. (1992), 'The rise of China', *International Economic Insights*, May/June, 17.

Sung, Y-W., Liu, P-W., Wong, Y-C. R. and Lau, P. K. (1995), *The Fifth Dragon: The Emergence of the Pearl River Delta*, Addison Wesley Publishing: Singapore.

Tan, A. (1996), 'PSA [Port of Singapore Authority] venture's China container terminal to be completed by 1998', *Business Times*, 6 December.

Teh Hooi Ling (1996), 'Singapore businesses to increase Qingdao investments', *Business Times*, 18 October.

Todd, D. and Zhang Lei (1994), 'Ports and coal transfer: hub of China's energy supply policy', *Energy Policy*, 22(7), 609–21.

Tracy, N. (1994), *The Making of a New Little Dragon: The Overseas Chinese and the Transformation of Guangdong*, Asia Research Centre, Murdoch University: Perth.

Tsui, K. Y. (1991), 'China's regional inequality, 1952–1985', *Journal of Comparative Economics*, 15, 1–21.

Urban Social and Economic Survey Organization (1990), *China: The Forty Years of Urban Development*, China Statistical Information and Consultancy Service Center: Beijing.

Vatikiotis, M. (1994), 'Romance meets reality', *Far Eastern Economic Review*, 22 September, 72–7.

Wang Chi (1992), 'Power structure and key political players in China', in Joint Economic Committee (ed.), *China's Economic Dilemmas in the 1990s: The Problems of Reforms, Modernization and Interdependence*, M.E. Sharpe: Armonk (Conn.), 29–47.

Wang Huijiong and Li Shantong (1995), *Industrialization and Economic Reform in China*, New World Press: Beijing.

Wang Xingchun (1991), '*Xiangzhen qiye xindai zhengce de huigu yu sikao* [Reflections on and review of rural enterprise credit policy]', *Nongye Jingji Wenti [Issues in Agricultural Economics]*, No. 10, 2–25.

Wang Xue-ming (1992), 'Guangdong: economic growth and structural changes in the 1980s', in T. Maruya (ed.), *Guangdong: 'Open Door' Economic Development Strategy*, Institute of Developing Economies: Tokyo, 18–49.

Wang Zhenquan (1996), 'Investors turn their focus to vast central resources', *South China Morning Post*, 12 September.

Watson, A. (1983), 'Agriculture looks for "shoes that fit": the production responsibilty system and its implications', *World Development*, 11(8), 705–30.

Watson, A. (1988), 'The reform of agricultural marketing in China since 1978', *The China Quarterly*, No. 113, March, 1–28.

Watson, A. (1992), *Conflict over Cabbages: The Reform of Wholesale Marketing in China*, USC Seminar Series No. 6, Hong Kong Institute of Asia–Pacific Studies, The Chinese University of Hong Kong: Hong Kong.

Watson, A. (1996), 'Conflict over cabbages: the reform of wholesale marketing in China', in R. Garnaut, Guo Shutian and Ma Guonan (eds), *The Third Revolution in the Chinese Countryside*, Cambridge University Press: Cambridge, 144–63.

Watson, A. and Findlay, C. (1995), 'Food and profit: the political economy of grain market reform in China', unpublished paper presented to the conference on 'Grain Market Reform in China and its Implications', East–West Center, Hawaii, September.

Watson, A., Findlay, C. and Du Yintang (1989), 'Who won the "wool war"?: a case study of rural product marketing in China', *The China Quarterly*, No. 118, June, 213–41.

Watson, A. and Wu, H. X. (1994), 'Regional disparities in rural enterprise growth', in C. Findlay, A. Watson and H. X. Wu (eds), *Rural Enterprises in China*, Macmillan: London, 69–92.

Wei, Y. and Ma, L. J. C. (1996), 'Changing patterns of spatial inequality in China, 1952–1990', *Third World Planning Review*, 18(2), 177–91.

Wong, C. (1992), 'Fiscal reform and local industrialisation', *Modern China*, 18(2), 197–227.

Wong, J. (1995), 'Finance and taxes: the half-way house', in D. Bloodworth (ed.), *The Risks and Rewards of Investing in China*, Times Academic Press: Singapore, 155–61.

Woo Tun-oy (1996), 'Regional economic development and disparities', in M. Brousseau, S. Pepper and Tsang Shu-ki (eds), *China Review 1996*, Chinese University Press: Hong Kong, 281–314.

World Bank (1992), *World Development Report 1992: Development and the Environment*, Oxford University Press for World Bank: New York.

Wu Minyi (1990), '*Guanyu difang zhengfu xingwei de ruogan sikao* [Some thoughts on local governments' behaviour]', *Jingji Yanjiu* [*Journal of Economic Research*], No. 7, 56–9.

Xu Xue-guiang and Li Si-ming (1990), 'China's open door policy and urbanisation in the Pearl River Delta region', *International Journal of Urban and Regional Research*, 141(1), 52–65.

Yamaguchi, M. (1993), *The Emerging Chinese Business Sphere*, Nomura Research Institute: Hong Kong.

Yan Changle (1994), *Report on Energy Development in China* [in Chinese],

Economic Management Press: Beijing.

Yang, D. (1990), 'Patterns of China's regional development strategy', *China Quarterly*, No. 122, 230–57.

Yang Jianwen, Zhou Yifeng and Zhen Li (1986), ' *"Wenzhou Moshi" yu Zhongguo nongcun jingji de tengfei* [The "Wenzhou model" and the take off of China's rural development]', *Shehui Kexue (Lu)* [*Shanghai Social Sciences*], No. 5, 30–4.

Yang, M. (1995), 'Technical Paper I: China's banking system', in D. Bloodworth (ed.), *The Risks and Rewards of Investing in China*, Times Academic Press: Singapore, 178–90.

Yang Xuguang, Xu Changzhong and Zhang Guangyi (1984), 'Regional economic and technical cooperation', in Xue Muqiao (ed.), *Almanac of China's Economy 1983*, Modern Cultural Company Ltd: Hong Kong, 237–40.

Yatsko, P. (1996), 'China's Tarim Basin is proving a big disappointment', *Far Eastern Economic Review*, 19 September, 68–9.

Ye Shun-zan (1995), 'Population growth and urbanization' [in Chinese], in Lu Da-dao (ed.), *Studies of Sustainable Development of China's Bohai Rim*, Science Press: Beijing, 224–8.

Ye Ruqiu (1996), 'Sustainable development in China and international trade', *International Environmental Affairs*, 8(1), 16–31.

Yeung, Y-M. and Hu, X-W. (eds) (1992), *China's Coastal Cities: Catalysts for Modernization*, University of Hawaii Press: Honolulu.

Young, S. and Yang Gang (1994), 'Private enterprises and local government in China', in C. Findlay, A. Watson and H. X. Wu (eds), *Rural Enterprises in China*, Macmillan: London, 24–38.

Yuasa, K. (1996), 'China telecom entity seeks partners for cable project', *Nikkei Weekly*, 15 June, 22.

Yue Qifeng (1994), 'Province must face second front of economic development' [in Chinese], *Heilongjiang Ribao*, 1 November, 1–2.

Zhang, J. X. and Wang, Y. (1995), *The Emerging Market of China's Computer Industry*, Quorum Books: Westport (Conn.).

Zhang Wenchang, Jin Fengjun and Rong Chao-he (1992), *On Spatial Transport Linkages—Theoretical Study, Empirical Analysis and Forecasting Methods* [in Chinese], China Railway Publishing: Beijing.

Zhang Xiaohe and Tracy, N. (1994), *The Third Foreign Investment Wave in Mainland China: Features and Implications*, Asia Research Centre, Murdoch University: Perth.

Zhongguo Nongye Nianjian Editorial Group (1986), *Zhongguo Nongcun Fagui 1984* [*China Rural Laws 1984*], Nongye Chubanshe: Beijing, 343–56.

Zhou Dadi (1993), 'Energy price management in China', in She Zulin (ed.), *Proceedings of UNESCO Round Table on Strategic Energy Issues in China*, Atomic Energy Press: Beijing, 92–9.

Zweig, D. (1992), 'Rural industry: constraining the leading growth sector in China's economy', in Joint Economic Committee (ed.), *China's Economic Dilemmas in the 1990s: The Problems of Reforms, Modernization and Interdependence*, M.E. Sharpe: Armonk (Conn.), 418–39.

Index

Acid rain, 5, 91, 93
administrative boundaries, and regional planning, 38, 44, 98
ageing population, 6
'Agenda 21', White Paper, 1
agricultural export development zone, 115; income and prices, 11, 22; production, 66, 72, 143, 202; water saving techniques, 136
agriculture, 11–12, 13, 93, 167–70
air pollution, 5, 91, 92, 152
air freight, 59
air travel, 54, 59, 62, 68
airports, 58, 68, 90, 112, 156
Anhui Province, coalfields, 64; trade, 100
Anshan: heavy industry, 24, 130; iron and steel, 138, 146, 148, 152; pollution, 134
Anshan Iron and Steel Company, 25, 127, 151
aquaculture, 115, 127
arable land, 2, 8, 72, 137
Asia–Europe fibre-optic cable, 56
Asian Development Bank, loans, 131, 156, 157; priority to inland areas, 200
Association of South-East Asian Nations (ASEAN), 95
authorized 'gateways', 58
Automobile Industry Corporation (Shanghai), 106

Banking: centrally controlled, 100; foreign involvement in, 10, 20, 102, 110, 201; mortgage schemes offered by, 105; reforms needed, 14, 136
bank loans for fixed investments, 43; for state-owned enterprises, 12, 13
Bank of Communications, 57
Baoshan (Shanghai), 109
Baoshan Iron and Steel complex (Shanghai), 29, 67, 106
Baotou Iron and Steel, 25
barter trade, 153, 159
Beihai, open city, 32

Beijing: air traffic, 59, 142; consumer tastes and preferences, 187; cross-border co-operation, 39, 125; driving force of Bohai Sea Rim region, 142; energy consumption, 49, 134; expertise available, 142; foreign investment, 18, 142; industry, 128, 130, 131–2, 138; per capita income, 30; pollution, 5, 134; pressure on space, 133; retailing, 10; service sector growth, 130; special privileges, 101; state-owned enterprises, 16; subsidence, 3, 132; telephone availability, 55; traffic congestion, 134; urban population, 123, 133; urban renewal, 133; water availability, 3, 132
Beijing: expressways to Dandong, 166; to Qinhuangdao, 139; to Shijiazhuang, 139
Beijing: railways to Baotou, 51; to Guangzhou, 48, 51, 54, 62, 69, 139; to Hanoi, 58; to Hong Kong, 62, 69, 117, 135, 139; to Shanghai, 48, 51, 54, 62, 70, 139; to Shenyang, 48, 51, 54, 145; to Shenzhen, 90; to Zhanjiang, 86
Beijing–Tianjin–Tangshan triangle, 23, 69, 129
Benxi, 130; iron and steel, 138, 146, 148, 152; pollution, 134, 153
Benxi Iron and Steel Company, 127
births and deaths, 6
'black' money recycled through Hong Kong, 17, 111
Bohai Sea, future transport across, 69, 139, 166; oilfields, 137
Bohai Sea Rim 123–43, 204; characteristics, 127–9; co-operation within, 136; definition of, 54, 123–4, 144; energy, 128, 133, 137, 143; environmental issues, 133, 134, 137, 141, 143; farmland diminishing, 127, 137; foreign investment, 17, 125, 134, 136; grain growing, 127; industrial areas, 129–31, 137; industry, 127, 128, 131–2, 135, 136, 137, 138, 143; infrastruc-

Pingshuo, opencast coal, 64
Pingxiang, railway border crossing, 58
pipeline, gas from Siberia, 70; gas from
Pinghu offshore field, 112
policy banks established, 13
polluting enterprises, impacts of closure,
4, 43
pollution, of air, 5, 49, 64, 91, 138; of
water, 4; legislation concerning, 5
population, 1, 6–7, 8; 72, 79; aim to
stabilize, 38
ports, 58, 65, 66–7, 109, 135
post office remittances system, 58
poverty, 1, 2, 36, 66; poverty line, 1, 7
power, electric, 48–9, 64, 71, 78, 91; see
also hydro-power, nuclear power
Poyang Lake Economic Zone, 117
private sector, 10, 77, 78
Project Grain Self-Sufficiency, 202
Pudong, 103, 104, 109–13; central government support, 98, 103, 110, 113;
counterweight to south-east, 206;
future prosperity, 113; inaccessibility,
105, 112; industry, 110, 112; international airport, 112; investment in,
41, 110, 111; links with Changjiang
Valley, 121; population, 108, 110;
prestigious symbol, 110; problems of,
112–13; state-owned enterprises supporting, 112; see also Jinqiao Export
Processing Zone, Lujiazui–Huamu
Finance and Trade Zone, Waigaoqiao–Gaoqiao, Zhangjiang High-Tech
Park
purchasing power parity (PPP), 1

Qilu (Zibo), petrochemical complex,
128
Qingdao (formerly Huangdao), 32, 52,
58, 59, 128, 130–1, 134, 138; water
shortage, 3, 132
Qinghai Province, 30, 44; impact of
Chongqing Municipality on, 40, 199
Qinghai Provincial Handicraft Company, 33
Qinghai, railway to Ürümqi, 25; to
Lianyungang proposed, 139
Qinhuangdao, coal line to Datong, 62,
135; coal port, 52, 62, 134, 135; expressway to Beijing, 139; open city, 32, 134;
railway to Shenyang, 139; water shortage, 132
Qinshan, nuclear plant, 64; thermal
power, 26
Qiqihar, industry, 24, 149, 151

quality of life, 7, 96
Quanzhou, 75, 78, 81, 83

Railway Development Fund, 62–3
railways, 26, 46, 47, 51, 54, 62–4, 70, 139;
border crossings, 58, 158; coal transport, 46, 62, 63; congestion, 51, 62,
155; central control needed, 63;
construction, 25, 46, 62; competition
from road transport, 70; congestion,
51, 59, 155; fares, 55; freight flows,
51–4, 62; investment in, 62–3; passenger journeys, 46, 54–5
reform programme, 22, 74, 77
regional development, 36–7; co-operation schemes, 33–4, 36; economic
policies affecting, 40–2, 43; growing
diversity of, 184; investment policies,
42–3
regional disparities in rural development, 167–90
regional equality, socialist objective, 29
regional linkages, 46, 52–4, 57, 57–8
regional planning: developing concepts
about, 23–37; goals of, 43–5; methodological framework for, 44
remittances from migrant workers, 58,
89
Report on Creating a New Situation in
Commune and Brigade-Run Enterprises, 170
Republic of Korea (ROK), investment
from, 134, 156
resource problems facing China, 1–4
restructuring, continuous process, 192
retailing, foreign involvement in, 10, 20,
201
river ports, 58, 61, 117
rivers, polluted, 4, 153
road system, 11, 59, 60, 64–6
road transport, 61
'Ruhr of China', north-east region, 24
rural and municipal credit unions, 57
rural economy, 76, 168, 169, 170–6, 184,
186, 188–90
rural employment, 8, 9
rural enterprises, 79, 168, 170, 171, 172,
176, 177, 172, 180, 190; see also town
and village enterprises
rural incomes, 11, 58, 168, 170
rural output, diversification of, 168
rural population, mobility of, 46, 171
rural poverty, 66
rural production diversification of, 171
rural reforms, 167, 169–71